REBEL BISHOP

Bishop Augustin Verot

Rebel Bishop

THE LIFE AND ERA OF

AUGUSTIN VEROT

BY

MICHAEL V. GANNON

WITH A FOREWORD BY

JOHN TRACY ELLIS

THE BRUCE PUBLISHING COMPANY • *MILWAUKEE*

IMPRIMATUR:

✠ Joseph P. Hurley
Archbishop, Bishop of Saint Augustine

July 28, 1964

Library of Congress Catalog Card Number: 64–23895

TO MY MOTHER

ABBREVIATIONS

AAB   = Archives of the Archdiocese of Baltimore
AANO = Archives of the Archdiocese of New Orleans
ADC   = Archives of the Diocese of Charleston
ADP   = Archives of the Diocese of Le Puy
ADSA = Archives of the Diocese of St. Augustine
ASBE = Archives of the Savannah Board of Education
ASCH = Archives of the Savannah City Hall
ASLA = Archives of St. Leo Abbey
ASS   = Archives of the Society of St. Sulpice, Paris
ASSJ = Archives of the Sisters of St. Joseph, St. Augustine
CHR = *Catholic Historical Review*
MCND = Manuscript Collection of the University of Notre Dame
NA   = National Archives
OR   = *The War of the Rebellion: A Compilation of the Official Records of the Union and Confederate Armies* (Washington, D. C.: Government Printing Office, 1880– 1901)
RACH = *Records of the American Catholic Historical Society of Philadelphia*

ACKNOWLEDGMENTS

IN A BIOGRAPHY based on original sources, the writer's debts are obviously many and varied. He is glad to acknowledge that he was afforded free access to archival materials in every diocese and library to which he presented himself and his purposes. Certain of these obligations are recognized in footnotes to the text. Here he wishes to thank in particular: the Most Rev. Joseph P. Hurley, D.D., Archbishop-Bishop of St. Augustine, who gave the writer free access to the archives of the diocese and encouraged him in his researches; the Rt. Rev. Monsignor John Tracy Ellis, Professor of Church History in the University of San Francisco, who first suggested Bishop Verot's career as an important field for historical inquiry and provided valuable corrections and suggestions as the manuscript took shape; Dr. Arthur W. Thompson, Professor of History in the University of Florida, under whose technical advice and judicious pencil the core of this study was written; and Drs. John A. Harrison, David L. Dowd, Franklin A. Doty, and George Bartlett, all of the University of Florida.

For the grant of access to diocesan archives acknowledgment is gratefully made to: the Most Rev. Paul J. Hallinan, Archbishop of Atlanta (at the time of the writer's researches, Bishop of Charleston), and the Rt. Rev. Msgr. Joseph L. Bernardin, Chancellor of the Diocese of Charleston; the Most Rev. Thomas J. McDonough, J.C.D., Bishop of Savannah, and the Rt. Rev. Msgr. Andrew J. McDonald, J.C.D., S.T.L., Chancellor; the Rt. Rev. Msgr. George L. Hopkins, Chancellor, and the Rev. Father John Joseph Gallagher, Archivist, of the Archdiocese of Baltimore; and the Rt. Rev. Msgr. Charles J. Plauché, J.C.L., Chancellor of the Archdiocese of New Orleans.

Similar acknowledgment for the use of original materials is made to the Rev. Father Thomas T. McAvoy, C.S.C., of the University of Notre Dame; the Rev. Father James Hennesey, S.J., of the Gregorian University in Rome (who also graciously read Chapter VIII and made numerous suggestions for its improvement); the Rev. Father William C. Repetti, S.J., Archivist of Georgetown University; M. l'Abbé Irénée Noye, P.S.S., Director of the Archives of Saint-Sulpice, Paris; Mr. Eugene P. Willging, Director of the Mullen Library, The Catholic University of America; the Rev.

Fathers Jerome Wisniewski, O.S.B., and Boniface Meyer, O.S.B., of St. Leo Abbey, St. Leo, Florida; Mr. Edward A. Egan, of Chicago; Mr. Frank Rossiter, of the Savannah *Morning News;* Mr. Walter Hartridge and Mr. Picot Floyd, of Savannah; the Rev. Father James M. Burns, S.S., Archivist of St. Mary's Seminary, Roland Park, Baltimore; the Rev. Father Lawrence E. Molumby of the Diocese of Richmond; the Rev. Father Finbar Kenneally, O.F.M., of the Academy of American Franciscan History, Washington, D. C.; Mr. Richmond D. Williams, Director, Eleutherian Mills Historical Library, Greenville, Wilmington, Delaware; and the Sisters of St. Joseph, St. Augustine, Florida.

Regrettably, the writer found no single large store of documents which might be called the Verot Papers. Most of the bishop's own manuscripts and letters received appear to have been lost or destroyed. The sources from which his life has been re-created in these pages are as scattered as the acknowledgments above. In lieu of a bibliographical essay on these sources, information on the nature and location of original and secondary materials used here has been included in the footnotes wherever pertinent.

For invaluable assistance of many kinds the writer expresses his gratitude to the Very Rev. Father John P. McCormick, S.S., Rector of Theological College, The Catholic University of America; to the Rev. Fathers John Smolko, James J. Kortendick, S.S., and Gerard S. Sloyan of the same university; to the Rt. Rev. Msgr. T. James McNamara, V.G., P.A., Rector of the Cathedral of St. John the Baptist, Savannah; to the Rt. Rev. Msgr. Richard C. Madden, St. Andrew's Church, Myrtle Beach, S. C.; to the Rev. Fathers Irvine Nugent, Chancellor, and Thomas R. Gross of the Diocese of St. Augustine; to Dr. Willard E. Wight of the Georgia Institute of Technology; to Mr. William E. May of the Bruce Publishing Company; to Mr. Gabriel Rebaf; and to his typists, Mrs. Phyllis Durell and Mrs. Ethel Reidy.

Responsibility for any errors of fact or judgment is, of course, the writer's own.

Mission Nombre de Dios
St. Augustine, Florida
February 4, 1964

FOREWORD

THREE MONTHS before the firing on Fort Sumter, Augustin Verot, Vicar Apostolic of Florida, preached a sermon in which he summarized Catholic teaching on human slavery and gave a spirited defense of the property rights of those who owned slaves. When the sermon was printed the Archbishop of Baltimore would not allow its circulation in his see city because, as its author told Bishop Lynch of Charleston, it was thought "it would create an excitement." During a fair portion of Verot's life he was charged with "creating an excitement" of one kind or another, a fact that accounts in part for the highly interesting character of Father Gannon's biography. Born in France and trained for the priesthood by the Sulpicians at their seminary in Issy, where he had as classmates Félix Dupanloup, the future famous Bishop of Orléans, and Henri Dominique Lacordaire, O.P., the noted preacher, Verot was ordained to the priesthood in 1828, and after joining the Society of St. Sulpice he was assigned by his superiors to the United States. His departure coincided with an historic moment for France, for two days before the young priest sailed on August 1, 1830, Louis Philippe, Duke of Orléans, was offered the lieutenant-generalship of the realm as a consequence of the July Revolution.

For the first twenty-eight years of his residence in the New World Father Verot served either as a professor in the Sulpicians' American seminaries where he usually taught science, or as a parish priest until his consecration, in April, 1858, as the first Vicar Apostolic of Florida. His advent to the South came at a time when the nation was moving inexorably toward the secession crisis, with the months between March and October of that year marked by the agitation over the Lecompton Constitution for Kansas, the Lincoln-Douglas debates, and the speech of Senator

William H. Seward which warned of an "irrepressible conflict" ahead. With many Americans' attention at the present time focused on the centennial of the Civil War, the appearance of this scholarly work, which reveals so much about the Catholic Church in the South during the slavery controversy, the war, and Reconstruction, is of more than ordinary importance.

According to Father Gannon, there were four issues or events during Verot's episcopacy (1858–1876) with which the bishop was conspicuously identified. Two of these were matters of major concern to the State as well as to the Church, namely, the Negro (both slave and free) and the Civil War. A third was a mixed problem that involved both Church and State in the relationship of private and religious schools to the public school system; but for the great majority of Americans the fourth issue, Vatican Council I, was only a remote ecclesiastial affair that touched them hardly at all. Given that Bishop Verot was prominent in these matters, some may wonder why he has had to wait until almost ninety years after his death for a full-length biography. The delay has been due to a number of factors, such as the relatively scant knowledge of the man even by historians of the American Church and Verot's personal idiosyncrasies, which have tended to create an image that has made it open to question whether he was worthy of serious investigation. There has also been a vague and widespread impression that the sources for his life were no longer extant; and the further fact that most of the really significant history of Catholicism in the past century was made in the North, not the South, has contributed to keeping Augustin Verot in the wings rather than permitting him to move to the center of the stage.

There is truth in all these points, but Father Gannon has proved that either in some cases it is only a half-truth or the impression has sprung from rumor and imagination. Undoubtedly Verot was a churchman worthy of a biographer's time and labor. While he might, indeed, be described as something of a "character," he was, nonetheless, a man of genuine integrity and high intelligence. His unconventional views — and the quite unconventional way he had of expressing them — invited opposition and even ridicule, but these opinions and judgments were at the same time sufficiently sound to recommend themselves today to more men than would be pre-

pared to accept the attitude and judgment of many of Verot's
episcopal contemporaries. Unfortunately, much documentary evidence has, indeed, disappeared, but the rewarding results of Father
Gannon's research are apparent throughout this work and offer proof
that if the historian is patient, persistent, and thorough, he can
at times turn up a body of data that others would have thought
impossible. As to the point about the most important Catholic
history being enacted north of the Mason and Dixon Line, that
is obvious. But it does not follow that southern Catholicism has
nothing to offer the historian and those who read what he writes.
In fact, the amount of first-rate history embodied in this volume
will, I suspect, come as a surprise to many. And in that connection,
one can be grateful that this lively material found its way into the
hands of one whose sensitive use of the English language has
enabled him not only to arouse the reader's interest but to sustain it.

It is not the purpose of a foreword to relate in detail the con-
tents of the book it is supposed to introduce, and I have no intention of violating that well-established rule. But I trust that it
will not be out of place to mention a few incidents that may serve
to illustrate why Augustin Verot might well attract any biographer.
For example, that he should have advanced the traditional teaching
of Catholic theologians that slavery was not *in se* evil was to be
expected. But Bishop Verot was far from consigning the slaves
to their fate and letting it go at that. In a pastoral letter of
January, 1861, he urged that a code be drawn up and adopted by
the Confederate government that would clearly define the slaves'
rights as well as their duties. "This will be the means," he said,
"of proving to the world that the South is on the side of justice,
morality, reason, and religion." That Father Gannon frankly recog-
nizes the bishop's failure to face up realistically to the fact that
the South's troubles were in good measure of its own making is
a further recommendation of his book. The author's avoidance of
an uncritical effort to sustain Verot on all fronts, such as the latter's
attempt to reconcile a theological defense of slavery and his political defense of the South's rights, as well as his later mistakes in
the heat of debate during Vatican Council I, increase the confidence
of the reader in Father Gannon's ability to write history and not
hagiography.

Needless to say, the invasion of portions of his ecclesiastical jurisdiction by Union armies greatly complicated Bishop Verot's task as, for example, when the northern troops occupied Florida early in 1862 and sent so many Catholic families into flight that the Sisters of Mercy's academy in St. Augustine was virtually deprived of its student body. The bishop thereupon undertook personally to move seven of the eleven sisters to Columbus, Georgia, and during the trip there occurred a number of extraordinary happenings, both comic and grave, including their being halted and investigated by the Union forces when a rumor spread through the countryside that Verot was transporting slaves into Georgia in the guise of Sisters of Mercy! The hardship of the war told on the bishop, as it did on everyone else, and in the autumn of that year he spoke of his war weariness to Bishop Lynch and he remarked, "Sometimes I wish I was in France to represent things there in their true light and cause perhaps an intervention from the Emperor [Napoleon III]." It is intriguing to speculate on what the reactions of Lincoln's Secretary of State William H. Seward and his aides would have been had they got wind of this!

But Bishop Verot's fatigue by no means led him to give up the fight. On the contrary, his pastoral letter of November, 1863, contained a stout refutation of the charges against the South by John Hughes, Archbishop of New York, that won praise for him and his fellow bishops of the Confederacy from the Richmond *Whig* as "warm supporters of the Southern cause, and zealous advocates of the justice upon which this war of defense is conducted." One of the saddest episodes of Verot's wartime experiences — and at the same time one of the most fascinating to read — involved the religious ministrations of himself and his priests at Andersonville, Georgia, where in the winter of 1863–1864 there came into existence the notorious prison camp. Verot estimated that Andersonville contained "Yankee prisoners to the number of thirty thousand, one fifth perhaps being Catholics." The description given by the bishop and his priests of the conditions at Andersonville that took over 10,000 lives between June and November of 1864 adds further grim details of the horrors of that dread spot.

Bishop Verot's concern for the spiritual welfare of all who came within his jurisdiction, such as the northern prisoners at Andersonville, had from his first days in the South embraced the Negroes, whether they were slaves or free men. Many months before the Second Plenary Council of Baltimore in October, 1866, issued its directives concerning the Negro apostolate, Verot had engaged Sisters of St. Joseph from his native town of Le Puy in France to come to teach the colored. In a letter to the superior on February 21, 1866, his aim was stated with unmistakable clarity. He said, "I want you to understand fully and clearly that it is for the Negroes and for them almost exclusively that I have arranged for the daughters of your Order to come into the diocese." Their arrival in August of that year enabled the bishop to anticipate the plenary council's legislation which, as it turned out, proved to be so ineffective in winning the Negroes for Catholicism. In fact, in describing these postwar Catholic efforts for the Negro in the South, Verot's biographer remarks, "The only success story in these years was in Florida and Georgia."

In March, 1870, Bishop Verot was transferred from the See of Savannah to that of St. Augustine. But before the change became fully operative his earlier labors to win public aid for the Catholic schools of Savannah were rewarded. He had made his first attempt in March, 1862, but it had ended in failure as had several subsequent efforts. But Verot never admitted defeat easily, and by reason of his persistence the Savannah Board of Education at length voted in May, 1870, to take in the city's Catholic schools, an arrangement which lasted until 1916, although attempts to win a similar arrangement for the Catholic schools in Atlanta and in Florida were not successful.

Finally, of the major movements and events with which Augustin Verot's name was associated, Vatican Council I afforded him, perhaps, the most colorful and dramatic interval of his eighteen years as a bishop. The opinions he expressed both within and outside the council shocked more conservative prelates and gave rise to rumors that he was not sound in his faith. At no time, however, was Verot, as some maintained, a liberal in the philosophical and doctrinaire sense of the term, even if he was correctly described as Gallican in his tendencies. Verot's thinking was definitely what one might call that of a progressive, and had he been present in the early stages of Vatican Council II, Pope John XXIII would have had no more enthusiastic supporter of his policy of the *aggiornamento* than this bishop from the American South. His interventions in the conciliar debates began with a speech on

January 3, 1870, and of this and his later appearances on the rostrum his biographer has said:

> Sometimes in exaggerated form, causing laughter or rebuke, sometimes careless of protocol and ceremony, but always straightforward and plain, Verot would give the assembled bishops a lesson in what it meant to be an American.

Thus in his speech during the debates on the schema *De Fide Catholica*, Verot urged the Fathers to assure the scientific world that no condemnation of science was contemplated. He hoped that the council would candidly admit the error of the seventeenth-century churchmen who condemned Galileo and have the Church vindicate the latter's reputation, and he would extend every liberty to geologists to discover what they could "about the age of the earth and about the actual duration of the 'six days' of creation." At the same time he lamented that so much of the council's time and energy should be given to the condemnation of German philosophical errors when, he maintained, it would be more to the profit of all concerned if the council would define that a Negro had a soul since there were those who denied that he had. It was little wonder that Verot's interventions should have attracted widespread attention and that the correspondent of the Chicago *Tribune* should have described his speech of January 3 as "the most remarkable ever heard in the Eternal City since the days of Rienzi. . . ."

Bishop Verot was vigorously opposed to the definition of papal infallibility on which the council began debate on May 13. Two weeks later the Bishop of St. Augustine spoke, and when some of his statements brought laughter from certain bishops, he coolly remarked, "It is easier to laugh than to answer." The ecumenists of Vatican Council II would applaud if they had heard him say in this speech of May 28:

> I confess frankly that this council gave me high hopes of obtaining some reconciliation for the Protestants — high hopes, to be sure, if the exposition of doctrine made by this council were made plain, mild, and soothing — as far as the truth will bear — concerning those points which are subjects of controversy between Catholics and Protestants. . . .

To Giulio Arrigoni, Archbishop of Lucca, Verot's effort on this occasion was but another of "his seriocomic discourses," but he had to concede that it held the "firm attention of the Fathers for an hour and a half."

That the Bishop of St. Augustine at times went too far was true as, for example, when he rose to speak on June 6, acknowledged that a cloture had been voted on the infallibility debate, but contended that as a bishop he felt he should spread the truth whenever the occasion presented itself. There then followed a detailed criticism of the preamble to the controversial decree, and to the proponents' declaration that what they proposed was the long-established faith of the Universal Church, Verot answered, "The truth is that the doctrine is not according to the long-established and persistent faith of the Church but according to the whims of Ultra-Montanists." That this should have occasioned "murmurs" in the council hall and a rebuke from the presiding cardinal was hardly surprising. Verot was still not dissuaded or discouraged, and on June 30 he became the last American to address the council in another hour and a half speech that rehearsed the reasons for his opposition. But it was all to no avail, and when the time arrived for the final vote on July 18, like so many of the other inopportunists, Verot was absent. In spite of defeat, however, he was among the first of the opponents to send in his adhesion to the newly defined dogma in a letter of July 25 addressed to the secretary of the council.

It is a pleasure, then, to welcome this scholarly addition to the literature on American Catholicism, and it is especially welcome by reason of the scarcity of serious and up-to-date works on the history of the Church in the South. The author has rescued from relative obscurity one of the most lively personalities in the Catholic story of the United States, a bishop whose integrity of life was, in a sense, reflected in the words of his cathedral rector who asked in his funeral eulogy:

Who ever heard him boast, speak of himself; who knew him proud, self-conceited; when did he ever complain, show even indignation, except when the cause of God and the Church was in question; what duty however painful did he not fulfill?

For the opportunity to become acquainted with such a man, students of American religious and social history will thank Father Gannon, as they will likewise be grateful for the combination of scholarship and literary skill that he has brought to his task.

JOHN TRACY ELLIS

Professor of Church History
University of San Francisco

CONTENTS

REBEL BISHOP

CHAPTER I

FROM FRANCE TO FLORIDA

ON FRIDAY, JUNE 9, 1876, Augustin Verot, first Bishop of St. Augustine, was aged 71 years, two weeks, and two days. He had just returned to his episcopal residence in the old Spanish city that was his see after a lengthy visitation of the far-flung Florida diocese — a visitation that was marked, wrote one of his aides, by "sleepless nights, protracted fasts, exposure, long and interminable rides through roads often impassable, in wretched and incommodious stage coaches." He said Mass at the usual hour and had a breakfast of eggs, but afterward complained of fatigue and of a mild "indisposition." He saw a doctor and retired to his room. At sundown, after praying his Office, he went to bed, and bade the priests who lived with him do the same.

The next morning, asked how he spent the night, the bishop answered with a smile, *"La nuit est longue à la douleur qui veille,"* and added that it was the anniversary day of his ordination to the order of deacon. He greeted two Sisters of St. Joseph who had come from their nearby convent to nurse him. He ate lightly, and during the course of the morning he appeared to improve. But at 1:30 in the afternoon, while one of the sisters in attendance left his room to summon a servant, the old man dropped his hands upon the bedspreads and watched the shadows rush together into a gloom that his eyes could no longer pierce. "He was a man," said the young Bishop James Gibbons of Richmond, "who literally died in harness, who succumbed to sickness only when he succumbed to death. And after fifty years' sacerdotal life, he descended below the horizon without a single cloud to darken his fair name."[1]

---

[1] Sermon at the consecration of Verot's successor to the See of St. Augustine, Bishop John Moore, Charleston, South Carolina, May 13, 1877; quoted in John T. Reily, *Collections and Recollections in the Life and Times of Cardinal Gibbons* (Martinsburg, W. Va.: Harold Print, 1892–1893), II, 109.

1

The future Cardinal Archbishop of Baltimore spoke as much in charity as he did in truth: clouds had indeed darkened the bishop's fair name, and they would prevail in some corners of the sky for many years to come. Perhaps no American bishop of his era, which was, strictly speaking, the decade 1860–1870, had been so blunt and straightforward in manner, so incorrigibly outspoken, as Augustin Verot. None perhaps had been, all at the same time, so uncompromising in his devotion to the Church, so committed to old political principles and to new social goals, so desirous to mitigate the traditional sharp separation in American Catholicism between a spiritual Church and the secular environment, and — the unpardonable sin — so in advance of his time. For all this Augustin Verot paid the price. He was criticized and ridiculed in his own time, and he was maligned by history and by memory. Union generals who had to deal with the bishop during the Civil War rebuked him for "disrespectful and unbecoming language" and described him as "captious rather than charitable," "purposely vexatious," "warped" in judgment, and "embittered" in expression. At Vatican Council I Bishop Verot's unexpected burst of oratory brought forth laughter and shouts of disapproval, and criticism that he was a "sarcastic orator" who "spoke absurdly" and uttered "buffooneries" that were "contumelious" and "foolish," that he possessed "an audacity . . . that sometimes went beyond the bounds," that his actions were "peculiar" — that he was the council's *enfant terrible.*

This last derisive title was later pinned on him for posterity by the first extensive treatment of the Vatican Council in the English language.[2] Among most people who have any acquaintance with his name, he is remembered by this *sobriquet.* Some remember him as the bishop who told the council that Negroes did not have souls, though what he said was in fact directly and explicitly the opposite. In sum, he became known popularly as something of a joke. Only a few historians have discerned his true character and genius. It was left to an historian of stated unfriendliness toward

---

[2] Cuthbert Butler, *The Vatican Council* (London: Longmans, 1930), I, 136. Roger Aubert, in his *Le pontificat de Pie IX (1846–1878)* (*Histoire de l'Eglise*), Vol. 21, Fliche et Martin, eds. (Paris: Bloud & Gay, 1952), also points to Verot's "enfantillages au concile du Vatican," 433. See also J. Ryan Beiser, *The Vatican Council and the American Secular Newspapers, 1869–70* (Washington, D. C.: The Catholic University of America Press, 1941), 30; Francis Dvornik, *The Ecumenical Councils* (New York: Hawthorn, 1961), 96.

the Vatican Council to make the first rectifying assessment of Verot's role in that event: "Verot," he wrote, "was interrupted by men of whom the majority possessed not half his learning, nor half of his practical achievements for the Church."[3]

The record discloses that, for all his bluntness and seeming imprudence, Augustin Verot was a man of high intelligence, of keen vision, of marked sanctity, and of driving zeal who spent one of the most fascinating ten years of life in the history of the American Church. While everything he did that was of consequence in the nation's religious life he did within the ten-year span of the decade 1860–1870, he crowded into those years sufficient accomplishment and vision in advance of his time to make him at home, had he lived, in any of the decades remaining of the nineteenth century — and even, it may be argued, into the present century.

In what were perhaps the four leading issues before the Church in that decade: (1) the Negro question, (2) Civil War politics, (3) the common, or public, school crisis, and (4) representation of American interests at the Vatican Council, no bishop was more conspicuous than Augustin Verot. He was among the first prelates to take serious notice of the challenge presented America and the Church by the freed Negroes; and by doing something about it he became the first important American Catholic figure who attempted a solution of that problem. He was apparently the first bishop since the founding of the American hierarchy in 1790 to take a public stand on a national political issue not directly affecting Catholicism. He was the first postwar prelate to achieve a major accommodation between the parochial and public school systems. And, at the Vatican Council, he was the most vocal figure in urging the Church's recognition of the pragmatic character of the new American society, and of the need for adapting the presence of the Church to the demands of the American scene. In each of these four categories Verot was a prophetic figure — a prototype who anticipated, in either large degree or small, the Catholic liberal movement of the 1890's, the social concern that characterized American Catholicism after World War I, and the "aggiornamento" demands that followed convocation of Vatican Council II.

Verot may also be described as a representative figure for his own

[3] George Gordon Coulton, *Papal Infallibility* (London: The Faith Press, Inc., 1932), 166.

time, at least for that decade between the outbreak of Civil War
and the opening of Vatican Council I. Other periods have fared
better at the historian's hand. Colonial and early national Catholicism (1565–1820), the early middle period Church with its nativist
troubles (1820–1860), the era of emerging liberal Catholicism
(1871–1900) have all been treated generously. Among both Catholic
and non-Catholic studies of the American Church the 1860's have
formed something of an ellipsis. One reason for this neglect lies
probably in the fact that historians of the American Church have
usually written a period's history around one man, or around one
group of men. In nineteenth-century studies these men have almost
always been bishops. Thus, John Carroll of Baltimore and John
England of Charleston are selected to epitomize Catholicism for
the early national period, John Hughes of New York for the early
middle period, and the celebrated company of James Gibbons of
Baltimore, John Ireland of St. Paul, John Lancaster Spalding of
Peoria, Bernard J. McQuaid of Rochester, and Michael A. Corrigan
of New York for the last quarter and *fin de siècle*.

For the 1860's there has been, seemingly, no comparable figure.
The Archbishops of Baltimore during these years, Francis Patrick
Kenrick (1851–1863) and Martin J. Spalding (1864–1872), were
nominal spokesmen for the American hierarchy.[4] But they have not
yet been seized upon as types for their times — perhaps for this
reason: that each man, in this important moment, took a position
at variance with the views of the majority of his fellow bishops.
Thus, in the Civil War, Kenrick chose to run with the fox and
hunt with the hound, when most of his fellow prelates had opted
vigorously for one side or the other. And Spalding, in the course of
the Vatican Council, radically changed his mind on what should
be the American position on papal infallibility, adopting in the
end a position that was not supported by most of his American
colleagues. In neither man has the historian so far found a prototype for an era in American Catholicism that was clearly distinguished by several great causes, and by an increasingly positive

---

[4] See John J. O'Shea, *The Two Kenricks* [the other being Peter Richard, Arch-
bishop of St. Louis] (Philadelphia: J. J. McVey, 1904); James D. Brokkage,
Francis Patrick Kenrick's Opinion on Slavery (Washington, D. C.: The Catholic
University of America Press, 1955); John Lancaster Spalding, *The Life of the
Most Reverend M. J. Spalding, D.D.* (New York: Christian Press Association,
1873).

attitude toward the place of Catholicism in American society. Perhaps the muse will feel more comfortable with Augustin Verot, Vicar Apostolic of Florida, third Bishop of Savannah, and, finally, first Bishop of St. Augustine.

On the left bank of the Loire, between the Borne and Dolaison Rivers, in the Department of Haute-Loire in south central France, stands the city of Le Puy. In 1805 it was a modest town of only several thousand people, most of whom were engaged in the manufacture of lace. Le Puy had been the see of a diocese since the earliest centuries of French Christianity, and it boasted in Notre-Dame du Puy one of the finest cathedrals of Roman architecture in France. The town was also a pilgrimage center of wide reknown: each year on August 15 tens of thousands of pilgrims wound through her ancient streets in processions honoring the Black Virgin. Dominating the town was a hill, Mont d'Anis, from which rose a towering shaft of bare rock that the natives called Corneille. Below the shadow cast by that rock, on May 23, 1805, Magdeleine Marcet gave birth to a son, Jean-Pierre Augustin Marcellin Vérot. The infant bore the same name as his father, a dealer in lacework.[5]

Of the young Verot's formative years in home and school at Le Puy there is no known record. At sixteen years of age he

[5] Baptismal register, Cathédrale Notre-Dame du Puy, May 23, 1805. The priest who baptized Verot mistakenly recorded his name as "Veron." The date of birth is given as May 2, 1804, in Henry Peter Clavreul, "A Sermon Delivered in the Cathedral of St. Augustine on Sunday, July 16th, A.D. 1876, by Rev. Father Clavreul, Rector of the Cathedral," Benedict Roth, ed., *Brief History of the Churches of the Diocese of St. Augustine, Florida,* Part 4 (St. Leo, Fla.: Abbey Press, 1923), 77. This eulogy formed the principal source for the following short biographies of Verot: Richard H. Clarke, *Lives of Deceased Bishops of the Catholic Church in the United States* (rev. ed. New York: The Author, 1888), III, 94–108; John Gilmary Shea, *History of the Catholic Church in the United States* (New York: The Author, 1886–1892), IV, 210–211; Charles George Herbermann, *The Sulpicians in the United States* (New York: Encyclopedia Press, 1916), 246–264; Louis Bertrand, *Bibliothèque Sulpicienne ou Histoire littéraire de la Compagnie de Saint-Sulpice* (Paris: Alphonse Picard et fils, 1900), III, 369–372; Richard J. Purcell, "Jean Marcel Pierre Auguste Verot," Dumas Malone, ed., *Dictionary of American Biography* (New York: Scribner's, 1936), XIX, 252–253. Two recent studies are Benjamin J. Blied, "Bishop Verot of Savannah," *The Georgia Review,* V (Summer, 1951), 162–169; and Willard E. Wight, "Bishop Verot and the Civil War," *CHR,* XLVII (July, 1961), 153–163. Verot is treated briefly in Benjamin J. Blied, *Catholics and the Civil War* (Milwaukee, Wis.: The Author, 1945), and at some length in Vincent de Paul McMurray, S.S., "The Catholic Church During Reconstruction, 1865–1877" (unpublished master's thesis: The Catholic University of America, 1950). Certain biographical details also

matriculated in grammar and the classics from the nearby college of Annonay, administered by the Basilian congregation.[6] On October 15, 1821, he entered the ecclesiastical seminary of Issy, near Paris, where he began philosophical and theological studies under the direction of the priests of the Society of St. Sulpice.[7] During his years at Issy, where he had for classmates Félix-Antoine-Philibert Dupanloup, later bishop of Orléans, and Jean-Baptiste Lacordaire, the soon famous Dominican preacher,[8] Verot decided to devote himself to education as a member of the Sulpician Society. He was ordained a priest on September 20, 1828, by Louis Hyacinthe de Quélen, Archbishop of Paris, and gave lectures on the natural sciences at Issy until sometime in 1830, when he was formally accepted into the Society of St. Sulpice.[9] On August 1, 1830, at the instance of the Sulpician superior general, Antoine Garnier, and under the persuasion of another Sulpician, Joseph Carrière, Verot sailed for America and a teaching post at the Sulpician college of St. Mary's in Baltimore. By plan, he was to stay in the United States for a seven-year tour of duty; as it happened he would stay for life.[10] His departure coincided with the July Revolution which drove Charles X from the throne and seated Louis Philippe in his stead. What the change from Charles' theocratic regime meant to the Church and to one of Verot's classmates was described much later by the liberal Comte de Montalembert: "In 1830 [before the Revolution of 1848] all the priests, the Abbé Lacordaire amongst others, were reduced to not going out into the street except in the

---

appear in the following obituaries: Jacksonville *Daily Florida Union,* June 13, 1876; New York *Freeman's Journal and Catholic Messenger,* June 24 and July 8, 1876; and Baltimore *Catholic Mirror,* July 1, 1876. The only published primary source for Verot himself is the bishop's diary, or "Record of the Episcopal Acts of Rt. Rev. Augustin Verot, Bishop of Savannah and Administrator Apostolic of Florida," kept August 18, 1861, to March 28, 1876, and printed in Roth, ed., *Churches of the Diocese,* Part 6, 153–178.

[6] Baltimore *Catholic Mirror,* July 1, 1876.

[7] Bertrand, *Bibliothèque sulpicienne,* 369. The Society of St. Sulpice was founded at Paris by Jean-Jacques Olier in 1642 for the purpose of educating aspirants to the diocesan priesthood. Priests of the Society came to the United States in 1791 to found a seminary at Baltimore, first of many Sulpician undertakings in this country.

[8] *Ibid.,* 369.

[9] Archives of the Grand Seminaire du Puy, citation courtesy of M. le chanoine Fayard, archivist.

[10] ASS, Paris, Verot to Très Honoré Père, September 3, 1852. These letters are translated by the author.

guise of a layman. . . . In 1848 that same Lacordaire appeared in a Dominican habit in the Assembly."[11]

Verot arrived at Baltimore after a 46-day voyage on October 14, 1830, and was immediately appointed professor of mathematics at the college.[12] St. Mary's College had begun as a seminary in 1781, became a college in 1799, and was chartered by the state of Maryland on January 19, 1805.[13] The enrollment in 1830 was 200 students. In the year following, Verot taught, in addition to mathematics, minerology, zoology, geology, and geometry.[14] In 1852, when the college closed, he was teaching mathematics, astronomy, and chemistry.[15] According to his contemporaries he enjoyed a considerable reputation as an instructor in the physical sciences, and some accounts describe him as a friend and advisor of Joseph Henry, director of the Smithsonian Institute, of Ferdinand Hassler, founder of the Coast and Geodetic Survey, and of Joseph Nicolas Nicollet, of the French Bureau of Longitude (at the time in the service of the United States Government). Although a search through the papers and writings of these men turns up no mention of Verot in confirmation of these accounts,[16] some brief quotation from the accounts may be of interest. One of Verot's students, A. Leo Knott, later Attorney General for Maryland and Assistant Postmaster General under President Cleveland, recollected in 1891:

---

[11] Address of Montalembert, Malines, Belgium, 1863, quoted in E. E. Y. Hales, *Pio Nono* (New York: Image, 1962), 279.

[12] Bertrand, *Bibliothèque sulpicienne*, 369. Verot's first faculties as a priest of the Archdiocese of Baltimore, dated the day after his arrival from France, are in the ADSA.

[13] Bertrand C. Steiner, *History of Education in Maryland* (Washington, D. C.: Government Printing Office, 1894), 274.

[14] James Joseph Kortendick, S.S., "The History of St. Mary's College, Baltimore, 1799–1852" (unpublished master's thesis, The Catholic University of America, 1942), 106. A mathematics textbook in Verot's own hand is preserved in the MCND; a photocopy is in the ADSA. Cf. the Baltimore *Chronicle*, February 5, 1831, which carried a long report on the college, with its "complete Philosophical and Chemical Apparatus," and its library "of about 10,000 volumes." "The instruction in the Physical Sciences is not confined to a popular exposition but is grounded on the solid base of Mathematical Analysis."

[15] Archives of St. Mary's Seminary, Roland Park, Baltimore, "The Calendar of St. Mary's College, 1851."

[16] The papers, including correspondence, of Joseph Henry (1797–1878) are in the archives of the Smithsonian Institute. The index to these holdings shows no entry under Verot's name. Similarly, there is no mention of Verot in Nathan Reingold, *Records of the Coast and Geodetic Survey, Preliminary Inventories,*

8 REBEL BISHOP

The Rev. Augustin Verot was for many years professor of higher mathematics, Astronomy, Chemistry and the Physical Sciences. He was well equipped for these functions and he discharged them with superior ability and success. He had what I have never observed in any other teacher of mathematics, the faculty of interesting while initiating his students into the obstruse studies they pursued under his direction. Conic sections grew eloquent under his treatment of them, and the curves of the parabola and hyperbola became indeed almost lines of beauty. His scientific reputation was not confined to the walls of the College, nor was his usefulness to his classes. Professor Hassler, the Founder of the Coast Survey Bureau, and Mr. Nicollet, who conducted for the Government of the United States, the exploration and first survey of the region of the Great Lakes, frequently visited the College to consult Professor Verot about the mathematical part of their important work. His counsel and assistance were given cheerfully and without reward.[17]

Notes and diaries of the period carry occasional mention of Verot's scientific work. Most of them were gathered together in 1928 by Father Arsenius Boyer (d. 1939) who, as Sulpician archivist, was in touch with men who knew Verot either as teacher or bishop. "How much chemistry was taught before 1837," Boyer's notes read, "I could not say; in that year a premium for chemistry. Rev. A. Verot was well versed in that branch. . . . Owing to his known proficiency in these branches [physics and higher mathematics] he was consulted by the learned societies of the country. Joseph Henry would write to him. . . . In 1842 a magnetic observatory was put up . . . under the advice of Mr. Nicolet [sic]. M. Verot corresponded with [Joseph] Henry of the Smithsonian Institute. Scientific reviews were received and the library supplied with good books."[18] Boyer also noted that Verot obtained for the

Number 105 (Washington, D. C.: National Archives and Record Service, 1938) which catalogs the official papers of Ferdinand Hassler (1770–1843); neither is there any mention in the Hassler private correspondence collected by Worthington Chauncy Ford, and preserved in the Manuscript Collection of the New York Public Library. The MS "Journals and Reports" of Nicollet (1786–1843) are in the Library of Congress; they do not record any contacts, personal or written, with Verot.

[17] A. Leo Knott, *Address . . . on the Occasion of the Celebration of the Centennial Anniversary of St. Mary's College and Seminary* (Baltimore: St. Mary's Seminary, 1891), 24–25. Also among Verot's students were two later governors of Maryland during the Civil War, Oden Bowie and August W. Bradford, *ibid.*, 28–33.

[18] Archives of St. Mary's Seminary, Baltimore, "Notes" of Arsenius Boyer, S.S.

college a transit, a refracting and reflecting telescope, and other scientific instruments.[19] One of Verot's colleagues, Joseph Paul Deluol, S.S., recorded in his diary for January 14, 1831: "M. Verot traces the meridian time so that St. Charles College [another Sulpician undertaking in Baltimore] may face due south."[20] But such mentions are few and meager and do not support the claim of Knott that Verot actually held a prominent place in the scientific community. Nor is there any evidence that he made any special contribution to the advance of scientific knowledge. They do help, however, to give some background in explanation of the practical bent of mind he exhibited later.

In his recollections of Verot, Knott said that "his polemical contributions to the press and periodicals of the day were frequent and were marked by a great logical power and a keen, sometimes a caustic wit, when its exercise was provoked by the display of any prejudice or unfairness on the part of his adversaries, as some of them felt to their cost on more than one occasion."[21] Because most Catholic periodical writing at the time was done anonymously or under pseudonyms such as "Veritas" or "Testis," it is not possible, except in three instances, to determine which articles Knott may have referred to.[22] In 1843 a two-part technical article on the history of the calendar appeared under Verot's name in the *United States Catholic Magazine*. It ended with an example of what Knott called Verot's "caustic" polemics:

> The *reformation* of the calendar took place in 1582, at a time when minds were greatly preoccupied with ideas of *reform*. The Church is not, then, adverse to reform, and she is the first to adopt it in those matters which admit of and require reformation, such as *human* periods and cycles, which, received at one time as correct, have proved incorrect by the accumulation of errors arising from the accumulation of centuries: thus the Church has reformed the place of the seasons, and the times of the conjunctions of sun and moon; but she cannot think of reforming the laws, dogmas, and practices handed down to us by the apostles and by Christ himself. Such, however, were the subjects on which certain men at the same

---

19 *Ibid.*

20 Archives of St. Mary's Seminary, Diary of Joseph Paul Deluol, S.S.

21 Knott, *Address*, 25.

22 Verot is not mentioned in Robert Gorman, *Catholic Apologetical Literature in the United States (1783–1858)* (Washington, D. C.: The Catholic University of America Press, 1939).

time exercised their zeal for reform. Time has shown the solidity of the two reformations: the reformation of the calendar has been admitted by all Protestant countries, whilst their pretended reformation, far from having made further progress, has been falling, and is still daily falling to pieces. The Greek Church is the only part of the civilized world which has not admitted the Gregorian reformation of the calendar: thus, according to the satirical but just remark of a judicious writer, they choose to the present day rather to be at variance with the sun, the moon, and the whole heavens, than to agree with the Roman pontiff.[23]

In the same year, Verot wrote two religious tracts for the Catholic Tract Society of Baltimore. The first of these included a rejoinder to the Know-Nothing movement:

> Some would scare the people, as if the Pope was on the point of invading the U. States at the head of an army and many imagine or have imagined to see evident signs of a fixed intention in the Pontiff to annex these States to his dominions. How supremely ridiculous is not such an idea! It has not even the *appearance* of any thing like reason, when we reflect that all the dominions of the Pope would scarcely form a larger extent than a few counties of our States, and that he is at least four thousand miles from us without a navy.[24]

A combative nature is also apparent in the other of his tracts, an historical and physical account of the appearance of comets. Here he treated, among other things, the Millerites.[25]

> All are aware that a certain Mr. Miller, assuming the prophetical trumpet, has threatened the world with a speedy destruction, and has specified the year and the month of that fearful event, about which no one knows, neither man nor angel. One would not have supposed that in this, so called, enlightened age, people would be credulous and stultified enough to give the least credit to these wild dreams; and indeed, it was but a just subject of mirth to hear that

---

[23] Vol. II (April, October, 1843), 51–53, 310–313. This magazine was published at Baltimore (1842–1849).

[24] *A Just Judgment on the Catholic Doctrines* (Baltimore: Murphy and Co., 1843), 11.

[25] Followers of William Miller, a New England farmer of Baptist background, who attracted a wide following when he predicted the end of the world for March 21 in the same year that Verot wrote. Miller's followers — variously estimated at from 50,000 to 1,000,000 — gathered on housetops and mountainsides on the dawn of the predicted day, many in "ascension" robes.

some deluded females were driven away by cold from the *ascension ground,* where they were provided with their *ascension robes:* but the farce has of late assumed an alarming aspect, on hearing that some deluded victims have lost totally that reason which they had partially surrendered at the voice of the prophet, and that others have hurried themselves into the *real* day, for fear of the *imaginary* one. We heard from a private correspondence that the prophet had read from the pulpit a letter in which the Pope was made to recant his former *superstitions,* and enrol [*sic*] himself a follower of Miller: an excellent counterpart to this would be a letter of Christ from heaven — via the Moon.[26]

Verot was never entirely happy with his situation at St. Mary's College, as his correspondence with his Sulpician superiors in Paris amply demonstrates. During the years 1848–1852 he allowed himself to complain at length about the local superior, about his colleagues, about the college itself, and about proctoring — which he detested. In 1848 the Sulpicians opened another college nearby, named St. Charles, to serve as a preparatory seminary for aspirants to the diocesan clergy. The changes in personnel that followed led Verot to fear that he would have to give up his concentration on teaching and take on some disciplinary post. In September, 1849, he wrote to the superior general of the Sulpicians in Paris: "I have lived and I continue to live constantly in the fear of receiving some supervisory assignment at the college. I have been so disgusted with the college during the last eleven years that the idea of having to supervise and punish these youngsters, and of having to live with them day in and day out, nearly makes me sick. I confess frankly my misery and my mortification: but I shall try, nevertheless, to do everything that is asked of me."[27]

What bothered Verot most, however, was not the fear of a disciplinary post (which never materialized), but the frustration of living and working under the directorship of the local Sulpician superior, Father Louis Régis Deluol, whom Verot described in his letter to Paris as being, "by reason of his age, his habits, and his turn of mind completely incapable of being superior of this house."[28]

His frustration mounting, the blunt-spoken professor wrote again to Paris in October. "In the state of crisis in which we find our-

[26] *The Comet: A Tract for the Times* (Baltimore: Murphy and Co., 1843), 2.
[27] ASS, Verot to Très Honoré Père, Baltimore, September 24, 1849.
[28] *Ibid.*

selves," he wrote, "I believe that I would be lacking in my duty if I did not tell you everything that I have in my heart." He proceeded then to give a personal assessment of his Sulpician colleagues, with special emphasis on Father Deluol:

> During the twenty years that he has been superior, he has governed the house in a totally absurd manner, never bothering himself about the rules, acting by worldly caprice, and working always with a vanity as silly as it is intolerable. Nevertheless, he has a good heart, he is affable on many occasions; he cheers people in conversation, and he has dealt fairly in the temporal administration of the house and in the handling of house funds. . . . On the other hand, as superior, he is absolutely incapable of giving any instruction whatever to seminarians. Although customarily he does not criticize at the reading, and although he no longer preaches (because of his throat, as he repeats ceaselessly), still he does explain the rule at present, and also the method of prayer. *Eh bien!* It is my duty to tell you that he speaks inanities without end.

As for Gilbert Raymond, president of the college for the past eight years and recently transferred to St. Charles, "he does not carry away the regrets of anyone," Verot wrote. "He has made so many mistakes that I could not possibly recount them." François Lhomme, professor of Latin and Greek, "is a man of regularity, of much order, and of great attachment to St. Sulpice." He has, Verot went on, "the airs of an heir presumptive, taking the better room and the better places." Oliver L. Jenkins, new president of the college recently transferred from St. Charles, "is full of good will and of virtue. If there is any means of giving new life to the college, I believe that he is the man who will do it." John Randanne, treasurer, "is seriously occupied with the well-being of the college." Peter Fredet, professor of history, "has the greatest reputation for virtue and for theological knowledge, and . . . he enjoys the most respect and esteem from his colleagues. I esteem and love him without measure." Verot concluded his long report: "Messieurs [Alexis J.] Elder and [Edward] Knight are American colleagues about whom I shall say nothing. They have had the ill fortune of having been formed in the ecclesiastical and Sulpician life by M. Deluol."[29]

In the following month, to his great surprise, Verot learned that

---

[29] *Ibid.,* October 15, 1849.

Deluol had been recalled to France. The actuality of his superior's departure wrung from Verot, who had long wished for the event, a touching reappraisal of the man. He wrote the superior general in Paris:

> [Deluol] told us that he had written you five times to resign his post and that at last he had succeeded, that he was aware that we were all tired of his authority — *nolumus hunc regnare super nos* — and that he asked pardon from everyone for the pain that he had caused us during his administration. . . . I confess that I have admired him more during these four days of preparation for his departure than I have during the whole course of my stay with him, and, to tell the truth, I would not have believed him capable of so much steadfastness and grandeur of soul. You have no idea of the heartfelt desolation that this news has brought to his numerous circle of friends . . . in the city [Baltimore]. The Archbishop [Samuel Eccleston] was as sorry as he could be. . . . My heart has been so rended that I have not been able to speak to M. D[eluol], and yet I see and I feel that M.D. could not continue as superior and . . . I rejoice at his leaving.[30]

In December, 1850, Paris announced the appointment of Father Lhomme to succeed Deluol as Sulpician superior in the United States. Verot had hoped for Father Jenkins, and so told the superior general. The promotion of Lhomme "surprised and offended" him, and he spent his Christmas retreat trying to resolve his antipathy toward the "dry, dogmatic, and incommunicative character" of François Lhomme.[31] By September, 1851, it was clear that he had not succeeded. "He is hard, dry, incisive, surly, and there is no one who can associate with him," Verot wrote. "A priest from outside said to me one day, 'What a man is M. Lhomme!' He's not a man, he's a bear."[32] Challenges more serious than personality conflicts were on their way, however. Toward the end of the school year of 1852, as Verot tells it, Lhomme one day entered the room of Father Jenkins, college president, "and told him brusquely: 'The college is suppressed, you will return to St. Charles.' "[33] Accordingly, after he had obtained more information, Jenkins announced to the press that St. Mary's "will be permanently closed for the future,"

30 *Ibid.*, November 5, 1849.
31 *Ibid.*, January 7, 1851.
32 *Ibid.*, September 11, 1851.
33 *Ibid.*, September 3, 1852.

and that, on instructions from Paris, the members of the Society
would henceforth "devote themselves exclusively to the education of
candidates for the Sacred Ministry" at nearby St. Charles.[34]

The news was no surprise to Verot, who, like the rest of the
American Sulpician company, knew since 1850 that Paris desired
them to concentrate on the original purpose of the Society, the
education of priests. It placed Verot at loose ends, however, and
made him wonder about the future. On August 5, following, he
received a letter from Father Joseph Carrière, new superior general
of the Sulpicians. Father Carrière invited Verot to transfer to the
Sulpician seminary at Montreal, Canada. It was bad enough to have
the college closed abruptly, Verot wrote back, but the invitation to
Montreal "completes my perplexity."[35] He was grateful to Father
Carrière for asking him to give his thoughts on the matter for
there was nothing he would less rather do than go to Montreal. He
reminded the superior general of the promises made to him twenty-
two years before:

> You are aware, M. le Supérieur, that the idea of coming to
> Baltimore in America did not come from me. I keep the letter of
> M. Garnier who made me the proposition, and in it he assures me
> that I might return as soon as I have shown a desire to do so. You
> remember that you yourself proposed that I go to Baltimore for
> seven years, and, look, I am here twenty-two years.

He was willing enough to stay on at his teaching post, he wrote,
so long as there was a college, despite the fact that he had grown
tired of the college and of college work. But now that the college
had been suppressed, "I had the thought that the time had come
for me to return from America. . . ." Certainly, he did not expect
to be propelled at once into another "temporary" North American
assignment. If he had absolutely to remain in teaching work on
this side of the Atlantic, then "I should much prefer to remain
at Baltimore where I have become accustomed to things, and where
I have begun to grow old, than to go off trying new things in an
unknown land, the more so as there will probably be a need here
[at St. Charles College] for a professor of mathematics and the
natural sciences."[36]

---

[34] Baltimore *American,* July 29, 1852; Baltimore *Daily Times,* July 29, 1852;
Baltimore *Sun,* July 30, 1852.
[35] ASS, Verot to Très Honoré Père, Baltimore, September 3, 1852.
[36] *Ibid.*

Verot mailed these remarks to Paris and awaited a reply. When it came, on October 19, he read with dismay that Father Carrière had rejected his proposals and the reasoning behind them. At once, Verot sat down to write again. He was now 47 years of age, at the divide between what he judged to be the waning enthusiasm of youth and the mounting resignation of old age. After a twenty-two year career of college teaching there seemed, at this point in his life, that no new conquests were likely. When the college closed, it was as though the best part of his life had closed, too. That he had spent these best years in a place for which he had no special liking, and from which he could not produce any examples of great accomplishment either for God or for man, only deepened his present anguish and sense of loss. He had, of course, no way of knowing of the high adventures that lay before him. He had no knowledge that the most enthusiastic, productive, and rewarding years of his life were not behind him, as he thought, but only a short distance ahead. And not knowing all of this, he wrote Father Carrière a second letter that was candidly revealing of his mental attitude and physical health at this critical turning point in his life:

I tried to prepare myself, I believe as best I could, for the reception of your letter. I went to kneel before the Blessed Sacrament before reading it, and after all of that, in reading it, not only have I not received either light or grace to enter into the views that you have suggested to me, but I have found there a source of insurmountable troubles, of extreme repugnances, and of frightful temptations. The series of processes by which I was induced to come to Baltimore is presented to me again, and I have seen the repetition of all that in the project of sending me to Canada. M. Garnier told me and wrote me that I might return to France when I desired, and you begin by telling me that those who are in America cannot be recalled to France. You tell me to go to America for seven years only, at the end of which I would return, and, look, twenty-two years later I cannot return. Thus, I find myself unable to believe what you tell me about going to Canada on a temporary basis.

. . . I will tell you now in a more particular manner the areas in which I have experienced repugnances and difficulties. I have contracted during a sojourn of twenty-two years at Baltimore certain habits of climate, of diet, of language, of personal relations, and of occupations that it will now be too painful to change. . . .

You seem to think that I would be useful to pastors in Montreal: I judge by that you mean that they would use me for preaching. But I pray you to recognize that I am growing old, and that I no longer have the vivacity and depth of spirit to improvise as once I was able. I could not preach in French. I do not have a single sermon written in French, and I do not feel that I am capable of picking up again in French where I left off. As for English, I would be able to preach more easily in English.

. . . I would not wish to leave you with the impression that the idea that I have begun to grow old is an exaggeration. I no longer hear well in one ear: the tympanum of the other is broken, so the doctor has told me. . . . I have no more teeth for chewing save one which is loose and is practically useless. I have lost the front teeth which are so necessary for articulation. It is true that I have been equipped with dentures. But the upper dentures which are the most essential for articulation are attached to a tooth that is broken in great part, that serves as a support only through mercy, so that within a short time I shall not be able to articulate distinctly. Furthermore, I must tell you that I am often aware of not being able to remember certain things. Believe me, M. le Supérieur, the life and the difficulty of a very painful and laborious mission during twenty-two years has just about worn me out.

. . . You speak of my reputation. I find it hard not to see a small joke in that. My reputation did not prevent the suppression of our college. I have no reputation at Montreal, and what good is there to have a reputation for ability in mathematics or physical science at establishments that people seem bent on suppressing?[37]

The poignancy of this letter, with its sounds of seeming defeatism, reminds us that Augustin Verot was no plaster saint. The letter fairly breathes with his humanity, and with his own private strain of outspokenness. Father Carrière was either moved to give up on the man or else favorably impressed, depending on how he viewed such independence in his priests, for he allowed Verot to stay on at Baltimore — Verot's preference short of returning to France. Verot was to teach philosophy at St. Charles. At the same time he received permission to devote part of his time to pastoral work at St. Paul's Church in nearby Ellicott's Mills, and at its adjoining Doughoregan Manor, ancestral home of Charles Carroll of Carrollton, only Catholic signer of the Declaration of Inde-

---

[37] *Ibid.*, October 19, 1852.

pendence.[38] As providence ruled, the new assignment was the watershed of Verot's life. It was in pastoral work that he would find himself at long last, and to everyone's surprise, including his own, enter into the sweep and challenge of great events.

In 1853 he secured release from his teaching assignment at St. Charles, and with the approval of Fathers Carrière and Lhomme, devoted himself full-time to parochial work.[39] The years that followed were an exhilarating period. He improved the Church of St. Paul at Ellicott's Mills, began construction of a new church at nearby Clarksville, and undertook instruction of the Negro slaves at Doughoregan Manor.[40] In September, 1853, he recorded that "I have been very much at peace and quite busy since I came to Ellicott's Mills, I have had a large number of First Communions, and I have been very industrious with the Negroes, who, thanks be to God, have given me their confidence."[41] In 1854 he expressed himself again as "very happy and busy in good works, above all for the poor Negroes."[42] In 1857 he wrote to a Sulpician colleague in Paris that his health was good, that his parochial programs were all going well, and that he had enjoyed great consolation in his new tasks. "What changes in the eight years since your last visit!" he wrote. "I hardly suspected anything like this at that time, above all with regard to me. Blessed be God for the fact that I am very busy; I have no time for musing about everything, as I used to do during the last years I spent at the Seminary." He expressed the hope that, despite his unworthiness, God would bring great good out of all his endeavors.[43] The future looked bright for really the first time.

What sort of man was Verot in temperament and general appear-

[38] *Ibid.*, December 6, 1852; September 9, 1853.
[39] *Ibid.*, Ellicott's Mills, September 9, 1853. Cf. Archives of St. Mary's Seminary, diary of François Lhomme, entry of September 9, 1853.
[40] *Catholic Mirror*, July 1, 1876. Verot's years at St. Paul's are mentioned briefly in Brother Fabrian of Jesus, *St. Paul's Church and Parish, Ellicott City, Maryland. Its Origins and Developments. A Sketch* (Baltimore: Foley Brothers, 1910), 12. The work is pietistic in character and of little historical value. The names of parishioners baptized by Verot are listed in an appendix. Of the first ten pastors of St. Paul's three were called to the episcopacy, Henry B. Coskery, who declined the See of Portland, [Maine], Verot, and John S. Foley, Bishop of Detroit.
[41] ASS, Verot to Très Honoré Père, Ellicott's Mills, September 9, 1853.
[42] *Ibid.*, August 7, 1854.
[43] ASS, Verot to M. Jaillon, Ellicott's Mills, March 3, 1857.

ance? The letters to Paris do not tell us everything; they were, after all, his own accounts. Physical descriptions are hard to find. A contemporary wrote of him: "In person he was under the medium height, with homely features, the embodiment of humility and meekness, without a particle of human vanity or ostentation."[44] A letter writer in 1887 said: "In height he was about five feet and had blue eyes, fair complexion."[45] A close aide to Verot in his later life described him as "indifferent to his personal appearance," but added that "his bearing never failed to impress those present." The same account went on: "In his sermons as in all of his writings, he was logical and forceful. His delivery was slow, clear, and distinct, with nothing emotional. He always addressed himself to the intellect of his hearers, whether from the natural bent of his mind or because of the long years he had given to teaching."[46] A Protestant in Savannah, Georgia, called him "saintly," and said: "He is a thorough Catholic, but he has too noble a heart to refuse love to those who differ from him in the matter of religion."[47] A newspaper article, date excised, but probably circa 1900, said: "This eminent prelate was a Frenchman — 'short, stout and unpolished,' as he used to style himself facetiously, though, in reality, few theologians of the land could compete with him in point of erudition, and he was withal a man of genial personality."[48] On his geniality and love for a good joke, all the witnesses were agreed — as would also be the 700 bishops at the Vatican Council in 1870, where Verot's droll nature became famous. William H. Gross, a successor to Verot in the See of Savannah, described him as he was in the period 1853–1858:

> You know that Bp. Verot was for many years pastor at Ellicott's City, Md. I was a little College boy at the petit séminaire — St. Charles. Bp. Verot edified us all by his assiduous care of the many slaves belonging to the Carroll family whose estates adjoined the

[44] Jeremiah J. O'Connell, *Catholicity in the Carolinas and Georgia* (New York: Sadlier & Co., 1879), 541.

[45] MCND, Mother M[ary] Lazarus to Professor Edwards, St. Augustine, Florida, November 1, 1887.

[46] Henry Peter Clavreul, *Notes on the Catholic Church in Florida, 1565–1876* (St. Leo, Fla.: Abbey Press, 1910), 21.

[47] Gallow Glass, in Savannah *Daily Herald,* January 19, 1865.

[48] Archives of the Diocese of Savannah, undated newspaper clipping under the title "The Bishops of Savannah." The style of type places it at about the year 1900.

College grounds. I remember him also as a great favorite among the College boys. His many anecdotes, his love for a good joke, and his hearty laugh endeared him to young hearts. . . . For his many saintly qualities, his unbounded zeal, his unsparing toil, and great asceticism he was regarded as a saint by all.[49]

As A. Leo Knott remembered him, from the same time:

Withal, he had the simplicity of a child. He had a ready interest, and would sometimes take an active part in our boyish sports. . . . He was a great and indefatigable pedestrian, as all of us in the classes of botany and geology had reason to know, who accompanied him in his scientific excursions around Baltimore.[50]

Father Boyer's "Notes" recall him as a frequent member of swimming excursions from St. Mary's College, particularly to the Patapsco River, where a small island, one mile west of Woodstock, still bears the name "Verot's Island."[51] On the occasion of his death in 1876, the Baltimore *Catholic Mirror* wrote:

Although rigid to himself, his piety was not of a demure or sullen cast; on the contrary, he was remarkable for his cheerfulness of manner, and even for his joviality in social intercourse. . . . His contributions to the *United States Catholic Magazine,* on various doctrinal matters, and his tract on the Comet in 1843 . . . were characterized no less by genial wit and humor than by varied learning and sound criticism.[52]

Father Verot's qualities did not go unnoticed by members of the American hierarchy. In March, 1856, Bishop John Hughes of New York sought to persuade him to assume the position of superior in a seminary that Hughes planned to build at Troy, New York.[53] How Verot reacted to the offer is not recorded, although he did not accept. In the following year Archbishop Francis Patrick Kenrick of Baltimore sent Verot's name to Rome as a candidate for Bishop of Savannah, a see vacant since the death in 1854 of Francis X. Gartland.[54] Rome did not choose him for that post but decided

[49] MCND, Gross to Richard Clarke, Savannah, March 16, 1884.
[50] Knott, *Address,* 25.
[51] Cited in Hebermann, *Sulpicians,* 247.
[52] July 1, 1876.
[53] Archives of St. Mary's Seminary, Lhomme diary, entry of March, 1856.
[54] MCND, Kenrick to Archbishop John Baptist Purcell of Cincinnati, Baltimore, May 5, 1857. Archbishop Kenrick had acceded to the See of Baltimore in August, 1851, following the death of Samuel Eccleston; he had earlier been Coadjutor

instead that Verot would make a suitable prelate for the new
Vicariate of Florida. On February 1, 1858, the pastor of Ellicott's
Mills received a letter from Archbishop Kenrick:

> I feel great pleasure in informing you that the Bulls of your
> appointment to the Vicariate of Florida are in my possession. The
> Cardinal Prefect of the Congregation of the Propagation of the
> Faith urges dispatch. I trust that you will recognize the divine will
> in this matter. It will gratify me to see you as soon as convenient.
> Dr. Lynch is appointed to the See of Charleston.[55]

Verot was astonished: "The news came to me like a bolt of
thunder."[56] He wrote to Paris: "I want very much to refuse. . . .
There is no order from the Pope to accept: but the Archbishop told
me that if I refuse, an express order will come. He has pushed me
hard to accept, and to accept *toute de suite.*"[57] To Bishop John
McGill of Richmond, Verot wrote: "I have not accepted the office
offered to me; neither do I feel at liberty to do so, before I hear
of the Superior of St. Sulpice in Paris. I would have refused at
once, had I not been afraid of going against the will of God, &
giving bad example, the post being one of labor, privation & suffering."[58] Verot gave as his principal reason for wanting to decline
the episcopacy the fact that "I have always wanted to live and
die a Sulpician."[59] He knew that it was Sulpician policy to require
those who were consecrated to the episcopacy to resign from the

---

Bishop of Philadelphia. John Barry was consecrated for Savannah on August 2,
1857, and died November 21, 1859, from which date another interregnum ensued
until the summer of 1862.

[55] ADSA, Kenrick to Verot, Baltimore, February 1, 1858. The Vicariate of
Florida was actually erected in early 1857 and offered to Francis Patrick Mc-
Farland, a priest of the Diocese of Albany [New York], on March 7, 1857. Mc-
Farland declined the honor only to be appointed Bishop of Hartford the following
year. See ADSA, Decretum Sacrae Congregationis de Propaganda Fide, Rome,
December 11, 1857. Lynch was Patrick Neison Lynch (1817–1882), consecrated
Bishop of Charleston on March 14, 1858. A great friendship would build up
between Verot and Lynch during the Civil War, when they were neighboring
prelates, at Savannah and Charleston, and of like minds concerning the justice of
the war.

[56] ASS, Verot to Très Honoré Père, Ellicott's Mills, February 4, 1858.
[57] *Ibid.*
[58] Archives of the Diocese of Richmond, Verot to McGill, Ellicott's Mills,
February 11, 1858.
[59] ASS, Verot to Très Honoré Père, Ellicott's Mills, February 4, 1858.

Society. "Is that not for me," he wrote to Paris, "sufficient motive to refuse in a peremptory manner?" He had other reasons, too:

> I sense an extreme reluctance at leaving my post, where I believe I have done some good, and where I have labored with tranquility and peace of spirit and of heart. . . . I am getting old [53 years]. I no longer have any upper teeth. I am a little hard of hearing; the tympanum of the right ear is torn. The heat bothers me terribly here during the month of July, when I have some difficulty in handling my affairs. What will it be like in Florida?[60]

Sulpician headquarters in Paris replied on February 16 urging Verot to accept the nomination. The letter reminded him, however, that he "must cease to be a member of the Society."[61] Verot did accept, sometime before February 27.[62] Accordingly, on Sunday, April 25, 1858, in ceremonies at the metropolitan church, or cathedral, of Baltimore, Archbishop Kenrick raised Verot to the dignity of titular Bishop of Danaba, *in partibus infidelium,* and Vicar Apostolic of Florida. Assisting the Archbishop were Bishops John McGill of Richmond and John Barry of Savannah. Newly consecrated Bishop Patrick N. Lynch of Charleston was present in the sanctuary. Father Benedict Madeore, pastor of St. Augustine, Florida, served as one of the chaplains to Verot. Seminarians from St. Charles sang the Mass in Gregorian chant. The sermon was preached by Father Charles J. White of St. Matthew's Church in Washington, D. C. As the Baltimore *Catholic Mirror* reported it:

> Toward the end of his discourse, the Rev. Preacher spoke in happy terms of his distinguished friend, who was that day clothed with the dignity of the episcopal office. It was, no doubt, real information to the majority of those present to hear that, more than two hundred years ago, our holy religion was in a flourishing condition in Florida, which then possessed many churches and convents, served and occupied by men of Apostolic zeal and piety. A few poor churches, and three or four laborious priests, are all the new diocese [*sic*] has to boast of at present. . . . The preacher happily predicted

---

[60] *Ibid.*

[61] ASS, M. Fauconges to Monsieur et Très Honoré Père, Paris, February 16, 1858.

[62] MCND, [Bishop] Martin J. Spalding [of Louisville] to Purcell, Louisville, February 27, 1858: ". . . Dr. Verot has accepted the Vicariate and is to be consecrated some time in April." Cf. MCND, Carrière to Purcell, Baltimore, March 2, 1858. Verot's episcopal faculties were sent from Rome on April 18, 1858; original is in the ADSA.

that the industry of Bishop Verot, with the blessings of Divine Providence, would soon make Florida, in religion, truly deserving of its beautiful name.[63]

Six years earlier it had seemed to Verot that the high-water mark of his career had passed into memory. Yet now he was *Bishop* Verot. New fields were suddenly thrust open to him, and responsibilities unlike any that he had known before were laid upon his shoulders. One week after his consecration, Bishop Verot took part in the Ninth Provincial Council of Baltimore, his first as a prelate.[64] And on May 22 he left for Florida accompanied by Father Madeore.[65] His departure was marked by numerous demonstrations of affection.[65] The scene at Doughoregan Manor was especially touching. The Negro slaves of the manor assembled in their best attire and sang of their loss in strains of sacred music. Each one brought a present. As the bishop walked among them, the slaves knelt reverently to receive his blessing.[66] Warm tributes and fond farewells were also paid him at St. Charles College, at Ellicott's Mills. Sykesville, and other communities that had known his ministry. The Young Catholics' Friend Society of Ellicott's Mills accompanied the bishop to his ship at the wharfs of Baltimore. There the members of the Society recalled to him the words of God to Abraham (*Genesis* 12:1): "Go forth out of thy country, and from thy kindred, and out of thy father's house, and come into the land which I shall shew thee."[67]

The land called Florida, discovered by Juan Ponce de Léon in 1513, was a state of the American Union in 1857. Geographically a peninsula, it was bounded on the north by Alabama and Georgia, east by the Atlantic, south by the Straits of Florida and Gulf of Mexico, and west by the Gulf and Perdido River. Its name of Florida was originally applied by Spanish discoverers and pioneers to continental territory extending northward to Virginia and westward indefinitely from the Atlantic. During successive Spanish,

---

[63] May 1, 1858.
[64] *Catholic Mirror*, May 8, 1858. Verot had taken part as a theologian in the Provincial Councils of 1843 and 1846, and as one of the three theologians to Archbishop Kenrick in the First Plenary, or National, Council in 1852; *Catholic Mirror*, May 15, 1852.
[65] *Ibid.*, May 29, 1858.
[66] Clarke, *Deceased Bishops*, 97.
[67] *Catholic Mirror*, July 3, 1858.

English, and American occupations, the territory of this name was delimited to the boundaries existing in 1857 and at the present. Ecclesiastically, the peninsula had been under the jurisdiction, successively, of the Dioceses of Santiago de Cuba (1565–1787), San Cristobal de Habana (1787–1793), and Louisiana and the Floridas (1793–1825 — although actual jurisdiction was disputed over much of this period, being exercised in fact by Havana from 1801 to 1819); the Vicariate of Alabama and the Floridas (1825–1829); the Diocese of Mobile (1829–1850); and the Diocese of Savannah (1850–1857). From 1821 to 1857 episcopal authority was exercised only sporadically, and visitations by the bishops or their delegates were few and far between.

Spanish pioneers under Don Pedro Menéndez de Avilés founded Florida's — and the American nation's — first permanent European settlement on September 8, 1565. Named St. Augustine, the Spanish colony was also the first Catholic parish within the present limits of the United States. Forty years before the English settled Jamestown, fifty-five years before the Pilgrims landed at Plymouth Rock, and 210 years before the American Revolution, the city and parish of St. Augustine were thriving centers of Christian faith and civilization in the American wilderness. From the pioneer Indian mission of Nombre de Dios at St. Augustine, priests and laymen year by year carried Christianity and the rudiments of arts and crafts into the trackless interior. By the middle of the seventeenth century they had founded a chain of twenty-four Indian missions that stretched like a belt across Florida from Nombre de Dios to the Apalache villages near the present site of Tallahassee. This chain was later destroyed by a force of Carolinians and Creek Indians under English Colonel James Moore in 1702–1704, and Catholic life in Florida retreated during the first half of the eighteenth century to the immediate vicinity of St. Augustine. The only break in Florida's long Catholic history came in 1763 when Spain ceded the territory to England for a twenty-year period. The entire Spanish Catholic population left for Cuba and Spain. Catholic Minorcans, refugees from an ill-fated English colony at New Smyrna, came to St. Augustine in 1777 and resumed the ancient city's Catholic life. Spain reoccupied Florida in 1783, and during the second occupation her priests built a large parish church at St. Augustine (completed in 1797), opened a free school in the city, and attempted, unsuccess-

fully, to revive the missions in the interior. In 1821 Spain relinquished Florida again, this time to the United States, which gave
the ancient mission country territorial status. Florida was admitted
to the Union as the twenty-seventh state in 1845.

At the change of flags in 1821, after thirty-eight years of renewed
Spanish effort, only two parishes stood in the vast territory, at St.
Augustine and Pensacola. Under American occupation the Catholic
population of St. Augustine very nearly lost its parish church, and
did in fact lose its episcopal residence (used by visiting auxiliary
bishops from Cuba); its Mission Nombre de Dios, site at the time
of a hermitage to the Blessed Virgin; and the long-unused Franciscan Convent of the Immaculate Conception.[68] In 1824 male members of the congregation formed themselves into church wardens and
succeeded in having the territorial government incorporate them as
trustees of the parish church.[69] The trustee device saved the church
building, but it became the cause of interminable difficulties for
thirty-five years thereafter. Off and on during this period the wardens
were unable to secure a priest to serve them. When they had one,
they insisted on ruling him with an iron hand. In 1830, because of
administrative disagreements, they ousted the pastor, Father Edward
Francis Mayne, and did without Mass or the sacraments for most
of the next six years. The problem would not have grown so severe,

---

[68] See *Report of the Solicitor of the Treasury, 30th Congress, 2nd Session,
Senate, Executive Document 21, January 30, 1849* (Washington, D. C.: Government Printing Office, 1849). The United States assumed ownership of these properties, or authority over their disposition, on the grounds (1) that the Spanish
Crown and not the local church was the proper original owner, and (2) that the
church had in fact relinquished actual use of the properties prior to the change of
flags in 1821. In 1849 the Catholics of the city, headed by their pastor, Father
Benedict Madeore, petitioned the federal government for return of the disputed
properties. The Department of the Treasury appointed Stephen Russell Mallory,
a Key West businessman and a Catholic, to arbitrate the dispute. Mallory, later a
United States Senator and Secretary of the Navy in the Confederate government,
decided against the Church. His judgment confirmed the United States in its
title to the properties with right to dispose of them as federal authorities saw fit.
The Franciscan monastery, converted into a barracks during the English occupation, continued to be used for that purpose under the United States. The sites of
the Mission Nombre de Dios and of the episcopal residence (corner of St. George
and King Streets) were confirmed to private ownership. The Mission site was
eventually purchased by Bishop Verot in 1868.

[69] The "Roman Catholic Congregation of the City of St. Augustine" was in-
corporated by an Act of the Legislative Council of the Territory of Florida on
July 2, 1823; copy in ADSA. Cf. William W. Dewhurst, *The History of Saint
Augustine, Florida* (New York: George P. Putnam's Sons, 1881), 149.

one presumes, if there had been a regularly exercised episcopal authority in the territory.

By 1858 there were three parishes in Florida, at St. Augustine, Jacksonville, and Pensacola. Pensacola, however, was excluded from Bishop Verot's new vicariate which had its northwest boundary at the Apalachicola River. Fathers Madeore and Edmund Aubril, French-born priests of the Order of Mercy, were stationed at St. Augustine. Father William J. Hamilton was pastor of the Church of the Immaculate Conception in Jacksonville. Mission chapels were located at Middleburg, Mayport, Mandarin, Fernandina, Palatka, Tallahassee, and Key West.[70] The largest building was the Spanish church of St. Augustine.[71] There was no school, convent, or educational facility of any kind. A negligible Catholic population lived in scattered parts of the vicariate, the largest number at St. Augustine, where the weekly St. Augustine *Examiner* estimated the total at 952 white and 376 Negro Catholics.[72] Most Catholics, like their fellow Floridians, were engaged in farming. Only about 2000 of the state's 110,000 people were employed in manufacturing, and less than 20 percent of the population lived in towns and villages. Negro slavery was a recognized institution, and much of the wealth of the state was represented by this human chattel. The leading tourist city was St. Augustine, where the Magnolia House and the Florida House drew both invalids and wealthy northerners who wished to luxuriate in the Old World atmosphere of the "Ancient City."[73]

Bishop Verot's ship arrived at St. Augustine at 8 o'clock in the evening of June 1. With him was Bishop John Barry who had come on board at Savannah to install the new bishop in his vicariate. The two bishops were met by the ringing of old Spanish bells from the Moorish belfry of the parish church, which dominated

[70] *The Metropolitan Catholic Almanac and Laity's Directory for the United States . . . for 1858* (Baltimore: John Murphy & Company, 1858), 84–85. Cf. Thomas A. Donohue, D.D., M.R., *et al.,* *The Catholic Church in the United States of America* (New York: Catholic Editing Company, 1909), II, 154–155.

[71] A good description of this church and of other Catholic sites and features of St. Augustine is in the Archives of the Sisters of Mercy, St. Vincent's Academy, Savannah: Father James H. O'Neill to Sister Agnes, St. Augustine, Saturday before Palm Sunday, 1853.

[72] August 18, 1860.

[73] Herbert J. Doherty, Jr., "Florida in 1856," *The Florida Historical Quarterly,* XXXV (July, 1956), 60–70. An excellent contemporary account of St. Augustine is George R. Fairbanks, *The History and Antiquities of the City of St. Augustine, Florida* (New York: Charles B. Norton, 1858).

the city's narrow streets, projecting balconies, verandas, and remains of ancient porticoes. A correspondent of the *Catholic Mirror* wrote: "No sooner did the bells of the church announce in joyful peals the glad tidings of the arrival of the Vicar Apostolic of Florida than all the streets of St. Augustine became quite lively. Men, women and children, white and colored, old and young, all joyfully flocked toward the church to see the Bishop and kiss his ring, the emblem of the solemn covenant which he has made with the Church in Florida."[74] It was, wrote Verot to Archbishop Kenrick, "a very warm and cordial reception."[75] A series of presentations and meetings followed, as, for example, on June 6 when the Catholic Negroes of the city presented him with a pectoral cross. On all these occasions Verot made appropriate responses in the course of which, we are told, "he delighted his new friends with several most happy allusions."[76]

During the first two months, Verot set about to learn as much as he could about the country and the people he had come to serve. The prospects, he discovered, were bleak. "The country is very poor," he wrote to Kenrick, "& the people are not like the North, fond of giving to the Church, even out of their poverty."[77] On August 28 he wrote a pastoral letter to call to the attention of his people how far the fortunes of the Church in Florida had fallen since Spanish days:

> Over an immense region including more than six degrees of latitude we have but three clergymen, but three missionaries to act as the co-operators of our ministry. How strange! How desolating is this statement for such a country as Florida: Florida which was originally discovered and settled by Catholics long before any establishment was even thought of in other parts of the American Union — Florida which bears almost everywhere marks, remembrances and tokens of its Catholic institutions — Florida which two hundred years ago possessed so many convents, in which men were trained in study and austerity for the labor of evangelizing the poor and the ignorant — Florida which abounded with devoted and self-denying missionaries who had set at nought everything that the world holds dear, for the sake of diffusing the light of

---

[74] July 3, 1858.
[75] AAB, 32-D-1, Verot to Kenrick, St. Augustine, July 4, 1858.
[76] *Catholic Mirror,* July 3, 1858.
[77] AAB, 32-D-2, St. Augustine, October 22, 1858.

heaven among those who were sitting in the shadow of death —
Florida which has been bedewed in the East and the West, in the
North and in the South with the purest blood of martyrs! O the
dreadful effect of human vicissitudes! O the desolating proof of
the instability of every thing here below![78]

Verot worked fast to correct these vicissitudes. In early 1859 he
tackled the lay-trustee situation in St. Augustine, where wardens
of the parish church still held a firm grip on the Catholic properties.
The bishop summoned together 117 members of the congregation
and had them "lease the Parochial Church and Burying Ground, and
all other property real and personal belonging to said Church and
also resign and depute the right of presentation of appointment of
Pastor, and management of the said Church, and said property unto
Augustin Verot, Roman Catholic Bishop of Florida, and his successors in office. . . ."[79] About the same time he made a swing
around the state to examine the few resources, mostly small mission
chapels, that belonged to the Church elsewhere. A correspondent
wrote: "The Bishop stated the regret and inexpressible grief he had
felt on being unable to grant a resident pastor to many places which
asked for one with such earnestness, such as Key-West, Tampa and
Tallahassee." He promised the Catholics in these places that he
would shortly go to Europe in an effort to find priests.[80] During

---

[78] *Pastoral Letter of the Right Reverend Bishop Verot to the Catholics of
Florida* (St. Augustine: n.p., August 28, 1858).

[79] Deed: "The Congregation of the Roman Catholic Church to Augustine Verot,
Bishop of Florida." Recorded in Book A, "Miscellaneous Records," on folios 124
and 125, Circuit Court of St. John's County, Florida. MS original in ADSA, dated
February 20, 1859. The spelling of Verot's first name was sometimes rendered as
"Augustine" by his subjects and by his fellow bishops. Verot himself never added
the final -e in his signature. After coming to the United States, he dropped the
acute accent in Vérot.

[80] *Catholic Mirror,* February 5, 1859. Verot sent a report of his findings on this
trip to the Societé de la Propagation de la Foi, in Lyons, France, a mission
organization from which over the course of the next seventeen years, he would
receive several thousand dollars in aid; see *Annales de la Propagation de la Foi,*
Lyons, XXXI (September, 1859), 426–442. For the history and work of this
Society in the United States, see Edward John Hickey, *The Society of the Propagation of the Faith, Its Foundation, Organization and Success* (1822–1922) (Washington, D. C.: The Catholic University of America Press, 1922). The *Annales* of
the Society were published in annual volumes, and each bishop receiving financial
aid was requested to contribute articles on the missions within his area of jurisdiction. The *Annales* are a largely untapped source of information on the nineteenth-century American Church. Verot contributed articles to Volumes 31 (1859),
35 (1863), 36 (1864), 37 (1865), and 44 (1872), the last through Father Henry
Peter Clavreul, pastor of St. Augustine.

Lent, Verot found it necessary to remind his people that special exemptions from Friday and Lenten abstinence that had been granted by the Holy See to Florida during its Spanish occupation no longer applied. "But we suspect," he added in a pastoral letter, "it is not so much to Spanish privileges that the violation of the law of the Church is attributable, as to the fact that many districts have long been deprived of the pastoral solicitude and fatherly vigilance of a resident clergyman."[81]

In 1859 Verot left for Europe in search of priests. It was his first visit to the continent since coming to the United States twenty-nine years before. He took passage on the steamship *Glasgow* and planned a trip to carry him to Ireland, England, and finally to France. Before sailing out of New York on May 14 he wrote a friend to describe a misadventure:

> I was very near falling into a trap on arriving in New York. A fellow came to me with great kindness & apparent zeal to take me to Merchant's Hotel where I wanted to go; he got my check, led me into a carriage & then into another carriage, & afterwards I found myself into [sic] a mean place in a small & wretched street. He had the boldness to tell me it was "Merchant's Hotel." I determined not to stay in such a place. I went about to get a hack, it was nine o'clock P.M. I had some difficulty & during that time & before, I wonder my baggage was not stolen. I saw afterwards that I had run a great danger of losing it & losing all the money I had. Fortunately I extricated myself & reached Merchant's Hotel . . . without any misfortune.[82]

In France Verot published a circular describing the needs of his vicariate.[83] This, together with his personal appeals, met with some success, and in late August Father Carrière, Verot's old Sulpician superior, wrote to Archbishop Purcell of Cincinnati: "Some time ago now Bishop Verot left us, taking with him, I believe, a rather good number of recruits. He has done well in his vicariate. May the Lord protect him!"[84] Verot's companions on

[81] *Lenten Pastoral of the Rt. Rev. Augustine [sic] Verot, D.D.* (Charleston, S. C.: Harper & Calvo, Printers, 1859).

[82] ADSA, Verot to Very Dear Confrère (Sulpician priest, probably at Baltimore), New York, May 14, 1859.

[83] *Circulaire sur le Vicariat apostolique de la Floride* (Paris: Bailly, Divry et Ce. 1859); copy in Archives of St. Leo Abbey.

[84] MCND, Carrière to Purcell, Paris, August 27, 1859.

the return voyage numbered six priests, four brothers, and two nuns — all French. The priests were Peter Dufau, Emile Hillaire, Charles A. Mailley, John Bernard Aulance, John Francis R. Chambon, and Silvain Joseph Hunincq. Another priest recruited at the same time would arrive the next year, Henry Peter Clavreul.[85] With the exception of Father Hunincq, who died during the yellow-fever epidemic at Key West in 1862, all these missionary priests would have important parts in Bishop Verot's story, the climax of which was the tumultuous decade just ahead.

Arriving at St. Augustine with the six priests in October, the bishop at once placed them under his personal instruction in the English language.[86] His skills as a teacher had not, apparently, suffered from disuse, for, as the local correspondent of the *Catholic Mirror* wrote in March of 1860: "Of the six missionaries whom Bishop Verot brought from France in October last, three have made such remarkable progress in English, that in the course of January last they preached in English to our astonished people. . . ."[87] In the latter part of 1859 Verot also succeeded in recruiting five sisters of the Order of Mercy from the Diocese of Hartford in Connecticut and three Christian Brothers from Canada to open a girls' academy and a boys' day school.[88] The local *Examiner* was not exactly sanguine about the appearance of sectarian schools in the city,[89] but visiting Bishops Hughes of New York and Lynch of Charleston encouraged Verot in his purposes.[90] And the *Examiner* itself, after the schools had been in operation for a year, and two free schools had been opened in conjunction with them, expressed itself more generously: "Too much gratitude cannot be felt by the Citizens of St. Augustine, to the Catholic Bishop and Priests, under whose auspices the schools connected with that Church have been established."[91] The correspondent of the *Catholic Mirror* was also moved

---

[85] St. Augustine *Examiner*, October 29, 1859; *Catholic Mirror*, November 12, 1859.

[86] AAB, 32-D-3, Verot to Archbishop Kenrick, St. Augustine, January 21, 1860.

[87] *Catholic Mirror*, March 3, 1860.

[88] St. Augustine *Examiner*, December 31, 1859, January 7, 1860; *Catholic Mirror*, March 3, 1860.

[89] February 11, 1860: "The moment our schools erect fortifications of *sect* and *ism* around them, from that moment, we honestly believe, they strike the first blow at their own ruin."

[90] *Catholic Mirror*, March 24, 1860.

[91] April 6, 1861.

to marvel at the rapid progress of the Church in Florida under Verot: "Two short years have scarcely elapsed since he came among us; how short the time! how great the work performed!"[92]

Verot's increasingly prosperous and somewhat idyllic mission life was not to last, however. Neither were his schools, which, only three years after their founding, would have to close their doors. A disquieting knowledge was abroad in the land in the fall of 1860. Its portents, we may suppose, bothered deeply the bishop who had written Paris in the decade just passed about the joys that he found in simple pastoral work. But a new decade was emerging, one in which Verot and his Church would both have to make new compacts, enter new arenas, fight new battles, and, in general, come of age. What we have seen of Verot's background — his vigor and zeal, his combative nature, his independence and wit — all these would show themselves again, and in high relief, during the decade that lay ahead. They were ten years that shook the Church, and they began ominously. On December 3, 1860, President James Buchanan addressed the Congress and interpreted the times in a fashion that Bishop Verot would duplicate a month later: "The long continued and intemperate interference of the Northern people with the question of slavery in the Southern states has at length produced its natural effects. The different sections of the Union are now arrayed against each other, and the time has arrived, so much dreaded by the Father of his Country, when hostile geographical parties have been formed."[93] Having exhausted all other means to avoid disaster, Buchanan proclaimed Friday, January 4, 1861, as a day "set apart for Humiliation, Fasting, and Prayer throughout the Union."[94]

---

[92] June 23, 1860.

[93] Annual Message to Congress, December 3, 1860. Quoted in George Tichnor Curtis, *Life of James Buchanan* (New York: Harper Brothers, 1883), II, 338.

[94] Proclamation of December 14, 1860; printed in *Pittsburgh Catholic,* December 22, 1860, and *Catholic Mirror,* December 22, 1860.

CHAPTER II

SLAVE OR FREE?

ON THE DAY appointed by President Buchanan, Bishop Verot rose to speak on "Slavery and Abolitionism" in the parish church of St. Augustine. The sermon he delivered was a rubicon in his personal life. More than that, it was a symbolic act in the general maturation of the American Church. Before 1861 the American bishops, Verot included, had tried to maintain a prudent aloofness from the political, social, and economic problems of the young nation. They had thought it unwise to submit a Church already suspect in American society for its "foreign" character to the further criticisms that would come from engaging in partisan politics.[1] Certain bishops, it is true, had spoken out occasionally before on issues directly touching the well-being of Catholicism, as in the "Know-Nothing" crises, and some had uttered thoughts on the moral issue of slavery. But few, if any, had deliberately launched themselves into passionate involvement with national political affairs having nothing directly to do with Catholicism, as Bishop Verot determined to do on January 4, 1861. His sermon of that day would soon be printed and disseminated throughout the South as a Confederate tract,[2] and would win its author the accolade and — in the North — the opprobrium of a "rebel bishop."

---

[1] See below, Chapter III.

[2] Rt. Rev. A. Verot, D.D., Vicar Apostolic of Florida, *A Tract for the Times. Slavery and Abolitionism, Being the Substance of a Sermon Preached in the Church of St. Augustine, Florida, on the 4th Day of January, 1861, Day of Public Humiliation, Fasting and Prayer* (Baltimore: John Murphy & Co., 1861), 14 pp. Actual publication occurred sometime after January 18, when Verot wrote that he had sent the manuscript to Baltimore; see AAB, 32-D-6, Verot to Kenrick, St. Augustine, January 18, 1861. The imprint was completed before May 7, when Verot informed Bishop Lynch that the invoice had arrived; ADC, Box 1861, Verot to Lynch, St. Augustine, May 7, 1861.

Standing in the pulpit of the old Spanish church at St. Augustine, Verot took a text from the Book of Proverbs: "Justice exalteth a nation; but sin maketh nations miserable (14:34)." He then announced that he had something to say about the critical state of public affairs to which the president had commended the nation's prayers. He would name the cause of the crisis and set it, as he saw things, in its proper perspective. "The political horizon has become gloomy," he told his congregation, "discord and disunion are rapidly spreading over the length and breadth of the land; horrors of war, and of the worst kind — of civil war — are staring us in the face." These dark designs on "our beloved country" are all the more terrible because "we have hitherto been a nation prosperous beyond even the most exaggerated conceptions of a wild imagination; productions of every kind lavished by our soil; an abundance, not to say an overflowing, of the circulating medium; extensive factories, an active commerce, and the rich and exuberant fruits of industry by sea and by land, have made the United States a paragon of riches — a sort of elysian fields, in which the overflowing population of Europe came to enjoy abundance, riches, peace, and freedom." Now, however, this national well-being has given way to mutual distrust, uneasiness, suspension of commerce, stagnation of industry, suffering, and the anticipation of evils yet worse to come. And what was the cause? The answer is plain: "Slavery is the origin of the present disturbances, and is the fatal sand-bank upon which the Ship of State has already made a total or partial shipwreck" — slavery, because one half of the nation refused to recognize and honor that legitimate institution.

In outlining what he would say about slavery, Verot set forth what was — perhaps to the reader's surprise — the common American Catholic opinion on the subject, North and South:

> I wish to show, on the one side, how unjust, iniquitous, unscriptural, and unreasonable is the assertion of Abolitionists, who brand Slavery as a moral evil, and a crime against God, religion, humanity, and society; whereas, it is found to have received the sanction of God, of the Church, and of Society at all times, and in all governments. On the other side, I wish to show the conditions under which servitude is legitimate, lawful, approved by all laws, and consistent with practical religion and true holiness of life in masters who fulfill those conditions.

In a letter several weeks afterward to Archbishop Kenrick, Verot would give another summary of the sermon, one which showed that his main concern at the time was moral and social, and that, as later events would bear out, he had a compassionate regard for the Negro slave:

> After having proved the legitimacy of slavery against abolitionists, I introduce the conditions to render it lawful and speak of many points which I deem very important and useful at this time where a Southern Confederacy will be formed. It would do a great service to the Negroes and to religion in general, if some social, moral and religious improvement were obtained for the poor slaves of our plantations.[3]

A review of Catholic positions taken earlier on the subject of slavery will show how closely Verot followed the classic Catholic treatments of the problem in this country. It will also explain how a northern Catholic newspaper of definite Unionist convictions could reprint his entire sermon after the war with only mild disclaimers.[4] In sum, official Catholic teaching, North and South, prior to the Civil War, held that the state of involuntary servitude was not necessarily evil. It taught that slavery, considered in the abstract, apart from possible specific abuses to human dignity, was not opposed either to natural or to divine law. Wherever circumstances permitted the slave to achieve better conditions on his own, the Church encouraged manumission; after the abolition movement gained momentum, however, Catholic masters became increasingly reluctant to grant this freedom.[5] Nevertheless, the theological sanction given to slavery did not mean approval of it as a natural necessity, much less as a divine one. The Catholic doctrine was one of "toleration," slavery being "not an evil *malum in se*,"

---

[3] AAB 32-D-6, Verot to Kenrick, St. Augustine, January 18, 1861.

[4] Cincinnati *Catholic Telegraph*, December 20, 1865. The sermon was also reproduced in the North during the war, by the New York *Freeman's Journal*, June 18 and July 9, 1864; but the New York journal showed consistent sympathy toward the South, and had a deserved "Copperhead" reputation.

[5] See Madeleine Hooke Rice, *American Catholic Opinion in the Slavery Controversy* (New York: Columbia University, 1944), 142. This is the best general treatment of the subject. Cf. John C. Murphy, *An Analysis of the Attitudes of American Catholics Toward the Immigrant and the Negro* (Washington, D. C.: The Catholic University of America, 1940).

but merely a "social evil to be tolerated until such time as it can be prudently replaced by another order."[6]

At the Council of Baltimore in 1840, the American bishops, among whom representatives of the slave states were in the majority, listened to a formal reading of an apostolic letter of Pope Gregory XVI (dated December, 1839), which condemned the slave trade in unequivocal language. Shortly afterward, John Forsyth, Secretary of State in the cabinet of President Martin Van Buren, attempted to use the Pope's letter in a campaign speech as proof that the American bishops, and Catholics in general, were aiding and abetting the abolitionist movement. Bishop John England, of the Diocese of Charleston, which included at the time North and South Carolina and Georgia, took this occasion to state the Catholic position in a series of public letters to Forsyth.[7] Having noted the fact that Pope Gregory condemned the slave trade only, and not domestic slavery as it existed in the Southern states, England set forth the outlines of what would thereafter be the common American Catholic viewpoint of slavery in pulpit and press, and the Catholic southerner's basic defense of it. The charge of consorting with abolitionists England considered hardly worthy of notice. He wrote: "I have been asked by many . . . whether I am friendly to the existence or continuation of slavery? I am not — but I also see the impossibility of now abolishing it here."[8]

While he was not enamored of what he found firmly established

---

[6] Baltimore *Catholic Mirror*, January 21, 1850. The same position was stated by the *Freeman's Journal* toward the close of the war: "The assertion that the Negro is not only *beset* now in subordination and compelled servitude to the white race — which we [*Journal*] hold, but that this must always in all cases be true, we consider as one of the narrow-minded Yankee notions;" March 4, 1865. The Catholic position differed essentially, therefore, from the "divine ordained" theory espoused by the Southern Presbyterians in May, 1857, and roundly condemned by the *Catholic Mirror*, September 19, 1857. Cf. Joseph Butsch, "Catholics and the Negro," *The Journal of Negro History*, II (October, 1917), 393–411.

[7] John England, *Letters to the Honorable John Forsyth on the Subject of Domestic Slavery* (Baltimore: W. George Read, 1844). Bishop England died April 11, 1842, having completed only the first part of his elaborately planned rebuttal. The letters, eighteen in all, appeared in England's diocesan paper, the *United States Catholic Miscellany* (hereafter cited as *Miscellany*), from September 29, 1840, through April 23, 1841. John England was born September 23, 1786, in Cork, Ireland, consecrated Bishop of Charleston in 1820, and came to his American see in the same year. One of the most respected of the early American prelates, he addressed the United States Congress in 1826.

[8] *Miscellany*, February 25, 1841.

in the South, England nonetheless advanced arguments in its favor of such force that they tended to give the institution ecclesiastical sanction. The existence of slavery as a social institution, he said, was supported by the natural law, by the slave codes of the Old Testament, by the attitude of Christ and the Church Fathers, and by the practices of the Christian Church during the first four centuries: "The right of the master, the duty of the slave, the lawfulness of continuing the relations, and the benevolence of religion in mitigating the sufferings . . . are the results exhibited by our view of the laws and facts during the first four centuries of Christianity."[9]

England's conclusion, with the means taken to arrive at it, received support in the moral theology treatise of the leading American Catholic theologian of the period, Francis Patrick Kenrick, Bishop of Philadelphia and later Archbishop of Baltimore. Writing in 1841, Kenrick agreed in substance with England's historical and scriptural proofs for the legitimacy of slavery, though he regretted that there should be so many slaves, and that, to guard against their movements, it had been necessary to pass laws prohibiting their education and, in some places, greatly restricting their exercise of religion.

> Nevertheless, such is the state of things, nothing should be attempted against the laws, nor anything be done or said that would make them bear their yoke unwillingly. . . . The Apostles have left us these rules; which if anyone should neglect and, through a feeling of humanity, endeavor to overturn the entire established order, he would in most cases but aggravate the condition of the slaves.[10]

Farther north, in New York, Archbishop John Hughes showed himself to be of the same mind, though for different reasons. The archbishop cared less for theological and historical arguments than he did for practical considerations. The slavery system in his view was an objective evil. Nonetheless, it was to be preferred to the conditions under which the Negroes lived in Africa.

---

[9] England, Letters, 50.

[10] Francis Patrick Kenrick, Theologia Moralis (Philadelphia, 1841), I, 255–257, translated in "The Catholic Church and the Question of Slavery," The Metropolitan Magazine (June, 1855), 267. Cf. Brokkage, Kenrick's Opinion, 242: "Certainly no theologian could have permitted slavery as it frequently existed in practice in America. There was equivocal use of the word slavery that should have been more clearly pointed out."

> While we know that this condition of slavery is an evil, yet it
> is not an absolute and unmitigated evil. . . . I have seen those
> masters impressed with the convictions of what they owed to these
> creatures, leaving nothing undone that kindness could prompt, at
> the same time that they provided for all their spiritual and tem-
> poral wants.[11]

The moral unanimity of the bishops on the slavery issue, South,
North, and border, prior to 1861 was reflected, with one exception,
in the Catholic press. Here the emphasis was not so much on
exposition of Catholic doctrine as it was on repudiation of the
abolitionist doctrine.[12] The *United States Catholic Miscellany,* organ
of the Charleston diocese, and oldest Catholic paper in the country,
took a firm stand against abolitionism from 1831 on. As Verot
was to do later in his sermon, the *Miscellany* linked abolitionism
directly with nativist attacks against Catholicism.[13] Two representative papers of the country, the New York *Freeman's Journal*
and the Baltimore *Catholic Mirror,* whose editors, John McMaster
and Courtney Jenkins, locked horns often on other issues, were
at one on the problem of "canting Abolition Puritans" (*Journal*)
and "the sophists of Abolitionism" (*Mirror*). Both papers were
sure what class was at the bottom of the sectional strife arising
from abolitionism: "Who but the Protestant clergymen?"[14] The
same sentiments ran through the pages of the New York *Metropolitan Record,* which would be ranked as Copperhead after 1860
along with the *Freeman's Journal;* and those of *Le Propagateur
catholique* of New Orleans, and of the Boston *Pilot,* whose editors
were particularly outspoken even during the prosecution of the
war.[15] The one notable exception to the Catholic press consensus
was the Cincinnati *Catholic Telegraph,* which condemned slavery
as immoral as early as February 6, 1841, and consistently thereafter, particularly during the war, declared that the moral issue

---

[11] Sermon of April 30, 1854, *Freeman's Journal,* July 3, 1854.
[12] See for the best study of the Catholic press during the period Cuthbert
Edward Allen, O.S.B., "The Slavery Question in Catholic Newspapers, 1850–
1865," *Historical Records and Studies,* XXVI (1936), 99–167. Cf. John Tracy
Ellis, *American Catholicism* (Chicago: University of Chicago Press, 1958), 92–94.
[13] E.g., September 12, 1835, June 30, 1838.
[14] *Freeman's Journal,* December 8, 1855. Cf. *Mirror,* September 15, 1860. "Each
paper can be considered at that time as a representative Catholic journal of the
North and South respectively"; Allen, "The Slavery Question," 99.
[15] See Murphy, *Attitudes of American Catholics,* 49–50.

gave a warrant to the abolitionist platform.[16] Generally, Catholic opinion associated abolitionism not with morality but with European "Red Republicanism," British do-goodism (a particular nettle in the side of the *Pilot, Freeman's Journal,* and *Metropolitan Record,* all organs of Irish-American opinion), and Protestant-nativist "infidels and fanatics," as Archbishop Hughes described William Ellery Channing, Theodore Parker, and other ministers of abolitionist persuasion.[17]

Despite the mounting controversy and the real danger of an armed conflict involving millions of Catholics, the bishops maintained the political insularity that had been their firm policy since the episcopate of the first American prelate, John Carroll of Baltimore (1790–1815). At the Ninth Provincial Council of Baltimore in May, 1858, the assembled prelates from both above and below the Mason and Dixon Line carefully refrained from interjecting any sectional appeals into the deliberations. Confident that "through her mild influence" the Church would eventually do away with the slavery system in this country, as she had rid it from Europe, the bishops determined not to endanger the peace of society "by following the theories of philanthropy." They did not, therefore, find it necessary "to modify our teachings with a view of adapting it to local circumstances." Because of the enormous political shape that slavery had taken by this critical date, and, one supposes, because the bishops felt themselves still irreversibly bound to a policy of political nonintervention, they gracefully abdicated any responsibility for moral leadership in the crisis at hand. If ever there was an instance of separation of Church and State, one finds it in this expression of transcendent concern:

> Our clergy have wisely abstained from all interference with the judgment of the faithful, which should be free on all questions of policy and social order within the limits of the doctrine and law of Christ. . . . Let the dead bury the dead. Leave to worldlings the cares and anxieties of political partisanship, the struggles for as-

---

[16] *Ibid.,* 51–52. Despite its vigorous stand against the thesis advanced by Bishop Verot, the *Catholic Telegraph* would reprint his complete sermon at war's end, December 20, 1865. In the South the most forthright Catholic challenge to the slave system on moral grounds during the prewar period came from a layman, Judge William Gaston, of North Carolina, in a speech at Chapel Hill, June 20, 1832, reprinted in *American Catholic Historical Researches,* VIII (April, 1891), 71.

[17] Letter of Hughes to Augustin Cochin, January 28, 1862, cited in Rice, *American Catholic Opinion,* 98.

cendency, and the mortifications of disappointed ambitions. Do not, in any way, identify the interests of our holy Faith with the fortunes of any party. . . .[18]

As though in explanation of the Baltimore decree, but apparently not connected with the decision of its authors in any direct way, the bishops of the Archdiocese of Cincinnati, meeting within a few weeks of Fort Sumter, and after Verot and several other prelates of the South had already made their move, issued a more reasoned declaration of Catholic nonintervention in the slavery controversy. The Cincinnati pastoral portrayed the Church as a law-abiding, unifying, and pacifying influence on the country at large:

> The spirit of the Catholic Church is eminently conservative and while her ministers rightfully feel a deep and abiding interest in all that concerns the welfare of the country, they do not think it their province to enter the political arena. They leave to the ministers of the human sects [Protestant] to discuss from their pulpits and in their ecclesiastical assemblies the very exciting questions which lie at the base of our present and prospective difficulties.[19]

Perhaps, as has been suggested,[20] the Cincinnati bishops acted with prudence in pursuing the neutral course they did, since the Catholic faithful were already by that time taking up positions on opposite sides of the barricades. But the year for leadership had been 1858, and the question of prudence would have to be asked about Baltimore as well. There, the decision to be silent stands in disconcerting contrast with the moral leadership exercised in later years by American bishops on the question of Negro rights, and is not extenuated by any immediate danger of armed conflict. In retrospect, it has the surface appearance of a failure of nerve. Yet there were at least two reasons to make the bishops' position understandable. For one thing, the fact that the issue was clouded by emotionally charged political and sectional loyal-

---

[18] Concilium Baltimorensis Provinciale IX, May 28, 1856, quoted in Frederick J. Zwierlein, *Life and Letters of Bishop [Bernard J.] McQuaid* (Rochester: Art Print Shop, 1925), I, 266–267.

[19] *Pastoral Letter of the Third Provincial Council of Cincinnati to the Clergy and Laity* (Cincinnati, 1861), 6; cited in Murphy, *Attitudes of American Catholics*, 57–58. A neutral stand in the slavery controversy had been recommended by other recent regional assemblies of American bishops. See the pastoral of the Third Provincial Council of New Orleans, *Catholic Mirror*, March 1, 1856, and the pastoral of the Provincial Council of St. Louis, 1855, *ibid.*, November 3, 1855.

[20] By Ellis, *American Catholicism*, 92.

ties probably caused the bishops to feel that the present was not
the most prudent occasion, nor the clearest circumstance, in which
to make an initial venture into civic moral leadership. Perhaps
the stronger reason was revealed in Bishop Verot's sermon. He
had taken part in the 1858 council, his first as a prelate, and
it is obvious that his own proslavery purpose gained from the
silence that reigned there. But so did the polemic advantage of
Catholicism as a whole. Many of the chief abolitionist voices belonged to Protestant ministers whose energies, only recently, had
been directed in nativist attacks against Catholicism. As shown
later, Verot could compare favorably the pacifying influence of
Catholicism with the "intolerance and bigotry" of the Protestant-
Nativist clergy, who "brought about this deplorable state of things."
As embarrassment to nativism seems to have served Verot's purpose, it may also have motivated the stand adopted at Baltimore
in 1858.[21]

---

[21] Since Verot's sermon will stress the link between northern nativists and the
abolitionists, it is important to ask if such a link actually existed. It is clear in
the first place that the majority of the Protestant clergy was favorable to the
anti-Catholic features of nativism in the period 1845–1860; see Ray Allen Billington, *The Protestant Crusade, 1800–1860* (New York: Macmillan, 1938), *passim*,
esp. 345–379. It is also accepted that, from 1845 on, when the various Protestant
bodies began to divide in North-South schisms, the northern Protestant clergy
became increasingly antislavery; see Dwight Lowell Dumond, *Antislavery: The
Crusade for Freedom in America* (Ann Arbor: University of Michigan, 1951), 349;
and Arthur Young Lloyd, *The Slavery Controversy, 1831–1860* (Chapel Hill:
University of North Carolina, 1939), 162–193. Louis Filler, *The Crusade Against
Slavery, 1830–1860* (New York: Harper Bros., 1960), finds that in the 1830's
and 1840's abolitionists were divided in their attitudes toward Catholics, but his
emphasis seems to fall on their leanings toward nativism. Speaking of such clergy-
men-abolitionists as Lyman Beecher, Samuel Crothers, George Bourne, William
C. Brownlee, and George B. Cheever, Filler writes: "The vindictiveness of these
enthusiasts cannot be overdrawn. The invective was not stinted when directed
at Catholics. In this they were at one with the political nativists of later vintage
(1850–56). . . ." For the period of political nativism (Know-Nothingism) immediately prior to the war, 1854–1860, Billington, *Crusade,* finds that "as passions
bred by the slavery controversy increased, northern Know-Nothing leaders openly
sought to align their party with the abolitionists" (425). Billington quotes a
typical Know-Nothing resolution of the time, condemning "Roman Catholicism
and slavery" as "natural allies in every warfare against liberty and enlightenment"
(425). Verot may have exaggerated the extent to which the northern Protestant
clergy who supported abolitionism in 1854–1860 were one and the same with those
who supported anti-Catholic nativism in the 1840's, but his recognition of a
general link between the clerical forces behind *northern* nativism and abolitionism
in the years directly prior to the war seems to be confirmed by Billington's
research.

Verot defined slavery as the state of dependency of one man upon another "so as to be obliged to work all his life for that master, with the privilege, in the latter, to transfer that right to another person by sale." As both theologians and lay scholars had shown, he said, men did not have an absolute domain over their own lives and limbs, but only the *usufruct* of them, "that is, a life-interest in them." Hence, a master, not being the true owner of his own life and limbs, could not be the owner or proprietor of the life and limbs of a slave, this high domain belonging exclusively to God. A master, however, could claim a right over the *usufruct,* or use of another person, "that is, a right on his labor and industry, and the labor and industry of his children." Verot set out to prove that this right had a warrant in four branches of law — natural law, divine positive law, ecclesiastical law, and civil law.

As to natural law, Verot conceded that nature did not establish slavery. "But natural law approves of reasons and causes by which a man may become the slave of another man." He linked the matter with property in land. Just as no land belonged to anybody by the right of nature, but legitimate titles constituted it the property of specific individuals, in the same way one man received clear title to the possession of another man's labor. Indeed, "any one, ever so little conversant with history, finds slavery established among all nations of antiquity, and it is not improbable that it is coeval with the division of property." Noting then that all men in whatever condition who labored under the wage system assigned the title of their labor to another, Verot laid down his principal argument: "A man may sell his labor and work for a day, a week, a month, or a year: why may he not sell it for all his life?" If it be answered that a sale required a consideration, an equivalent between the contracting parties, the master in fact did offer this, in the form of food and clothing, security at all times, and assistance in sickness and old age. "The equivalent given by the master may be a sufficient inducement for some individuals to offer their work and liberty forever." The bishop did not make clear in what sense the slaves might be said to have "offered" their work and liberty. But he was anxious that men appreciate the certainty of security that the slaves in fact possessed:

— a certainty which many distressed and starving families in Europe, and in the large cities of America, would indeed appreciate highly, as they know what a source of interminable care, anxiety, and solicitude, this matter is for them. It is truly remarkable how gay, cheerful, and sprightly are the slaves of the South. I do not hesitate to say that they seem to be better contented than their masters; assuredly more so than the sullen and gloomy population found in the work shops and factories of large cities. The master therefore gives an equivalent.[22]

The bishop then proceeded into an examination of other means by which men had gained legitimate title to the liberty of others, including (1) capture in a just war; (2) condemnation to slavery for crimes committed; (3) impressment for failure to pay debts; (4) birth from a mother in the state of servitude (for which he cited the ancient axiom *partus sequitur ventrem*); and (5) long possession in good faith. He expressed gratification that Christianity had introduced milder legislation to replace the first two. With reference to the third, he was not certain that the "spirit of philanthropy" of modern legislators was wiser than the stern justice of earlier times. The last two means he considered still lawful and valid. Interestingly, he did not mention the slave trade, which was the original means of gaining title employed by slave owners in the South, and the only means of title really at question. More curious still, in the second part of his sermon, Verot would condemn the slave trade as, next to murder, "the grossest violation of justice that can be conceived." Perhaps he felt that, while the

---

[22] Verot uses here the "wage-slave" antithesis popularized by John C. Calhoun of South Carolina. For a summary of similar argumentation on the southern side, see William Sumner Jenkins, *Pro-Slavery Thought in the Old South* (Chapel Hill: University of North Carolina, 1935). A recent attack on this form of argument is Kenneth M. Stampp, *The Peculiar Institution; Slavery in the Ante-Bellum South* (New York: Knopf, 1956). Laudatory of the "kindly feeling" of Florida slave masters is Edwin L. Williams, "Negro Slavery in Florida," Part II, *The Florida Historical Quarterly*, XXVIII (January, 1950), 203. In Part I, *ibid.* (October, 1949), Williams numbers the slave population in Florida in 1850 at 61,745, compared with 77,746 whites and 932 free Negroes, or 43.9 percent of the population. There are no figures for the total number of Catholic slaves in Florida. However, slaves attended missions administered for them at Cowford (Jacksonville), Fernandina, Key West, and St. Augustine. Most, if not all Catholic slaveholders, had their Negroes baptized in the Catholic Faith. Henry P. Clavreul in *Notes on the Catholic Church in Florida, 1565–1876* (St. Leo, Fla.: Abbey Press, 1910) wrote that, in 1858, of the nine hundred Negroes in St. Augustine "fully one half are Catholic" (31).

original enslavement was wrong, its continuation was justified by "long possession in good faith."

What Verot had to say about divine positive law and ecclesiastical [Canon] law reproduced in great part what Bishop England had written. "It would be tedious," he wrote, "to adduce all the proofs of my assertion which could be extracted from the Old Testament," but he adduced enough to show, as he thought, that "every page of Holy Writ," it seemed, "contains some statement to demolish the false and unjust principles of Abolitionism." As regards the New Testament, while this higher dispensation did abrogate many functions of the Old Law, it contained not one word to prohibit slavery; "but there are, on the contrary, plain and evident approbations of it." St. Paul, particularly, supported this judgment, and Verot catalogued the many instances in which that missionary confirmed the slaves of the Mediterranean world in obedience toward their masters. Canon law likewise contained no general proscription against slavery, "but has kept up the teaching and examples of the Apostles on this point, leaving masters at liberty to keep or to manumit their slaves, as they thought proper." It was the place now, the bishop said, to consider the civil law:

> As for the United States, it is plain, that the Constitution framed after the War of Independence, recognizes the relations of master and slave, and that the law of the United States gives a right to the master to reclaim and seize his fugitive slave, wherever he may be found within the United States. These statements are undeniable, and there is no occasion for me to dwell on a point known to everybody. Those states which have enacted laws against the constitution and the Legislation of the United States have sapped the very foundations of social order, and are the true and responsible causes and agents of the misfortunes which have already befallen the nation, and of the greater calamities with which it is threatened.[23] The words of my text receive here their application: "Justice exalteth a nation: but sin maketh nations miserable."

The fact was, the bishop declared, there had been in the northern United States an actual conspiracy against justice and truth. And

---

[23] Cf. Augusta (Georgia) *Daily Constitutionalist,* December 17, 1861, reporting an address by Verot in that city on December 14: "He spoke of the violation of the Constitutional rights of the South by the North, in their various State nullifications of the Fugitive Slave law, and claimed that they were the Rebels — not we of the South."

the responsible agents of that conspiracy, sorry to say, were the same "fanatical preachers" and "zealots" who earlier had assailed, calumniated, and vilified the Catholic Church. They were the responsible parties. And Verot named their deeds: the burning of the Ursuline Sisters' convent at Charlestown, Massachusetts, in 1834; the Philadelphia riots of 1844; "and so many other acts of crying injustice, cruelty and barbarity, during that religious excitement from which we are just now emerging, I mean the movement of Know-Nothingism." The leaders of that dismal cause, who inflamed the press against Catholics, who spread slanderous stories against the clergy and religious "as in the case of Maria Monk," had kept on their course of violence, deception, and misrepresentation; they seemed quite incapable, he said, of learning any lesson from truth, moderation, and justice.[24]

> Those blind leaders, quitting the sphere which they seem to claim, when they style themselves reverend, have sent remonstrances to Congress on points evidently within the pale of political and civil legislation; they have also invaded State legislatures, and in those places have disgraced their proceedings by iniquity and injustice. It is the same party, which, baffled in its attempts against the Catholic Church, . . . has opposed only patience, silence and prayer to its unholy attacks, and exasperated by the rebuke it received from the nation (for it could not destroy the sense of justice so deeply engraved in the American breast), has now turned its weapons against the South, advocating, in the name of the Bible, the liberation of slaves. But the South has not been, and will not, as a Nation, be as patient as the Catholic Church.

As an additional proof that the abolitionists were identical with the nativists, Verot recalled a fact asserted by Bishop England in his letters to Forsyth, namely that the abolitionists of England presented regularly every year two petitions to Parliament, one

---

[24] Verot is not thinking here of the nativists ("Americans") in Florida. Political nativism in Florida, which had reached its high-water mark in the state and national elections of 1856, consistently avoided any overt hostility toward Florida Catholics, and never made Catholicism an issue, possibly because the number of Catholics in the state was not significant. Florida nativists avoided close association with national Know-Nothingism, and concentrated their fire mainly on "foreignism." See Arthur W. Thompson, "Political Nativism in Florida, 1848–1860: A phase of Anti-Secessionism," *The Journal of Southern History*, XV (February, 1949), 39–66. For the best recent study of nativism nationally, from 1860 forward, see John Higham, *Strangers in the Land: Patterns in American Nativism, 1860–1925* (New Brunswick, N. J.: Rutgers University, 1955).

to ask that the American slaves be set free, the other to ask
that the penalties enacted against Irish Catholics be executed and
strictly enforced. Verot then closed his case with a peroration that
was at once a searing condemnation of abolitionism, a significant
defense of the position taken by the Catholic hierarchy, and an
eloquent tribute to the Republic:

> In the United States, it will be properly and clearly religion and
> bigotry that will have destroyed the beautiful fabric of Washington
> and the other great men who wished so much to keep the govern-
> ment and religion separate from each other. The Catholics of
> America have scrupulously adhered to those constitutional pro-
> visions, and have interfered only by praying for the republic, the
> general peace and welfare of their fellow citizens.[25] As for the
> Protestant Clergy, with, of course, honorable exceptions, they have
> brought about this deplorable state of things, in which the South
> is arrayed against the North, and in which war, bloodshed, and all
> the atrocities of civil discord may yet have their sad exhibition.
> Protestant intolerance and bigotry have demolished this beautiful
> edifice, which wisdom, moderation and prudence had reared to
> political liberty.[26]

Bishop Verot had completed only the first part of his remarks,
however. There was another side to the coin of slavery. If slavery
as an institution had certain rights to exist, it also was invested
with corresponding duties and obligations, which were of equal
vigor. In a dramatic turn — and in the strongest language used
by any American prelate prior to the Civil War — Verot now
lashed out against slave masters who had abused their slaves,
violated their slaves' inherent rights, and thereby given occasion
to the abolitionists' spleen. "A man, by being a slave, does not

[25] Cf. *Catholic Mirror*, May 10, 1862: "The observative [*sic*] and just people
of this conservative country have looked upon the course of the Catholic Church
in regard to our national troubles with profound respect. Certain it is, she has
never fanned the flames of discord."

[26] Cf. *Freeman's Journal*, December 8, 1855: "Who, but the Protestant clergymen? . . . Who have irritated and exasperated the North and poured obloquy and
misrepresentation on the South? Who have sundered their own Church organizations upon a North and South dividing line? . . . They are the true fomenters
of the mischiefs which imperil this union." Cf. also *Catholic Mirror*, September 15,
1860: "There are men in these United States, in clerical garments who, by neglect
of their own business, and meddling in that which was not, and is not theirs,
have done evils to this country which they cannot repair . . . and which may
yet prove fatal to this now glorious and powerful union of States."

cease to be a man, retaining all the properties, qualities, attributes, duties, rights and responsibilities attached to human nature, or to a being endowed with reason and understanding. . . . A master has not over a slave the same rights which he has over an animal and whoever would view his slaves merely as beasts, would have virtually abjured human nature, and would deserve to be expelled from human society." Verot then proceeded to lay down the various conditions that he maintained had to accompany a legitimate possession of slaves.

The first such condition was the slave owner's repudiation of the slave trade, which is "absolutely immoral and unjust, and is against all laws natural, divine, ecclesiastical and civil." Although his stand here against the slave trade jeopardized his earlier argument that the southern slave owners possessed their slaves under just title, Verot himself appears to have seen no contradiction:

What right has any man to steal another man and enslave him? This, next to murder, seems to be the grossest violation of justice that can be conceived. It is no palliation of this trade to assert that the condition of those poor creatures will be bettered by selling them to Christian masters in America: for evil is not to be done in order to obtain a good result. . . . It is not an excuse for the trade, but an additional monstrosity, to say that those negroes are sold to the captains of vessels by other tribes who have captured them in war: for the war is for no other reason than to make prisoners; it is not a war but an abominable plunder of human beings.

The slave trade was prohibited by nearly all the European governments, by the United States,[27] and by the apostolic decree of Gregory XVI, "which was solemnly read in the council of American Prelates held in Baltimore in the year 1840." It must be, he added, a cause of regret and mortification for all true friends of the southern cause that some people had wished to revive this trade. "Indeed if a Southern Confederacy was to authorize this worst of piracies, we would predict with certainty its speedy downfall, because it would not be founded on justice . . . but there is not the slightest or remotest fear of this," he concluded hopefully.

[27] Only the importation of slaves from abroad was prohibited by the United States; interstate and intrastate trade in slaves was legal and common. See Frederic Bancroft, *Slave-Trading in the Old South* (Baltimore: J. H. Furst Co., 1931).

The second condition of legitimate slavery was that the rights of free colored persons be respected. "The moment some colored people have acquired, or possess lawful exemptioṅ from slavery, it is as unjust to enslave them again as it would be to enslave a white man, because *the ground of slavery is not in the color of the skin,* but the titles which make one the legitimate servant of another."[28] He praised the South Carolina legislature (meeting in Charleston) for refusing to pass a bill that would cause all free Negroes to be sold back into bondage — "the report does great honor to the head and heart of those who lead politics in Charleston" — and he hoped that the escutcheon of Florida would not be sullied by such a statute.[29]

The third condition he offered in the names of public decency, religion, and Christianity: "It is that the whites do not take advantage of the weakness, ignorance, dependence, and lowly position of colored females, whether slaves or not — availing themselves of the impunity which, hitherto, laws in the South have extended to this sort of iniquity."

> I am a sincere and devoted friend of the South, to which Divine Providence sent me, and I am ready to undergo any hardship — to make any sacrifice — for the true welfare of the people among whom I live; still I must say it for conscience sake — who knows whether the Almighty does not design to use the present disturbances for the destruction of frequent occasions of immorality, which the subservient and degraded position of the slave offers to the lewd. I hope I am a false prophet: but, at the same time, I must admonish my countrymen that obscure, secret, and hidden crimes often call for an open, public, and solemn chastisement at the hands of the Supreme Moderator of events. . . . The Southern Confederacy,

[28] My emphasis. Verot differs sharply from his fellow Catholic, Chief Justice Roger Brooke Taney, whose Dred Scott decision in 1857 found that the Negroes' subordination to the white slaver was grounded in their stature as an "inferior class of being, who had been subjected by the dominant race, and whether emancipated or not, yet remained subject to their authority." See Henry Steele Commager, ed., *Documents of American History* (New York: F. S. Crofts, 1947), 339–345.

[29] The number of free Negroes in Florida declined from 932 in 1850 to 804 in 1855, but rose again to 1032 in 1860. See Williams, "Negro Slavery in Florida," Part II: "So rigorous did the regulation of the free Negroes become that many a free Negro must have felt that he would be better off as a slave under a kind master" (183–184). There were relatively few escapes: 18 fugitive slaves in 1850 and only 11 in 1860 (187).

if it should exist, must rest on morality and justice, and it could
never be entitled to a special protection from above, unless it
professes to surround Slavery with the guarantees that will secure
its morality and virtue.

While masters had, indeed, a right to the labor of their slaves,
and could justly require of them obedience, respect, and service,
they were not their masters in such a way that they could forbid
them marriage or proscribe it at pleasure. Hence Verot's fourth
condition for a legitimate slavery required masters to promote
marriage among their slaves according to the norms of Christian
morality, all the while respecting the slaves' freedom to choose
partners of their liking. The paragraph ending this section would
be quoted by southern newspapers during the last year of the war:[30]

> Slavery, to become a permanent institution of the South, must
> be made to conform to the laws of God; a Southern Confederacy
> will never thrive, unless it rests upon morality and order; the
> Supreme Arbiter of nations will not bless with stability and pros-
> perity a state of things which would be a flagrant violation of
> His holy commandments.

Another condition arose from the nature of connubial society:
husband and wife had a right to remain joined together until
death parted them. "There ought to be, therefore, a provision made
and sanctioned by the civil law, to be a bar against cupidity, that
families shall never be separated, and specially, that husband
and wife will be looked upon as one person, inseparable and
indivisible." Verot had in mind the forcible sundering of husbands
and wives and parents and children, a widespread practice in the
South which had formed the most damaging body of evidence
in Theodore Dwight Weld's 1839 antislavery tract, *American
Slavery As It Is*.[31] Verot continued:

> Legitimate gains from slaves cannot be censured . . . but gain
> at the expense of morality, religion, and humanity, is a horror which
> can but bring to a speedy ruin a fabric that would rest on it and
> admit of it. The separation of families is frought with evils and
> inconveniences which shock the moral sense of everybody at once.
> . . . What a dreadful responsibility for any master who has not

---

[30] See Richmond *Daily Dispatch,* January 30, 1865; Charleston *Daily Courier,*
February 6, 1865.
[31] New York, 1839.

yet extinguished altogether in himself the fear of his Supreme Judge!

Another condition "scarcely necessary to mention" was the master's obligation to provide adequate food, clothing, and shelter. Here Verot found the masters in general not guilty. It was indeed a striking feature of the South, he said, that the slave was better fed and clothed than the free Negro. There had been much misrepresentation and calumny resorted to on this point by abolitionists, but their appalling stories were no more than a malicious fiction. "If there have been cruel, tyrannical, tiger-hearted masters, it is only a proof that there may be monsters in the human race — but such monsters are found as well in free and in slave regions." The spirit of Christianity, if inculcated as it ought to be, he continued, would teach the master to treat the slave with humanity and kindness, as a fellow being, and as a partaker of the same promises of eternal life. Reverting to the Protestant clergy, he hazarded the opinion that if they endeavored to spread genuine Christianity among the masters they would "do incomparably more for the relief and the happiness of the slave than all the fanatical efforts of abolitionists."

The last condition he laid down was that slaves must be provided with the means of knowing and practicing religion. This was a sacred, indispensable, bounden duty of every master. And Verot, whose solicitude for the spiritual well-being of the slaves had been striking to those who knew him at Doughoregan Manor, and would be all the more impressive after Appomattox, clearly put his whole energy into the task of driving this duty home:

> He [the master] has, with regard to that, the same obligations which parents contract with regard to their children. Hence it would be a great crime, and a great folly at the same time, in masters to keep their servants in ignorance of every religious doctrine; those lost souls would cry out to heaven against them for vengeance, and this flagrant injustice against the souls of slaves, would be the sure way to render slavery an untenable and ruinous institution, deserving the contempt of men, and the malediction of God. It would be treating slaves like beasts. . . . and God would owe it to his mercy, wisdom, and justice, to bring about the speedy ruin of such an iniquitous institution.

With these sentiments, the bishop concluded. It was an important

effort. What were its effects? While Verot felt strongly that southern
constitutional rights were in process of violation by the northern
states and while he promised to earn himself, as he did, the
reputation of a "true friend of the South," the principal long-run
effect of this sermon was not the justification of slavery, but the
intelligence, widely disseminated in the South, that the slave system
must be ameliorated. That such may have been the primary
effect hoped for by the author himself is suggested by Verot's letter
to Archbishop Kenrick, written January 18, where he stated his
desire to have some improvement obtained "for the poor slaves
of our plantations." In the same letter Verot told Kenrick that
he had sent the manuscript to Baltimore for publication by John
Murphy and Company. He went on to suggest to the archbishop
that "this matter be a subject of some special and formal legislation or declaration in the next council, if it be in your view to
convene one this spring."

Such a council was not called, owing to hostilities,[32] and probably would not have been called anyway, as Kenrick was apparently not prepared to take a stand on slavery one way or
the other. This is apparent from the archbishop's reaction to Verot's
sermon. In the letter of January 18 Verot had concluded: "I direct
Mr. Murphy to send you a proof of my Tract as soon as practible
[sic], and if you wish to have the manuscript, you are at liberty
to take it, and I submit everything to your judgment in which I
have the fullest confidence."[33] Kenrick's letter book for February 7
shows notice, in Latin, of this curt reply: "I wrote to A. Verot,
Vicar Apostolic of Florida, suggesting that his tract on slavery
be suppressed."[34] Kenrick's actual letter is not extant, but something more of its tone may be discerned from Verot's explanation
to Bishop Lynch of Charleston: "John Murphy of Baltimore printed
for me a tract for the times which was not published in Baltimore
because the Most Rev. Abp. thought it would create an excite-

---

[32] "I was of the opinion that the Council should be held. I wrote about it in
time to the Most Rev. Abp. who answered that the thing was out of the question
in the present political excitement." ADC, Box 1861, Verot to Lynch, St. Augustine,
May 7, 1861.

[33] AAB, 32-D-6, Verot to Kenrick, St. Augustine, January 18, 1861.

[34] AAB, Kenrick Letterbook, p. 215: "1861 Feb. 7. Scripsi ad A. Verot Ap. V.
Florid. suggerens ut supprimatur libellus de servitute."

ment."³⁵ Verot complained to Lynch that, as of May 7, he had not yet received the printed copies.

> The edition was sent to me, via Charleston on one of the steamers that ply between your city & Baltimore care of Thornwell? (You introduced me to him on the streets of Charleston). I have not received the bundle. If it be not trespassing on your time & kindness, I would be much obliged to you, if you would inquire after that bundle, & in case you find it, please to open it & take from it a copy of the said tract, & tell me whether the circulation of it would be calculated to do some good.³⁶

There is no record of the date when the copies were received, nor is there any record of the number distributed and the area covered. On November 9, however, Verot, who by this time was Bishop of Savannah, wrote to Archbishop Jean Marie Odin of New Orleans, expressing gratification that the tract had made a favorable impression there. "I willingly give you permission," he wrote Odin, "to reprint and translate it [into French]. I enclose some copies."³⁷ Two editions, one in English and one in French, were subsequently published on December 8 and 9, respectively, by the press of *Le Propagateur catholique*.³⁸ Father Napoléon Perché, editor of the *Propagateur,* and an ardent secessionist, applauded Verot's sermon as proving the teaching of the abolitionists

---

³⁵ ADC, Box 1861, Verot to Lynch, May 7, 1861. Kenrick's reaction to Verot's tract perhaps showed less a disagreement than it did a desire simply not to get involved. By 1861 Kenrick's views on slavery were studiously, if not purposely, vague. On March 1, interestingly, Kenrick wrote to the Holy See to criticize Father Napoléon Perché, editor of *Le Propagateur Catholique* in New Orleans, for his vindication of the rights of the southern states to secede; Archives of Propaganda Fide, Rome: *Scritture Riferite nei Congressi, America Centrale,* 1861–1862, Vol. 19, fols. 118r and 120r, Baltimore, Md., March 1, 1861.

³⁶ ADC, Box 1861, Verot to Lynch, May 7, 1861. James Henley Thornwell (1812–1862) was a noted Presbyterian divine with whom Lynch had debated on theological questions. See Jeremiah J. O'Connell, *Catholicity in the Carolinas and Georgia* (New York: Sadlier & Co., 1879), 308.

³⁷ AANO, Box 1861, Verot to Jean Marie Odin, Savannah, November 9, 1861.

³⁸ The English edition was identical with that of Baltimore, except that to Verot's name on the title page was added, "and now Bishop of Savannah." The citation for the French edition is as follows: *Esclavage & abolitionisme. Sermon prêché dans l'église de St. Augustin, Floride, le 4 Janvier 1861, jour d'humiliation, de jeûne et de prières publiques, par Mgr. Vérot, Vicaire Apostolique de la Floride, aujourd'hui Évêque de Savannah* (Nouvelle Orléans: Le Propagateur catholique, 1861), 24 pp.

to be false and criminal. He rejoiced that Verot had supplied southern Catholics with an effective proslavery argument.[39] There are no records to suggest the extent to which these editions, like that of Baltimore, were distributed. As shown later, however, the sermon was certainly known in Charleston, Richmond, New York, and Cincinnati by 1865. Georgia and Florida, which were the areas under Verot's jurisdiction, would be acquainted with the sermon as a matter of course. Father Henry P. Clavreul, who was stationed at Fernandina, Florida, remembered later: "The sermon created quite a sensation throughout the South."[40]

Before sending the manuscript to Baltimore on January 18, Verot had altered the text of the next to last paragraph to bring the spirit of the sermon into conformity with Florida's secession from the Union, which had occurred on January 10. By that time he was politically committed to the Confederacy, which was then in process of formation. The interpolation also gave him the occasion to press again for reformation of the slave system, his apparent primary concern. The amended paragraph read:

The subject which I have presented today to your consideration, beloved brethren, is one of great importance, and is to have a powerful influence over the stability of the Southern Confederacy. Such a Confederacy will, to all appearance, be formed, and such is the rapid march of events that the dismemberment of the Union is already consummated, and the faint hopes of a permanency of the Union which existed yet when the first pages of this paper were written have altogether vanished, and the new flag of the Southern Confederacy is now given to the breeze, and waves under my eyes.[41] Now if that Confederacy is meant to be solid, durable, stable, and permanent, it must rest upon justice and morality. "Justice exalteth a Nation: but sin maketh Nations miserable." It is undoubtedly true that the law of God does not reprove Slavery; it is undoubtedly

---

[39] *Le Propagateur catholique,* December 21, 1861; January 4, 1862.

[40] *Notes,* 17.

[41] Verot mistook the flag of Florida for the Confederate banner. On January 7, three days before Florida's formal secession, the ladies of St. Augustine began raising funds for a flagpole to fly the "national flag of Florida" in the plaza. The flag was properly hoisted and subsequently replaced by the Confederate banner sometime after February 4, when the formation of the Confederate government was announced. See Omega G. East, "St. Augustine During the Civil War," *The Florida Historical Quarterly,* XXXI (October, 1952), 75, 86. By January 18, when Verot sent off his manuscript, South Carolina, Mississippi, Florida, and Alabama had seceded; Georgia would secede the day following.

true that now the sudden and abrupt manumission of slaves would be a misfortune of appalling magnitude, more so yet for the slave than for the master. Let then the wise and the virtuous unite and combine their prudence, their patriotism, their humanity, and their religious integrity to divest Slavery of the features which would make it odious to God and man. Now is the time to make a salutary reform, and to enact judicious regulations. I propose as a means of setting the new Confederacy upon a solid basis, that a servile code be drawn up and adopted by the Confederacy defining clearly the rights and duties of slaves. This will be the means of proving to the world that the South is on the side of justice, morality, reason and religion. This will be a just indication of Southern views sanctioned by the Great Arbiter of Nations; this will be a most triumphant confutation of the charges which bigotry, ignorance, fanaticism and malice, cloaked under a reverend garb, have for years heaped against Southern Institutions.

A student of Catholic attitudes during the slavery controversy states that, for the Catholic hierarchy and clergy, Bishop Verot "probably set the pace when he exhorted the Southern people to ameliorate the slave system."[42] Equally significant, Verot's "servile code" probably set the pace for the southern states as well. A recent study dates the initiation of the first serious attempts to propagandize slavery reform from the summer and fall of 1861, when the *Church Intelligencer,* a periodical of the Episcopalians, sought to stir up sentiment in favor of granting legal sanction to slave marriages. It places the next effort "early in 1862" when the *Southern Churchman,* another Episcopal journal, declared itself against the separation of married slaves.[43] But Verot's ringing call for these and other reforms antedated both these instances. By 1865 the Richmond *Daily Dispatch* and the Charleston *Daily Courier* were quoting from the second part of Verot's sermon.[44] Indeed, the whole South by that year was caught up in a self-conscious movement to purge slavery of its patent abuses, and to

[42] Rice *American Catholic Opinion,* 148.

[43] Bell Irvin Wiley, "The Movement to Humanize the Institution of Slavery during the Confederacy," *The Emory University Quarterly,* V (December, 1949), 208. That the pioneer character of Verot's effort went unrecognized is due, probably, to the fact that Wiley took his information on Verot's position from an extract of the 1861 sermon appearing in the Richmond *Daily Dispatch* four years afterward, on January 30, 1865 (217).

[44] February 6, 1865.

humanize the institution generally. Reform sentiment had gathered such strength from 1863 on that in both the secular and religious press the southerner of 1865 could find all the "conditions" that Verot had set down in 1861 as necessary for a just and lawful slavery.[45] The eventual failure of the reform agitators to secure passage of remedial laws and of the "servile code" that Verot was the first to propose was attributable to the fact that state legislatures were too occupied with the more pressing problem of self-preservation to give much time to any but emergency defense measures.[46]

On June 18, 1864, the New York *Freeman's Journal* reprinted Verot's sermon and praised its author editorially: "We know Bishop Verot to be a very soundly instructed theologian. He is of the *old school* walking in the straight paths marked out by the Saints and Doctors of the Catholic Church, who have all treated slavery — 'servitudo' — as a human arrangement for the common good." Such a proslavery interpretation was not surprising from the copperheading New York paper. More surprising was the generous treatment given the sermon after the war by the Cincinnati *Catholic Telegraph*, which had come out emphatically for emancipation in 1863, and had condemned those Catholics who wished to be "jailors of their fellowmen." On December 20, 1865, the *Telegraph* printed the sermon in its entirety, saying that the subject was "Rights and Duties of Slaveholders." Not too adroitly, the editors attempted to camouflage the obvious links which Verot had drawn between slavery and its concretization in the South:

> The proof of this first point [the justification of slavery by human law] would admit no contradiction, if the Right Rev. Prelate had shown that the law of GOD, whether Natural or positive, or the Ecclesiastical law, sanctioned Negro slavery as it existed in the South. But this the Rt. Rev. sermonizer does not pretend, or intend to do — so that all this first-point is irrelevant, superfluous. We may say of it — *"transeat."*

In the second part of the sermon the *Telegraph* found much to admire, and it offered it to its readers as "our own complete justification for our unqualified condemnation of Negro Slavery." One

---

[45] Wiley, "The Movement to Humanize," 211–220.
[46] *Ibid.*, 219.

can only conjecture how curious Verot would have felt had he known in 1861 that his defense of slavery would be used only four years later in the service of its unqualified condemnation. The *Telegraph* concluded: "We had underlined and made comments on some of the Bishop's remarks, in which, as a Southern citizen, he touches lightly on some of the shortcomings of the South, but we prefer to present his remarks as he has uttered and printed them."

The ambivalence of the sermon, dividing its force between the justification of slavery in the abstract, and the condemnation of certain of its concrete features, was revealing of the difficult position Verot found himself in at the beginning of secession. Theologically, he was convinced of the legitimacy of slavery. Politically, he was convinced that southern constitutional rights were in serious jeopardy, and he was prepared to fight for the Confederate cause. On the other hand, he realized that the present difficulties of the South were largely her own doing; widespread abuses of the slavery system were threatening to bring down the wrath of the Arbiter of Nations. Caught between two convictions, propounded with equal vigor, his argument understandably left several large openings for rebuttal. Certainly one of the "underlines" that the *Catholic Telegraph* thought of making would draw attention to Verot's failure to include the slave trade in his catalog of means that could be used for obtaining just title over a slave. The later section condemning the slave trade stood in curious confrontation with that lapse. One suspects, however, that Verot was not overly concerned about the contradiction, for, as the war progressed toward its humiliating conclusion, his mind would be drawn more and more to the plights of the slaves as opposed to the rights of their masters.

In all events, it was clear from his celebrated sermon that for Augustin Verot justice was the supreme imperative in human affairs. For him it was not a question where injustice most prevailed, whether among abolitionists or among slave masters, but a question of how long injustice could prevail among *either* before divine retribution descended on the country at large. Toward the beginning of his sermon he compared the nation's prospects with those of the later Roman Empire, and in so doing showed chilling prescience of the terrible swift sword that was soon to fall:

The great Doctor of the Church — the patron of this city and congregation — St. Augustine, in his admirable work, "Of the City of God," undertook to show the true reason of the unexampled prosperity of the Roman Empire. That Empire was the most extensive and the most prosperous that ever existed: it extended itself to the remotest corners of the known universe. Even the wild nations that could not be reached by its authority respected and dreaded the very name of the Roman. That illustrious Doctor does not hesitate to say that this temporal prosperity of the Empire was the reward of the moral virtues which illustrated the Roman nation in the first centuries of her existence, and which were never more conspicuous than in the men whom she placed at the head of her armies, and to whom she gave the direction of her civil and political affairs. They have left us admirable examples of justice, integrity, and fortitude, on most trying occasions. . . . As long as this love of justice lasted, the Supreme Ruler of events gave success to their arms, and extended their conquests far and wide, until the whole earth was under their sway. But at a later period, injustice, iniquity, ambition, covetousness, and bribery crept into the Empire, and were found disgracing even the leaders of the nation. It was then that Almighty God permitted that hordes of barbarians should invade that Empire, now fallen from its pristine justice and integrity; and those Barbarians devastated and overturned the colossal Empire, and swept its authority, its grandeur, and its very name from the earth.

Such is then the plan of Divine Providence in the government of this world. If iniquity, injustice, rapine, and bloodshed seem sometimes to meet with success, it is only temporary and ephemeral, similar to the devastation produced by a swollen torrent, but such causes cannot establish, settle, and place on a permanent basis, any civil and political institution: any government that rests upon injustice must necessarily crumble with its tottering foundation. "Justice exalteth a nation: but sin maketh nations miserable." Our beloved country is now undoubtedly under the operation of that stern and inflexible rule of justice at the hands of the Author of justice.

CHAPTER III

A VENTURE IN POLITICS

WHEN, in his January, 1861, sermon, Bishop Verot attacked the
"states which have enacted laws against the Constitution and the
Legislation of the United States," he did something that few other
American Catholic prelates had done before him — he entered the
ring of national politics. Besides this, it can be said that Bishop
Verot seems to have been the first prelate to enter national politics
on an issue not directly affecting Catholicism as such.[1] How unusual
the moment was, and why, from the establishment of the native
episcopate in 1790, the American bishops had followed a policy
of official abstention from political questions, can be learned from
a close reading of American Catholic history from 1830 to 1861.[2]
It will be seen that the bishops had more than one reason for
clerical aloofness. For one thing, Catholics formed only a small
minority of the national population; only 318,000 in 1830, Catholics
by 1860 numbered 3,103,000 (chiefly because of immigration), yet
were still less in number than Negro slaves.[3] It was an unpopular

---

[1] In the 1840 Harrison-Van Buren presidential campaign Bishop John England
of Charleston had defended the integrity and freedom of the Catholic voter against
the slanders of General Duff Green and other leaders of the Whig party, but had
remained aloof from the political campaign as such. He scrupulously turned down
invitations to speak before rallies of Harrison and Van Buren alike. See Joseph
L. O'Brien, *John England — Bishop of Charleston, The Apostle to Democracy*
(New York: The Edward O'Toole Company, Inc., 1934), 127–152; Peter Guilday,
The Life and Times of John England, First Bishop of Charleston, 1786–1842
(New York: The American Press, 1927), II, 524–528. In 1841 Bishop John Hughes
of New York had entered a "Catholic ticket" in the New York City elections in
an effort to obtain public funds for Catholic schools. The ticket was "a temporary
expedient brought on by the attitudes of the two regular parties rather than an
entrance into politics as such." Ellis, *American Catholicism* (Chicago: University
of Chicago Press, 1958), 167, n. 37.

[2] For the bibliography for this period cf. John Tracy Ellis, *A Guide to American
Catholic History* (Milwaukee: Bruce, 1959). See also the valuable summary of
this period, relating the American State to all the various religious denominations,
in Anson P. Stokes, *Church and State in the United States* (New York: Harper,
1950), II, Chaps. XIV and XV, 3–249.

[3] The best general studies of European immigration during this period are

minority: from the mid-thirties onward, Catholics were under continual fire from nativist groups, which carped at "Romish doctrines," the Church's supposed threat to American institutions, and the foreign cast, lent to it by immigration, of Catholic membership.[4] The bishops understandably shied away from any political action that would tend to enlarge hostility. Even had they decided to speak in the political forum, they could hardly have expected to improve substantially the position of the Church, already bountifully blessed by a Constitution which, because it ignored differences in religion and inequalities in population, was decidedly favorable to the Catholic minority. Coincidentally, it was when that Constitution was thought to have been violated that the southern bishops led the break away from the established policy.

Other reasons, too, can be adduced in explanation of the bishops' position. The flood of Irish and German immigrants that set in during the 1830's presented the young Church with enough internal problems to occupy her whole attention and to persuade her that official participation in public affairs would only draw away energies needed in the task of assimilating (ecclesiastically) the incoming groups. The bishops who assembled at the First Plenary Council of Baltimore in May, 1852, numbered thirty-two, of whom only nine were native-born. Thus the bishops themselves, with the Irish dominating, mirrored the immigrant nature of the young Church. More than that, the bishops' own immigrant backgrounds formed one of the chief reasons why no prelate during this period encouraged Orestes Brownson's view that Catholicism and Americanism were not only compatible but complementary, and that the Church should proceed at once to "Americanize" itself.[5] Actually, some Americanization had already occurred among German and Irish

---

Marcus Lee Hansen, *The Atlantic Migration* (Cambridge, Mass.: Harvard University, 1941); Oscar Handlin, *The Uprooted* (Boston: Little, Brown, 1951); and Maldyn Allen Jones, *American Immigration* (Chicago: University of Chicago Press, 1960).

[4] See Billington, *The Protestant Crusade, 1800–1860* (New York: Macmillan, 1938), *passim*.

[5] See, e.g., Brownson's essays during 1854 and 1857 in his *Brownson Quarterly Review* (New York). Cf. the study of Brownson in Ralph Henry Gabriel, *The Course of American Democratic Thought* (New York: Ronald Press, 1956), 57–61. Gabriel sees Brownson and his disciple Isaac Hecker, later founder of the Paulists, as the first Catholics of importance to attempt to "harmonize Catholic doctrine and the American democratic faith" (58).

Catholics in the frontier regions of the Middle West, and was reflected in the artificial, imported character of the nativism prevalent
there.[6] But Bishop John Hughes of New York, who spoke for the
Irish-born bishops on this point, believed that Irish origins and
the practice of Catholicism in English-speaking countries were so
intimately conjoined, if not one and the same, that Brownson's idea
amounted to a betrayal of the Faith. Hughes rebuked the "Yankee"
Brownson publicly in 1856.[7]

There were also during these years the tasks of establishing a
uniform system of ecclesiastical discipline and practice, of maintaining purity of doctrine and ritual, and of arranging for the
inauguration of new dioceses and provinces. The lay-trustee controversy was at its height, and bishops had to deal with recalcitrant
congregations which insisted on control of church property and
final authority on the appointment of pastors. Not wishing to add
any more difficulties, the hierarchy understandably refrained from
taking any official public positions that might aggravate the
sectional and national differences already existing among the
Catholic population. Their few corporate statements on political
matters emphasized that politics was an interest of lay people
only. The bishops attending the Fourth Provincial Council of
Baltimore in May, 1840, on the eve of the bitterly contested
Harrison-Van Buren election, stated in a pastoral letter to their
people: "We disclaim all right to interfere with your judgment in

---

[6] George M. Stephenson, "Nativism in the Forties and Fifties, with Special
Reference to the Mississippi Valley," *Mississippi Valley Historical Review,* IX
(December, 1922), 185–202.

[7] Henry F. Brownson, *Orestes A. Brownson's Later Life from 1856 to 1876*
(Detroit: The Author, 1900), 65–75. By failing "to see the advantages of a quicker
Americanization," one authority on the period has estimated, Hughes "set back
the progress of the Irish immigrant at least a generation . . ."; Thomas T.
McAvoy, C.S.C., "The Formation of the Catholic Minority in the United
States, 1820–1860," *The Review of Politics,* X (January, 1948), 26. Cf. Archbishop
John Ireland of St. Paul, speaking in 1894: "No one need remind me that immigration has brought us inestimable blessings . . . [but] Priests foreign in disposition and work were not fitted to make favorable impressions upon the
non-Catholic American population, and the American-born children of Catholic
immigrants were likely to escape their action. . . . Even priests of American
ancestry ministering to immigrants, not infrequently fell into the lines of those
around them, and did but little to make the Church in America throb with
American life." Quoted in Gabriel, *The Course of American Democratic Thought,*
69.

A VENTURE IN POLITICS 59

the political affairs of our common country, and are far from
entertaining the wish to control you in the constitutional exercise
of your freedom. . . ."[8]

As it happened, most Catholics, and the Catholic press as well,
were aligning themselves with the Democratic Party, which appeared, from its "professions of attachment to liberty and equality,"[9] more fitted to the aspirations that the immigrants had
brought from Europe. The discovery that the Whigs were in con-
sort with Nativists only confirmed the Catholics in their Democratic affiliation. The bishops, all the while, had done nothing to
direct that choice. Harriet Martineau, the English reformer, could
say in 1837: "The Catholic body is democratic in its politics, and
made up from the more independent kind of occupations. The
Catholic religion is modified by the spirit of the time in America;
and its professors are not a set of men who can be priest-ridden
to any fatal extent."[10] At the First Plenary Council in 1852 the
bishops issued a declaration that was typical of their fear lest
any occasion be given to political attack on the Catholic body:
"Show your attachment to the institutions of our beloved country
by prompt compliance with all their requirements, and by the
cautious jealousy with which you guard against the least deviation
from the rules which they prescribe for the maintenance of public
order and private rights."[11]

In the South, Catholic abstention from politics was more difficult
to maintain. Abolitionism in the North, and spreading antislavery
sentiment in the upper South, caused Catholics to become anxious
about the political possibilities in store for them. Still, the bishops
in this area consistently refrained from introducing into their
pastoral letters or diocesan synods any overt political counsels,
and they seem to have grown stronger in that resolution as North-
South relations worsened.[12]

---

[8] Peter Guilday, ed., *National Pastorals of the American Hierarchy, 1791–1921*
(New York: Macmillan, 1923), 87.

[9] Boston *Pilot,* November 1, 1856; cf. *Freeman's Journal,* June 21, 1856.

[10] Harriet Martineau, *Society in America* (London, 1837), III, 237, cited in Ellis,
American Catholicism, 81.

[11] Guilday, *National Pastorals,* 192.

[12] See, e.g., pastoral of the bishops of the Province of Baltimore, in Louisville
Catholic Guardian, June 5, 1858; pastoral of the diocesan synod of Natchez,
April, 1858, in *Freeman's Journal,* June 5, 1858; Bishop William Elder, pastoral
to the clergy and laity of Natchez, October 28, 1858, in *Freeman's Journal,*
November 13, 1858.

The eleven states which eventually formed the Confederacy were governed ecclesiastically through eleven Catholic dioceses: the Archdiocese of New Orleans with its five suffragan sees of Galveston, Natchitoches (Alexandria), Little Rock, Natchez, and Mobile; Nashville (of the Province of St. Louis); and the following sees of the Province of Baltimore: Wheeling, Richmond, Charleston, and Savannah, the last comprising Georgia and the Vicariate Apostolic of Florida. Only three of the bishops were American by birth: Richard Whelan of Wheeling and William Elder of Natchez, both of whom had been born in Baltimore, and John McGill of Richmond, who had grown up in Philadelphia. Four prelates came from France originally: Jean Marie Odin of New Orleans (after 1861), and Verot, Augustus M. Martin, and Claude Marie Dubuis (after 1862) of Savannah, Natchitoches, and Galveston, respectively. The four remaining prelates, James Whelan, Andrew Byrne, John Quinlan, and Patrick Lynch, of Nashville, Little Rock, Mobile, and Charleston, were born in Ireland.[13] Since by far the greater number of Catholics resided in the North and were already coalescing into strong urban units,[14] it was clear that political rebellion on the part of the southern bishops would divide Catholics into two extremely unequal groups. Probably for this reason and for the added reason that southern institutions were receiving as much vocal support in the northern Church as in the southern,[15] and simply because it was the established episcopal policy, the prelates of the South tried as hard as their northern colleagues to stand apart from the nation's political troubles. The majority kept their own counsel up to the fateful guns of April 12, 1861.

A warning note was sounded by Bishop Quinlan of Mobile in a pastoral letter issued January 1, 1861. Quinlan strongly defended the Union, "our noble edifice," but added vaguely that "we would not purchase union at the expense of justice." He continued: "It is only as a security for just, independent rights — and the noble

---

[13] For a summary of the names and sees of the American hierarchy during the period 1860–1865, see Blied, *Catholics and the Civil War* (Milwaukee: The Author, 1945), 50–53.

[14] Gerard Shaughnessy, S.M., *Has the Immigrant Kept the Faith?* (New York: Macmillan, 1925), 114–145. Cf. Philip Hughes, "The Catholic Pioneers," *The Atlantic*, 210 (August, 1962), 107–108.

[15] See above, Chapter II.

character of the constitution is, in letter and in spirit, all of this
— that we love the union of the states, and pray for its con-
tinuance. Let us, then . . . as long as hope remains, faint not in
our efforts for its preservation."[16] Three days later, Bishop Verot
delivered his sermon on "Slavery and Abolitionism," bluntly condemning the North's violation of the Fugitive Slave Act, and promising that the South "will not, as a Nation, be as patient as the
Catholic Church."[17] With this stroke the American Church moved
awkwardly into the political arena. It was followed in short order
by a small widening of the breach: on January 10, Bishop Elder
of Natchez directed that prayers would no longer be said for
the civil powers in Washington as those authorities could no longer
claim the allegiance of Mississippi's people.[18] On February 4,
Elder wrote to Bishop James Duggan of Chicago, declaring that
he was ready to "contribute means and arms" to the new con-
federation.[19] By this date, Verot, too, was hailing the proposed
Confederacy and outlining plans how it should conduct itself on
the issue of slavery. But the other bishops of the country, North
and South, were still, not strangely, silent. In pastorals, in sermons,
in official announcements, the hierarchy held fast to their accustomed platform above the smoke, and up to the fall of Fort Sumter,
limited their voices to pleas for peace.[20]

Only after guns began to roar, when it appeared that they could
no longer stand apart from the civil agony and still claim the
full loyalty of their subjects, did the remaining bishops commit
their miters to the fire of politics and war. It was a strange
moment for the Church that had "left to worldlings the cares
and anxieties of political partisanship."[21] Some of the bishops
yielded easily to the new order, like Lynch of Charleston and
Archbishop John Purcell of Cincinnati; others gave in more re-

---

[16] Reprinted in *Freeman's Journal*, March 2, 1861. By January 1, 1861, only
South Carolina had seceded.

[17] See above, Chapter II.

[18] Blied, *Catholics and the Civil War*, 55.

[19] Quoted in *ibid.*, 56.

[20] See the survey of episcopal pronouncements in the six months prior to Fort
Sumter in Joseph R. Frese, S.J., "The Hierarchy and Peace in the War of
Secession," *Thought*, XVIII (June, 1943), 293–305. The author omits mention of
Verot's sermon, and concludes that the hierarchy's attitude was characterized by
sorrow over the disruption of the Union and by desire for peace.

[21] Concilium Baltimorensis Provinciale IX, May 28, 1856.

luctantly, like Hughes of New York and Nashville's James Whelan.[22]
For most, that choice was not hard to make: the bishops simply
lined up along geographical lines, as everyone else was doing.
Excepting border state prelates, like Kenrick of Baltimore, who
heeded the exigencies of that delicate position,[23] the southern
bishops, "whose worldwide system of government was attuned to
support any secular establishment under which they were living,"[24]
found themselves by nature supporting the Confederacy, and declaring northerners "no longer our countrymen."[25] The northern
bishops, for their part, preached loyalty to the Union.

Despite the satisfaction that Bishop Verot took in the justification of the war, he could take little satisfaction in the course
of the war itself. In Florida and neighboring Georgia the war went
badly from the start. During the fall and winter of 1861–1862
Union warships and troop transports ranged at will along the
coasts of the two states. Landings were made against ineffectual
resistance at Port Royal, South Carolina, a short distance above
Savannah, on November 7, and scores of frightened Savannahians
fled into the interior at the news.[26] At Savannah itself five months
later Union cannons tore apart the "impregnable" brick walls of
the city's famous Fort Pulaski, forcing the surrender of Savannah's
elite garrison.[27] The defeat threw the city into panic again, one
correspondent recorded — "women are leaving and property of all

[22] For Whelan's peculiar difficulties, see Victor F. O'Daniel, *The Father of the
Church in Tennessee, Richard Pius Miles, O.P.* (New York: Frederick Pustet,
1926), 573.

[23] For Kenrick's difficulties see James Cardinal Gibbons, "My Memories,"
Dublin Review, CLX (April, 1917), 165; Ellis, *American Catholicism*, 94.

[24] E. Merton Coulter, *The Confederate States of America, 1861–1865* (Baton
Rouge: Louisiana State University, 1950), 521. Cf. Augusta *Daily Constitutionalist*
(hereafter cited *Constitutionalist*), July 10, 1864: "The reason [why the Roman
Catholic Church] has been as steadfast to the cause of Southern Independence as
the fiercest of us could desire . . . is apparent from the history of the church.
For nearly a thousand years there has been no material change among this class
of Christians, and the Church has always frowned upon all innovations, changes
and isms."

[25] Edward McPherson, *The Political History of the United States of America,
during the Great Rebellion* (2nd ed.; Washington, D. C.: Philip & Solomons, 1865),
516–517.

[26] Alexander A. Lawrence, *A Present for Mr. Lincoln, The Story of Savannah
from Secession to Sherman* (Macon, Ga.: Ardivan Press, 1961), 36–37.

[27] *Ibid.*, 51–65.

kinds is being sent off."[28] Capture of the city would wait, however, for William Tecumseh Sherman two and a half years later. In Florida, Union forces landed with ease at Fernandina (March 2), Jacksonville (March 12), and St. Augustine (March 11). Fernandina and St. Augustine would remain in federal hands for the duration of the war. Jacksonville would be occupied off and on four separate times. In all, it was not an auspicious beginning for the southeast corner of the Confederacy. During the two years prior to 1863, when the main body of his political writing would appear, the bishop found no reason to be encouraged by his wartime experiences. Already in July, 1861, he was writing apprehensively to Archbishop Kenrick about "the present very gloomy storm."[29]

At a solemn consistory held at the Vatican on July 22, 1861, Pope Pius IX announced the transfer of Augustin Verot to the See of Savannah, vacant since the death of Bishop John Barry on November 21, 1859.[30] Verot was named third Bishop of Savannah and Vicar Apostolic of Florida. Thus, in addition to Florida which he retained, Verot had also to care now for some 8000 Catholics in neighboring Georgia. His new diocese, like the vicariate to the south, covered the entire state. Verot learned of the appointment on August 18 while in Baltimore:

> August 18th, 1861, the Sunday within the Octave of Assumption, being in Baltimore for the business of the Florida missions, I heard in the evening from Rev. M. [Joseph P.] Dubreul that he had seen a great piece of news for me in the "Ami de la Religion," namely that I was appointed Bishop of Savannah. The next day at the Archbishop's, the news of the appointment had come from

---

[28] New York *Herald*, April 19, 1862.

[29] AAB, 32-D-7, Verot to Kenrick, St. Augustine, July 12, 1861.

[30] The appointment was actually signed on July 16: ADSA, Decretum Sacrae Congregationis de Propaganda Fide, Rome, July 16, 1861. Verot had written to Lynch on May 31 proposing the names of Fathers Henry F. Parke of Parkersburg, Virginia, and Bernard J. McManus of Baltimore as possible successors to the See of Savannah; ADC, St. Augustine, May 31, 1861. Correspondence of Verot to the Holy See on this matter of his transfer to Savannah is in the Archives of Propaganda Fide, Rome: *Scritture Riferite nei Congressi, America Centrale;* 1861–1862, Vol. 19, fols. 325rv and 326rv, Baltimore, Md., August 28, 1861; fol. 508rv, Savannah, December 21, 1861; 1863–1865, Vol. 20, fols. 71rv and 72v, St. Augustine, January 28, 1863.

Rome without my bulls and the Archbishop compelled me to act upon them and to accept the office which I wanted to decline.[31]

Hearing that an old friend, Bishop Jean Marie Odin, had been promoted at the same time from Galveston to the Archdiocese of New Orleans, Verot wrote him: "Your change has been a fore-gone conclusion for a long time; mine has come following the remonstrances of the Archbishop of Baltimore, who has placed me under obedience pure and simple. God be blessed."[32] On September 1, Verot left Baltimore for his new see in the company of Father Jeremiah F. O'Neill, Sr., rector of the Cathedral of Savannah, and Michel V. Regnouf, a subdeacon of the diocese.[33] He traveled by way of Fortress Monroe and Norfolk in Virginia, where he was allowed to cross the battle lines under a flag of truce.[34] A number of strangers attached themselves to his party as he made his passage through the lines: on September 3 his pass included the designation "three young persons and Miss Jones," and his pass for the following day included the names of still three more ladies.[35] He passed through Charleston and reached Savannah by the middle of the month:

> Sept. 15th, 1861, Sunday, Octave of Nativity of the B.V. I took possession of the See of Savannah. The ceremony was performed as prescribed in the ceremonial. I was received at the main door [of the cathedral] and received the Clergy by the kiss of the ring; there was High Mass and I preached on the Legitimacy and Authenticity of the Mission of Catholic Bishops and Clergy, from the words of our Lord to St. Peter: "Thou art Peter, Etc."[36]

As William Makepeace Thackeray had found it in 1856, Savannah was a "tranquil old city, wide-streeted, tree-planted, with a few cows and carriages toiling through the sandy road, a few happy negroes sauntering here and there, a red river with a tranquil little fleet of merchant-men taking in cargo, and tranquil ware-

[31] "Episcopal Acts," 153. Cf. Savannah *Daily Morning News,* September 2, 1861.
[32] AANO, Box 1861, New Orleans Papers (photostat), Verot to Odin, Savannah, September 24, 1861, in French.
[33] "Episcopal Acts," 153.
[34] Baltimore *Catholic Mirror,* September 6, 1861.
[35] See *The War of the Rebellion: A Compilation of the Official Records of the Union and Confederate Armies* (Washington, D. C.: The Government Printing Office, 1880–1901), Series II, II, 55, September 3, 1861, and 34, September 4, 1861. (This compilation is hereafter cited as *O.R.*)
[36] "Episcopal Acts," 154.

houses barricaded with packs of cotton."[37] Not everything was out
of an antebellum picture book, however. There were a couple of
iron foundries and cotton compresses and shipyards to spew smoke
and odors over the venerable squares and picturesque waterfront.
Three railroads connected the city with other points in the Confederacy. A population of 13,875 whites and 8417 slaves and free
Negroes had been counted in the city in 1860. Now in the fall
of 1861 many were in military service. Those who remained,
according to all accounts, were ardent secessionists.[38]

Verot must have been heartened on his arrival at Savannah to
find the Catholics of that city offering funds for Confederate arms[39]
and praying against "the aggressive invasion of Northern barbarians."[40] Indeed "no religious group at Savannah embraced [the
Southern cause] more warmly than the Catholics."[41] In equal degree it must have disheartened him to see those same Catholics
fleeing the city in panic only weeks later, after federal troops
landed at Port Royal, twenty-five miles to the north.[42] "The people
here," Verot wrote Archbishop Odin, "are leaving the city in
droves: It is a veritable 'stampede.' The Yankees are only a day's
march from Savannah. I must not leave my post. . . ."[43] In
December, after the situation in Savannah had eased, Verot managed to get Augusta, where he delivered "a most excellent discourse on the present civil war," pointing out to his listeners that,
since the North had violated the Fugitive Slave Act, "they were
the rebels — not we of the South . . . that the war was just and
proper on our part, but no matter how just and proper, war was
the greatest scourge with which a people could be afflicted."[44]
On February 10, 1862, at Savannah he published a Lenten pastoral
in which he encouraged his people to accept in a penitential spirit
"the many privations, sufferings and calamities entailed upon us

[37] Quoted in Walter Charlton Hartridge, *Savannah, Etchings and Drawings by
Christopher Murphy, Jr.* (Columbia, S. C.: Bostick and Thornley, 1947), 1.

[38] See Lawrence, *A Present for Mr. Lincoln,* 3–33.

[39] T. Conn Bryan, "The Churches in Georgia during the Civil War," *Georgia
Historical Quarterly,* 33 (December, 1949), 287. Cf. Savannah *Republican,* July 9,
1861.

[40] Savannah *Daily Morning News,* June 11, 1861.

[41] Lawrence, *A Present for Mr. Lincoln,* 150; see also 7–8.

[42] *Ibid.,* 36–39.

[43] AANO, Box 1861, New Orleans Papers (photostat), Verot to Odin, Savannah,
November 9, 1861, in French.

[44] *Constitutionalist,* December 17, 1861.

by the war in which we are now engaged for the preservation of our just liberties and legitimate possessions."[45]

A month later, in St. Augustine, a Confederate soldier attending Mass in the parish church was handed a message which read: "The Yankees are landing." Pandemonium broke loose. Confederate troops quickly absented themselves from the city, and many of the residents, Catholics among them, were not far behind. A letter writer said: "The Catholic congregation left en'mass [sic], not heeding the remonstrance of Father Lance."[46] In Georgia at the time, Verot was spared this sight. He soon learned, however, that federal forces had occupied St. Augustine, where they would remain for three years, and that some of the landing troops had broken into the church at Fernandina and stolen its vestments and a sacred vessel.[47] When many Catholic residents of St. Augustine, with their children, fled into the interior, the Sisters of Mercy were compelled to close St. Mary's Academy for lack of both funds and students. In these circumstances Verot thought it best to remove seven of the eleven sisters stationed there, and reassign them to Columbus, Georgia, where presumably they could do more good.[48] He left Savannah for St. Augustine on July 2, 1862. A month and a half later, with the sisters in tow, he set out on the return trip. The journey was a pure classic for error and misadventure and deserves retelling here from an account left by one of the nuns.[49]

St. Augustine was garrisoned by the Seventh New Hampshire

---

[45] *Lenten Pastoral* (Augusta: F. H. Singer, 1862), 11.

[46] Harriet B. Jenckes to Martha Reid, St. Augustine, March 10, 1862, quoted in East, "St. Augustine During the Civil War," 79. The priest was John Bernard Aulance, whom Verot had brought from France in 1859. The event took place on March 10, 1862, and is described in Herron, *Sisters of Mercy*, 236–237, who mistakenly places the event in June.

[47] See *O.R.*, I, XIV, Brigadier-General Alfred H. Terry to Colonel R. Rich, Ninth Maine Volunteers, Hdqrs. U. S. Forces, Fort Pulaski, Key West, etc., St. Augustine, Florida, August 2, 1862: "The Roman Catholic bishop of Florida has complained to me that some time since the Catholic Church at Fernandina was broken open and the vestments of the priest and a valuable chalice were stolen. Such an act of sacrilege must be detected and punished. . . . If necessary open every knapsack in your command and examine every house in the city."

[48] Member of the Order, ed., *Leaves from the Annals of the Sisters of Mercy* (New York: P. O'Shea, 1895), IV, 334–336. In a letter to Lynch, Verot wrote that he took out seven sisters; ADC, Savannah, September 2, 1862. In his "Episcopal Acts," he mentioned only five sisters (155). The sisters closed their academy in May, 1862; *Leaves*, IV, 334.

[49] *Ibid.*, 335–343.

Volunteers, Colonel Lewis Bell commanding. The Union troops erected picket lines along the west and south flanks of the city, and a breastwork, or embankment, along the north. At the road leading north from the city gates was a passageway carefully guarded by a picket post.[50] When Verot arrived in the city he discovered that the defenses were as efficient in keeping rebel bishops in as they were in keeping rebel cavalry out. Although he was ready to depart with his sisters by August 7, he was prevented from doing so for ten days. Verot complained to Bishop Lynch: "I have been a prisoner of the Yankees for ten days for they refused to give me a pass to return to Savannah, though at last they granted it."[51]

August 17 dawned hot and rainy — not a promising day for travel. But early that morning the bishop informed the sisters: "Our passports are signed for today, and rain or shine we must go." At eight o'clock the travelers mounted their transportation, which consisted of an old wagon drawn by a mule recently broken, a tent wagon covered by a ragged carpet, and two dump carts drawn by mules in rope harness. As one of the sisters described the procession, "the wagon with the frisky mare contained the bishop, two trunks, a box of provisions and Cooper, a white lad of fifteen, for driver. The tent-wagon had three sisters and a trunk of provisions with Rev. Father [Peter] Dufau for driver. The two dump-carts had each two sisters, one trunk on which they sat, and a white boy of fourteen to drive." Before this unlikely procession reached the passageway in the picket line north of the city the travelers were thoroughly drenched. A long delay ensued at the picket post where Verot showed his passports to the officer on duty. Finally allowed to pass, the procession squeaked and rattled out onto the muddy road that led through the pines and palmettos toward Jacksonville, 35 miles to the north. The bishop had trouble with his mare, which periodically stopped dead and refused to move on despite the prelate's coaxing, shouting, or whipping. When this happened, "the Bishop tied a rope about her neck and fastened the other end to the dump-cart, and in this way pulled her on

---

[50] Recollections of E. C. F. Sanchez, *St. Augustine Record,* April 30, 1912. Cf. John E. Johns, *Florida During the Civil War* (Gainesville: University of Florida Press, 1963), 68–69.

[51] ADC, Box 1862, Verot to Lynch, Savannah, September 2, 1862. Cf. "Episcopal Acts," 155.

for awhile." Except for this difficulty, the journey was uneventful
for the first four hours of travel. Then, suddenly, there was a
shout to the rear: "Halt! . . . We will fire into you!" The procession stopped. Down the road behind the travelers came gallop-
ing a detachment of Union cavalry, sabers drawn. The captain in
charge drew his horse alongside Verot's wagon. As one of the
sisters recalled:

> The Captain told the Bishop a report had reached headquarters
> that he was taking into Georgia slaves dressed as Sisters of Mercy!
> Hence the rapid pursuit. The soldiers dismounted, looked into the
> faces of the Sisters, and examined their hands. Mother Liguori
> Major, a Virginian, was rather dark; so was a charming Cuban,
> Lugarda Tray, Sister M. Frances, who had recently joined the
> Sisterhood. But even excited Northern men could see that the rich
> brown tint of their complexion was not due to any admixture of
> negro blood, and their hands, especially their nails, proved them
> to be of the Caucasian race. The examiners were soon satisfied on
> that point; and the other Sisters were extremely fair.

Allowed again to go on, Bishop Verot was soon startled to see
a man in ragged clothing step out of the woods ahead of his
wagon. The bishop stopped and asked if the man needed help.
The wretched fellow's reply was that he was an invalid and that
he had been chased by Yankee soldiers. Weak from his long run,
he was anxious to get to his brother's house about a mile distant.
On helping the man into his wagon, Verot allowed himself to
complain, "why [Confederate] Captain Westcot did not come out
and give these cavalry battle."[52] The remark would give Verot a
great deal of trouble three days later.

Twenty miles short of Jacksonville the bishop ordered a stop
for the night at a deserted house near the roadway. After supper,
he helped bring in wood to make a fire to dry the clothes of his
party. Conveniences for the night were taken from the trunks.

> In one room was a large bedstead with two mattresses. Boards
> placed on stools, a mattress spread over them, made a comfortable
> bed for the Bishop. The Sisters took turns keeping up the fire to
> scare off the mosquitoes and dry the clothing they had washed,
> resting occasionally on the large bed. About midnight the sleepers

---

[52] John Westcot organized a company of Partisan Rangers early in August, 1862.
It was part of the Confederate Department of East Florida, General Joseph
Finegan commanding.

were aroused by a crash in the episcopal chamber. The boards had given way, depositing his lordship on the floor, where he wisely remained for the rest of the night.

At daybreak the bishop offered Mass and the sisters prepared a modest breakfast. After grace was said, the bishop's first words were: "Did you hear me fall last night?" When no one answered, he said, "I know you did, for I heard you laughing." He told the sisters that when he heard the noise caused by his tumble, "he thought a bombshell had exploded under the house, and he was terribly frightened — to his own great amusement, for the old rookery that afforded . . . shelter was entirely out of the line of warfare." The party mounted their crude wagons and resumed the journey north. The rain had stopped, but the road was still muddy. At one point a shallow stream had thickened to a good-sized water hole, and the episcopal equipage became stuck in the middle of it. The bishop decided that he could spring to the opposite bank if the young lad Cooper would get out and stand in the water, bend over, and let his back serve as a stepping-stone. The bishop was in his fifty-eighth year and rather stout, while poor Cooper, though strong and wiry, was lean as a ramrod. The episcopal foot had scarcely touched the boy's back when the waters opened to receive both bodies. There was then another long pause in the trip while clothes were changed and dried out.

It was early evening and already quite dark when the bishop's party reached the ferry that would take it across the St. John's River to Jacksonville. The two youths unloaded the fleet of wagons and carts and then left to take the conveyances back to occupied St. Augustine. The bishop and sisters, meanwhile, went aboard the ferry and arranged their trunks in the center of the boat as a barricade against possible rifle fire from Confederate defenders mistaking them for Union troops — Jacksonville had been abandoned temporarily by Union forces on the previous April 2.[53] It was good thinking. Shortly after the ferry pushed off toward lights that glimmered on the opposite shore, a volley of rifle balls struck the vessel. Verot and the sisters huddled behind their trunks. Another volley fell hissing into the water alongside. Then one of the boatmen raised a lighted lantern on a pole and waved it to signify that the boat carried friends. At this, the firing ceased.

[53] See Johns, *Florida During the Civil War*, 67.

The landing was uneventful, and about nine in the evening the party reached Jacksonville itself and the home of a Catholic family where they stayed for a night and a day. On August 20 Verot took his sisters on board the train to Lake City, Florida. There was no direct railway connection between the east coast cities of Florida and Georgia.[54] In order to get to Savannah, Verot would have to travel westward halfway across the Florida peninsula on the Florida, Atlantic and Gulf Central line, then travel north by stage from Lake City to catch another train to Savannah at the Georgia border. After about three hours on the train to Lake City, Verot had the last and most threatening experience of his ill-starred journey. So far he had been "a prisoner of the Yankees," had been pursued and stopped by Union cavalry, had fallen out of bed and into swollen streams, and had been shot at by rebel rifles. Now he would have to deal with Captain John Westcot's Confederate guerrillas, probably the unkindest cut of all.

John Westcot had only that month organized a company attached to the 1st Battalion Partisan Rangers guarding the interior defense line along the St. John's River. His men were adventure-seeking guerrillas, eager, proud, spoiling for a fight — even if it meant taking on a bishop. Three hours west of Jacksonville, at a depot platform, as the nun-diarist recorded:

> The train was stopped and boarded by Captain Westcot's guerillas, who swarmed on the platform and crowded the aisles of the compartment — wild-looking fellows in bandit costume, red shirts, black pantaloons, leathern belts with huge daggers and pistols stuck in them, and broad-brimmed straw hats. With them, we grieve to relate, was the wretched looking man whom the Bishop had taken into his wagon, and with whom the Sisters had shared their scanty rations. To the terror of all, Westcot, in a most arbitrary manner, ordered the Bishop to come out, and answer for some remark he had made about himself and his troops. The conductor refused to let the Bishop out of his custody until the captain had pledged his word that no harm should come to him. Turning to the ladies the gallant official said: "Do not fear; I will answer for the Bishop's life with my own." He then followed the Bishop to the platform, and confronted the irate officer. Loud words and angry threats followed, but . . . the Bishop return[ed] unmolested, about an hour afterwards. All this trouble came from the spy who had reported

[54] *Ibid.*, 135–136.

at headquarters the Bishop's remark: "Why does not Captain Westcot bring out his men and fight these Union soldiers?"

The train reached Lake City without further incident, and there Verot's party spent the night. At daybreak they took a stagecoach north toward the Georgia border. After traveling all day and most of the night they arrived at four o'clock in the morning of August 22 at the headquarters of Brigadier General Joseph Finegan, commander of the Confederate District of East Florida, and "an Irish gentleman well-known to the Bishop."[55] Finegan showed his guests a princely hospitality. At seven in the evening, after a good supper at the general's table, the bishop and sisters continued their journey by stage. In the early hours of the next day they reached the Georgia railhead. By eight that evening they were in Savannah.

Safe again in his residence at Savannah, and doubtless grateful that his excursion into the war-contested countryside had been comic opera instead of tragedy, Verot ordered a *Te Deum* of thanksgiving for Confederate victories of that summer to be sung in all the Catholic churches of Georgia and Florida, "with the exception of St. Augustine."[56] Though thankful for these things, he was plainly discouraged, too, as a result of what he had seen and experienced at Savannah and St. Augustine, for he wrote to Lynch a few days after returning: "How long will be [*sic*] the war last? What frightful amount of evil does it not entail upon the people. Sometimes I wish I was in France to represent things there in their true light & cause perhaps an intervention from the Emperor."[57] His discouragement mounted still further when he heard the news from Jacksonville six months later.

A "fine south wind" was blowing over Jacksonville on the morning of March 29, 1863, as the Eighth Maine and Sixth Connecticut regiments prepared to evacuate the city. Jacksonville had not proven to be an advantageous point from which to raid the Confederate interior, and Union strategy now called for it to be abandoned for the third time. As the Union troops marched toward their vessels a number of them broke ranks to loot private dwellings, stores, and business offices. Soon flames were seen bursting

---

55 *Ibid.*, 70.

56 Savannah *Daily Morning News*, September 11, 1862.

57 ADC, Box 1862, Verot to Lynch, Savannah, September 2, 1862.

up from several points in the town, and the looting troops, who
had now become an uncontrolled mob, swept toward the Church
of the Immaculate Conception. The next day a correspondent of
the New York *Tribune* described what happened:

> Yesterday the beautiful little cottage used as the Catholic par-
> sonage, together with the church, was fired by some of the soldiers,
> and in a short time burned to the ground. Before the flames had
> fairly reached the church, the soldiers had burst open the doors
> and commenced sacking it of everything of value. The organ was
> in a moment torn to strips and almost every soldier who came out
> seemed to be celebrating the occasion by blowing through an organ
> pipe.[58]

The sacrilege would live in Verot's memory all the rest of his
life.[59]

By 1863 many of the bishops in the country had delivered
themselves of some opinion about the cause, justice, and course
of the war. What Verot heard about the opinions of the influential
Archbishop of New York troubled him. He had written about it
to Lynch: "I often hear that Bishop Hughes is & speaks against
the South. I do not believe what I hear. Still I would like to
hear his arguments against the justice of the Southern side."[60]
During the spring and summer of 1863 Verot collected his thoughts
for a rebuttal of Hughes's position, as he understood it, and as
it must have been made known to him in greater detail by Lynch.[61]

---

[58] New York *Tribune,* April 8, 1863; cf. New York *Herald,* April 27, 1863;
Boston *Journal,* April 10, 1863; *O.R.,* I, XXVIII, II, 11–12.

[59] See Chapter VI.

[60] ADC, Box 1862, Verot to Lynch, Savannah, September 2, 1862. Hughes had
already given his argument in a letter to Lynch: ". . . The constitution having
been formed by the common consent of all parties engaged in the framework and
approval thereof, I maintain that no state has a right to secede, except in the
manner provided for in the document itself." New York *Daily Tribune,* September
5, 1861. For the best study of Hughes at this period, see Mzyck Andrews, *Archbishop Hughes and the Civil War* (Chicago: University of Chicago, 1935). The
devotion of Hughes and of Archbishop Purcell of Cincinnati to the Union cause
is recognized by James Ford Rhodes, *History of the United States* (New York:
Macmillan, 1929), III, 372; and by John G. Nicolay and John Hay, *Abraham
Lincoln* (New York: Century, 1890), VI, 325. Purcell is treated briefly in Stokes,
Church and State, II, 226; the *Constitutionalist* called him "very violent" (January 11, 1865). Verot is chosen as the representative southern bishop during this
period by Coulter, *Confederate States,* 521–522.

[61] The archives of the Diocese of Savannah contain no correspondence to Verot
from any source. Most of the older archival materials was accidentally burned
some twenty years ago. Hence, it is not known how complete an account of

Hughes had contended that secession from the Union, for any cause or in any manner not provided for in the Constitution, was opposed to that Constitution and therefore patently illegal.[62] In November of 1863 Verot published a *Peace Pastoral* in which he replied indirectly to Hughes. His argument was fairly representative of the state-rights doctrine held in common by the seceded states. "Whatever opinion be maintained on the nature of the contract which bound the States of the former Union together," he wrote, "and although it would be admitted that each state was not at liberty to retire without cause and without reason, still it is evident that if a majority of the States break the social compact, the minority is not bound to stand by it."[63] This is exactly what has happened, said Verot. The "peculiar institutions" of the South had for many years past been an "apple of discord," threatening the dissolution of the Union, because the North would not trouble itself to understand them. The political consequences thus far had been these:

A compromise received, some years ago, the sanction of the whole

---

Hughes' view Lynch transmitted to his colleague. Lynch did not keep a letter book. Lynch and Hughes engaged in a lengthy correspondence on the constitutional legality of secession, which was printed in full in the New York *Daily Tribune,* September 5, 1861; New York *Herald,* September 4, 1861; and in Lynch's diocesan organ, *Catholic Miscellany,* September 14, 1861, a copy of which Lynch may have sent to Verot.

[62] For the northern view on the constitutional legality of secession, see Abraham Lincoln, "First Inaugural Address," March 4, 1861, in Roy Prentice Basler, ed., Abraham Lincoln, *Collected Works* (New Brunswick, N. J.: Rutgers University, 1953–1955), IV, 262–271; Hermann von Holst, *The Constitutional and Political History of the United States* (Chicago: Callaghan and Co., 1891–1892), I, "State Sovereignty and Slavery." For the view that secession was not primarily a constitutional matter, see James G. Randall, *Constitutional Problems under Lincoln* (rev. ed.; Urbana: University of Illinois, 1951). For a summary of southern views, see Charles M. Wiltse, *John C. Calhoun* (Indianapolis: Bobbs-Merrill, 1944–1951), 3 vols.; Dwight Lowell Dumond, *The Secession Movement, 1860–1861* (New York: Macmillan, 1931); Alexander H. Stephens, *A Constitutional View of the Late War Between the States* (Philadelphia: National Publishing Co., 1868–1870).

[63] *Peace Pastoral* (Augusta, Ga.: F. H. Singer, 1863), 7. The pastoral was dated November 22, 1863. In this excerpt Verot refers to the question whether the federal government was created originally by a compact between the states or directly by the people as a whole. The "compact" theory was first promulgated in the Virginia and Kentucky Resolutions of 1798, and was thereafter the common opinion of the South, receiving its full flowering in the antebellum state-rights school of John C. Calhoun, of South Carolina. In this theory what the states conferred on the federal government they could also recall, if any of the con-

country, and became a law of the land;[64] it was a law cementing
the Union of the States, and was understood by all as such. That
law gave the Southern man a right to recover his fugitive slave
wherever he found him, even in the Northern States. In the face
of that law, which in the circumstances in which it was framed,
was tantamount to a provision of the Constitution, many of the
Northern States in their legislatures and by judicial enactments
having among them the force of law, decreed imprisonment and
fines against the master who would pursue his right secured to him
by the law of the United States.[65] These enactments of State Legislatures against the law of Congress constituted a true rebellion,
which was, however, unchecked, either by armies or by blockades.
This was tearing the social compact. No reliance could be placed
any longer upon a faithful compliance with the conditions of the
Union, and the Northern States having thus themselves broken the
Union, the Southern States were not bound to stand by it, and they
vindicated only their plain right when they formerly abjured a
Union which had already been virtually dissolved. These principles
would hold good, even in monarchical governments; how much more
so in a republic where all admit that the right of the people to
govern themselves is paramount to all constitutions.[66]

federated parties failed to meet the terms of the compact. See Dumond, *Secession
Movement*, 2–4.

[64] This was the Compromise of 1850, engineered by Henry Clay of Kentucky,
which, together with provisions favoring "free soil" interests, palliated the South
by passage of a stringent fugitive slave measure requiring return of all runaway
slaves to the owners and authorizing masters to pursue them in the northern
states. See Randall, *Constitutional Problems under Lincoln*, 421.

[65] States which enacted statutes nullifying the provisions for pursuit in the
Fugitive Slave Act included Maine, Vermont, Connecticut, Rhode Island, Massachusetts, New Hampshire, Indiana, Michigan, Wisconsin, Ohio, Pennsylvania, and,
by extension, New York and the Territory of Kansas. A summary of the nature
of these statutes, or "personal liberty laws," is given in J. G. Randall, *The Civil
War and Reconstruction* (Boston: D. C. Heath, 1953), 167–169.

[66] *Peace Pastoral*, 7. Verot's argument is substantially that used by the secessionist convention of South Carolina in its declaration of December 24, 1860, on
the causes of secession. Having named the states which enacted laws nullifying
the Fugitive Slave Act, the convention concluded: "Thus the constitutional compact has been deliberately broken and disregarded by the non-slaveholding states;
and the consequence follows that South Carolina is released from her obligation. . . ." Henry Steele Commager, ed., *Documents of American History* (New
York: F. S. Crofts, 1947), 373. It may be argued that Catholicism in both sections
of the country, prior to the war and after, was marked by a distinct state-rights
orientation and by a tendency to oppose any broadening of federal powers. This
is the opinion of Stokes, *Church and State*, II, 188; also that of Rice, *American
Catholic Opinion* (New York: Columbia University, 1944), 155, who ascribes the
main cause to memories among the immigrants of Church-State conflicts in Europe.

Verot assured his readers that "the justice of our cause is clear; clear enough to admit of no doubts in our mind." He insisted that it was important to stress this, since there were some, presumably Archbishop Hughes included, who looked upon the Southern people as "presumptuous culprits and impudent wretches." How much circulation this effort received in the South is not known. Neither is it recorded that Hughes ever saw it. The Richmond *Whig*, however, plainly hoped that he had:

> The tone of these sentiments, particularly as they relate to the justice of our cause, is creditable to the candor and good judgment of the venerable prelate who has pronounced them. It shows that while Archbishop Hughes has exercised his influence in behalf of the cause of our enemy, in violation, according to Bishop Verot's opinion, of every principle of justice, the Catholic Hierarchy of the South are warm supporters of the Southern cause, and zealous advocates of the justice upon which this war of defense is conducted.[67]

In order to give wider circulation to his opinions on the correctness of southern politics and on the course of the war generally, Verot went to Augusta in the latter part of August, 1864, and "countenanced the intention of two young men to publish a Catholic paper."[68] The men in question were Leopold T. Blome and Patrick Walsh, both residents of Augusta, journalists, Catholics, and spirited secessionists.[69] As joint editors and publishers, Blome and Walsh brought out on October 8, 1864, the first issue of the *Pacificator*, "A Journal Dedicated to the Interests of the Catholic Church in the Confederate States," the only such paper published in the South during the war years.[70] Published "with the appro-

---

[67] Richmond *Whig*, quoted in *Constitutionalist*, January 8, 1864.

[68] "Episcopal Acts," 161.

[69] Blome was an editor of the *Constitutionalist* prior to 1863. In 1868–1870 he published the *Banner of the South*, which served as Verot's diocesan organ at that period. A member of the city council for 30 years, he died in October, 1891. Patrick Walsh was also an editor of the local *Constitutionalist*, and a collaborator on the *Banner*. He later became mayor of Augusta, United States senator from Georgia, and editor and publisher of the Augusta *Chronicle*, dying in March, 1899.

[70] The Charleston *Catholic Miscellany* had ceased publication after its presses were destroyed in the fire that swept one sixth of the city in late 1861. See ADC, Box 1865, Lynch to . . . Propagation of the Faith, Lyons, September 7, 1865. The *Pacificator* had four pages of five columns, 11½ by 17 inches, and carried, besides Catholic intelligence, news articles, stories, poetry, and advertisements. It was printed on the presses of "J. T. Paterson & Co., Job and Newspaper Printers and Lithographers . . . Augusta, Ga." Publication was interrupted in

bation of the Bishop of Savannah,"[71] the first issue of the four-page weekly announced editorially that it would serve as an organ for the bishops of the South. "As to our political views . . . we are conscientiously bound to give our support to the cause of Southern Independence."[72] Across the top of the front page, under the masthead, the editors ran a motto that, according to the paper, Pius IX had used in a statement to some "federal citizens" who applied to him for a photograph: *Mitte gladium tuum in vaginam et Deus Pacis erit tecum* — "Put up thy sword into its sheath, and the God of Peace will be with thee." During the eight-odd months of its existence, the *Pacificator* would achieve "an extensive circulation through the South."[73] One of Verot's contemporaries would claim it as "the most widely read journal in the Confederacy,"[74] though this was probably an overstatement. Whatever its actual circulation, it served as an expedient platform from which Verot could broadcast to a large audience, North, perhaps, as well as South, his thoughts on the war and on the political

March and April, 1865, owing to a loss of circulation following Confederate surrender. A brief attempt at revival failed, and the last issue was published on July 20. The present writer has discovered that another attempt was made to revive the paper in April, 1866, by Walsh, who secured a renewal of Verot's approbation, but published no issues. See ADC, Box 1866, Verot to Lynch, Savannah, April 16, 1866. Present holdings of the *Pacificator* are meager and scattered; they are listed in Eugene P. Willging and Herta Hatzfeld, "Catholic Serials of the Nineteenth Century in Georgia," Part X, *RACH*, LXX (September, December, 1959), 116. The writer is indebted to Edward A. Egan, 7626 Colfax Avenue, Chicago, who has gathered photostats of the extant issues and made them available to him. Most earlier citations of the *Pacificator* have named Abram J. Ryan, so-called "Poet-Priest of the Confederacy," as its editor. See, e.g., Shea, *Catholic Church in the United States*, IV, 460; O'Connell, *Carolinas and Georgia*, 565; Joseph R. Frese, S.J., "Pioneer Catholic Weeklies," *Historical Records and Studies* (United States Historical Society, New York), XXX (1939), 143–144. Egan has demonstrated to the writer, from evidence in his possession, that Ryan could not have been in Augusta at the time in question. Ryan's name, furthermore, appears nowhere in any of the extant issues, while the names of Blome and Walsh appear regularly as "Editors." The present writer has corroborated the revision by discovery of a letter from Blome in which the publisher traces briefly the founding and the career of the *Pacificator,* and makes no mention of Ryan; see ADC, Box 1865, Blome to Lynch, Augusta, November 28, 1865. The poet's later association with the *Banner of the South* is probably the reason for earlier confusion on this point.

[71] *Pacificator,* June 24, 1865.

[72] *Ibid.,* October 8, 1864.

[73] Walsh obituary, Augusta *Chronicle,* March 20, 1889.

[74] O'Connell, *Carolinas and Georgia,* 565. O'Connell ascribed the popularity of

issues involved in it. Accordingly, he chose the first issue in which to launch a three-part series under the title: "An Address to the People of the United States in Behalf of Peace."[75] The "United States" was, of course, the North.

The war that had changed America, formerly so prosperous, into "a bloody field and a heap of smoking ruins" was a misfortune of such magnitude, Verot wrote, that he was required by this circumstance to "submit to the reflection and meditation of thinking people both North and South some plain and, in my opinion, irresistible arguments, showing that the war, and particularly the continuation of the war, against the Southern States, is unjust, unbecoming and ruinous." He would consider the matter under three headings: *an liceat* — is it lawful? *an deceat* — is it becoming? *an expediat* — is it expedient? The writer described himself as "tolerably well acquainted with persons and things on both sides of the line." Therefore he sensed no hesitancy in setting forth the true nature of the political controversy that had brought on the present conflict. Verot then proceeded to enlarge upon his state-rights argument that the northern states had abrogated the Constitution by passage of "personal liberty" laws contravening the Fugitive Slave Act.

Hence, Buchanan, in his last message, admitted the fact — declared these laws of the Legislatures unconstitutional, and asked for their repeal, though he contented himself with saying that they were null and void, as being against the laws of Congress.[76] All this shows that the Union was virtually dissolved. . . . Tell me, my friends, what would be your decision in the following case submitted to your arbitration? Five merchants enter into an association for mercantile purposes, and draw up by-laws to direct the company. Three of these merchants violate these by-laws and agreements, and wish to govern the firm without any reference to those

the paper to "its strong advocacy of Southern rights." The *Constitutionalist* said of it that "in point of beauty and style it is not excelled by any weekly in the Confederacy," February 24, 1865.

[75] October 8, 1864. Verot's "Address" was published simply as "By a Catholic Divine," but internal evidence clearly demonstrates that it was written by Verot. It was the custom of southern journals at this time to address the "United States" as a foreign country. The Charleston *United States Catholic Miscellany* had dropped "those two obnoxious words" on December 29, 1860, becoming simply *Catholic Miscellany*.

[76] President James Buchanan, Fourth Annual Message to Congress, December 3, 1860; see Dumond, *Secession Movement*, 154–155.

by-laws. Are the two other merchants bound to remain in the firm, although they are only two against three? You will say, no; unless you wish to repudiate reason and justice. . . . Apply the example and conclusion . . . in your present struggle against the South.

Basing his argument for the justification of secession on what he conceived to be an abstract right founded on the sovereignty of the individual states, Verot claimed that the most that could be alleged against that right was that it was "doubtful, as would be the right of the North to urge a continuation of the Union." In the present instance the question of right was more than abstract, however, since the North had actually practiced aggression against the South by enacting statutes openly at variance with the compact that bound the states together. Verot thus represented himself as holding the common southern, state-sovereignty view that secession was a just and peaceful act that had been resorted to solely as a defensive measure against statutory aggression. He probably felt it necessary to stress the point of aggression as opposed to the abstract right of secession, for which he had produced the simplistic example of a merchantile contract, because of the many legal complexities bound up in the Constitution itself, and in the history of its ratification by the states.

The question of the constitutional validity of secession was freighted with sufficient vagueness to permit both North and South to engage in elaborate discussion of the point both prior to the war and for many generations after its close. Further obscuring these discussions was the fact that secession was probably not primarily a constitutional problem at all, but a social and economic one. It could be argued, that is, that secession was not pursued for its own sake in answer to abstract rights that the South believed itself to possess: it was pursued because it was desirable in the light of certain social and economic pressures. The North, too, rested its constitutional interpretation upon a motive, namely, that the union was necessary to the country's welfare.[77] Aware that it was considerations of this kind that probably dominated the secession crisis and sustained the morale of the warring parties, Verot was willing to recognize that some question prevailed on the intentions of the men who framed the Constitution:

The Constitution does not say, or at least does not say clearly

---

[77] See Randall, *Constitutional Problems*, 1–25.

where the supreme authority resides, whether in the separate States that have formed the Union, or in the Government resulting from that Union; and, hence, there have been two opinions coeval with the Constitution itself concerning this supreme and paramount sovereignty. . . . It has been interpreted both ways by great minds.

But Verot was writing a political tract, and therefore was guided by both the exigencies and the failings of that medium. Laying aside the nebulous and the questionable, the blunt-speaking prelate got back down to cases:

> But the Union is broken, and you, my friends of the North, have broken it. If you wanted to maintain Union at all hazards you ought to have opposed the Legislatures that annulled the Fugitive Slave law; opposed John Brown's raid; opposed Abolitionism. The General Government ought to have sent armies and fleets against the States that denied its sovereignty and assailed its laws. . . . But again you will tell me the interests of the North require that it should be united with the South, and the welfare of the country requires there should be but one flag over the whole of it. But, my friends, do you not see the fallacy of this argument? You assume that your interest constitutes justice. This is Machiavelism [sic] not Christianity. The South tells you, also, that her interest requires that she should be separated from the North. If interest constituted justice, the rich man might appropriate to himself the yard and house of his poor neighbor, as it is his interest to enlarge his own premises. Do you say also that might is right? The unity of the flag over very extensive countries becomes an impossibility, but at any rate it is subservient and secondary to justice. Would it not be a ridiculous theory that there must be but one flag over the whole of North America? Why do you not try this theory first on Canada?

The uneven development of Verot's words indicated that, unlike his other published writings, he was writing here *currente calamo*, as his thoughts came to mind. Not a few times he repeated his thoughts, though always in different language. The most repetitive sequence he devoted to proofs that the South was engaged in a "just war." The emphasis placed on this point showed that he was concerned to prove that the carnage being committed in the name of opposing political principles was necessary and just on the southern side, despite the fact that "the roar of the cannon has added no strength to the arguments on either side." The justice of Confederate arms, he said, rested on the "defensive" posture of the South. While an offensive war required for its legitimacy a cause that was not only probably or dubiously just but a cause that was certainly and evidently just, a defensive war was justified if its cause was only "dubiously" just. As Verot did not elaborate further on his moral principle, many of his readers were doubtless led to wonder if he meant to qualify the merits of southern justice as only "dubious" — in light, perhaps, of the attack he had made in 1861 on the sins of slaveholders.

In all events, the war on the southern side was a defensive war, "and for this reason . . . the President of the Confederacy would not allow the army [after the battle of Manassas, July 21, 1861] to march then on Washington, which might have been easily taken and destroyed. Although I am no judge of military operations, as I was in Washington soon after . . . I think I do not make in this a rash statement." (Verot was misinformed.[78]) He closed these thoughts with a catalog of instances where federal forces had not obeyed the rules of civilized warfare, and had thus demonstrated the "injustice" of their cause; and his peroration was a charge that the Union conduct of the war was an affront to the principles of free republican government:

> What are we to think of the act confiscating the property of the Southern people? . . . Again, promises made even to an enemy who surrenders must be complied with. I know of places, such as St. Augustine, Florida, that surrendered to the United States under the promise of protection. What was that protection? The people were made to take an oath of allegiance which they detested, and were soon after driven from their homes in the winter, under the plea that they had relatives in the Confederate army.[79] This is, indeed, a gross and unpardonable violation of justice and good

---

[78] Verot erred in the reasons he adduced for the failure of the Confederate forces to advance on Washington. General Joseph E. Johnston, commanding the Confederate forces at Manassas, wrote that his army was "more disorganized by victory than that of the United States by defeat." Quoted in Randall, *Civil War and Reconstruction,* 277. Davis gave no orders such as those Verot described, although the Confederate propaganda mill may have circulated such a story.

[79] This event took place in the summer, not the winter, of 1862. Lieutenant Colonel Louis Bell, commanding the federal garrison, received orders to "drive out of your lines all persons, without reference to sex, who have not taken and shall refuse to take the oath of allegiance." *O.R.,* I, 356, Major Charles G. Halpine to Bell, June 20, 1862. Most residents of the city had relatives in the Confederate Army and refused the oath. A great number were therefore ordered to sell their property, then were sent by ship to Jacksonville, where the order was later rescinded. See East, "St. Augustine During the Civil War," 87–88.

faith. Again, all authors and writers on war state that innocent
persons — children, women, old people and non-combatants — must
not be harmed, and are not to be an object of attack. How do you
reconcile this with the direct and deliberate shelling of cities? But
what shall I say of the right your Generals claim of sending the
people of the cities they capture into exile? I had the bad fortune
of advising some of the people of Atlanta to stay, even if the city
should be taken, as even in that case I thought they would not be
molested, and the inconveniences of wandering through the Confederacy would far exceed those of staying. I judged so from what
I had seen in other parts of the country that had fallen into your
hands. What a sad disappointment! The people of Atlanta must
go into exile, leave their homes and all their property, and choose
an exile either South or North.[80] This way of acting assuredly ren-
ders the war unjust; and it is of no use to allege necessity, or the
interest of the Government, for the Government is for the people,
not the people for the Government. Autocrats and despots might
bring in such a plea; a Republican government cannot, without a
flagrant contradiction of all its principles. . . . The injustice of the
way of carrying on the war would reach its culminating point if the
North claimed the right of subjugation and extermination. . . . Subjugation can have a meaning only in the ways and measures of a
King, of an Autocrat, of a Czar, or of a Sultan, but subjugation is
a piece of absurdity in a Republic; it is a contradiction in terms, a
heresy in popular government. It is the first axiom of a Republic
that the people are the real sovereigns, and this right is deemed
anterior to all constitutions and all laws; and hence the people in
a Republic are to be governed by persons who receive their appointment and office from the people themselves. To try to infringe this,
is to abjure Republicanism; to abjure the Declaration of Independence; abjure the Constitution of the United States; abjure all sense
of propriety and justice. . . . What a crying injustice and a mon-
strous iniquity if the North would conquer and treat the South as
the Czar of Russia treats the Poles!

Bishop Verot's political vocabulary was not the language of a
theorist or treatise writer. It was the language of the stump. It
was blunt, hyperbolic, and popular. Reading the first of the
Pacificator articles, one is struck by the distance the American
hierarchy had traveled in three short years: from a carefully culti-

---

[80] Atlanta was taken by General William T. Sherman shortly over a month
before Verot wrote, on September 2, 1864.

vated indifference to political matters to a forum where bishops, North and South, were charging each other's subjects with constitutional illegality and civil injustice. Almost everywhere the hierarchy had become involved — though only a few, like Purcell of Cincinnati, reached Verot's level of passion — and two of the bishops went on missions abroad in service to their respective sides in the war.[81] In the South, the political allegiance of the bishops to the Confederacy was recognized by the secular press to be "as steadfast to the cause of Southern independence as the fiercest of us could desire."[82] The Richmond *Daily Whig* was glad to hear that Bishop Verot was fighting for liberty and justice;[83] and the Augusta daily paper, despite its editors' "Protestant views, education and feelings," praised his "powerful and original" article in the *Pacificator*.[84] But Verot was concerned with more than liberty and justice. Somehow he must persuade the North to make peace, and to "stop the awful bloodshed that has now stained the land for 3 long years."[85]

From the fall of 1863 onward, Verot began to sense with increasing keenness that the social good of both North and South depended on an early peace. He began to plead for a cessation to hostilities, and these pleas ran side by side with his polemics, giving to the latter their rationale. Verot was after a negotiated settlement that would guarantee southern independence. He was not interested in peace at any cost, especially at the cost of subjugation. In his 1863 *Peace Pastoral* he wrote:

> Some also there might be, who could see no possible end of the war except by the subjugation of the Southern portion of the country, and in their views to pray for peace would be identical with

[81] On April 4, 1864, Bishop Lynch of Charleston was appointed special commissioner of the Confederate States of America to the Papal States, by order of Judah P. Benjamin, Secretary of State. In Rome Lynch was disappointed not to be recognized by the Vatican as an emissary of a sovereign state. After the war he had considerable difficulty gaining readmission to the United States, finally obtaining a presidential pardon. His adventure is related in Leo Francis Stock, "Catholic Participation in the Diplomacy of the Southern Confederacy," *CHR*, XVI (January, 1930), 1–18. Hughes, of New York, went as an unofficial envoy to Paris and Rome for the Lincoln administration in 1862. See Benjamin Blied, *Catholics and the Civil War* (Milwaukee: The Author, 1945), 93–96.

[82] *Constitutionalist*, July 10, 1864.

[83] January 2, 1864; cited in Coulter, *Confederate States*, 521.

[84] *Constitutionalist*, November 5, 1864.

[85] ADC, Box 1864, Verot to Lynch, Savannah, March 22, 1864.

praying for that subjugation. But . . . peace cannot come by subjugation. Subjugation will not change the minds of the millions,
and of the immense majority, not to say unanimity, of the people
who have irrevocably decreed their separation from the northern
portion of the country, and the formation of an independent government. Subjugation, therefore, if it were possible, would not be
peace, but would be the beginning of an interminable war, worse
even than the one which is carried on now openly. It would become
a war of implacable rancor and relentless enmities — of murderous
revenge and hatred, of midnight assassinations, and other secret
cruelties and infamies, worse than the present state of things.[86]

Verot noted at the same time that he and several other of the
southern bishops, assembled accidentally at New Orleans toward
the beginning of the war, had written to Pius IX explaining the
justice of the southern cause. The pope wrote back to Archbishops
Odin of New Orleans and Hughes of New York, enjoining them
to employ their influence for the restoration of peace. The Richmond
Times, after the war, referred to the pope's letters and approved
them heartily since they "gave counsels for peace at a time when
peace meant the victory of secession."[87] This appears to have been
Verot's line of thought and main motive: peace would not only
stop the bloodletting, it would achieve the aims of southern independence. In October, 1863, he called on all the bishops of the
South to set aside a certain period for prayers to this end,[88] as
was subsequently done.[89] To his own people he addressed a fervent
appeal for prayers in behalf of peace — "to arrest the further
effusion of blood which has already deluged our land, and rescue
thousands from grief, distress, privations and sufferings which
language is inadequate to describe."

God, in his ordinary providence, can remove all impediments to
peace. He may grant victories to our armies which will dishearten
our enemies and make them desist. He may enlighten those who
rule over our destinies so as to make them conceive, mature and
execute counsels of peace. He may change the minds and dispositions
of our adversaries and make them desire peace, and become afraid

[86] *Peace Pastoral,* 6.
[87] Cited by *Constitutionalist,* March 10, 1866.
[88] ADC, Box 1863, Verot to Lynch, Savannah, October 5, 1863.
[89] See Blied, *Catholics and the Civil War,* 54. The period designated was December 1–20, 1863.

of the horrors of war; he may cause the abettors and authors of this war to appear by a premature death at the bar of his justice; he may suggest to foreign nations sympathy for our cause, and incline them to become our protectors and allies. . . . Nothing is hard or impossible to God, and he can even by the apparently natural course of human events defeat the best contrived plans of crafty politicians, profound statesmen and invincible warriors.[90]

In the second installment of his "Address to the United States" Verot urged: "Put then an end to a war which is so absurd, so unbecoming, so unnatural, and which decency alone requires you to stop, if justice did not command it imperiously."[91] And in the final installment[92] he treated the subject, *an expediat?*, "Or, in technical American phraseology, 'Will it pay?'" He advised the North that it would not. Despite the reputation that "your nation" had acquired and justly earned for keenness in devising and conducting profitable enterprises, in this instance "you have deviated, woefully deviated, from your usual standard. . . ." For one thing, the glory and military laurels that would accrue to the North from her conquests would pass away as rapidly as the sound from the cannons, particularly since the Union forces, as everyone knew, possessed an overwhelming advantage of men and industry from the start. "But you, with every advantage in your hands, have yet, after four long years, done nothing, or next to nothing, in putting down the so-called rebellion that had no arms, no navy to bring them from abroad, no military supplies. . . ." Nor had the war paid the North any better in land. "If you wanted land, you could have bought more land in the South with the money you spend in one day to keep all those places, than you possess now." There was an abundance of land in Florida, Verot noted, at a half dollar an acre. Financially, the North had assumed an unprecedented debt and a burdensome tax load, and it was unlikely that anyone would find that the battles had paid off in that category, either. "The South fights through necessity, and must submit to the sad consequences, having no choice in the matter; but you fight through choice, and you must be blind indeed if you do not see the folly that has made you contract, for nothing, an enormous debt. . . ." His final sally was directed at the North's

---

[90] *Peace Pastoral,* 10.
[91] *Pacificator,* October 15, 1864.
[92] October 22, 1864.

refusal to reach for the only laurel available to her, a negotiated peace guaranteeing southern independence. This, he said, was the only sensible and honorable policy for the North to pursue.

Verot was, of course, not alone in seeking peace for the South. Various defeatist groups in Alabama, Arkansas, and North Carolina had clamored for peace as early as 1862,[93] and the Confederate administration had sought a negotiated settlement from the very beginning, but with independence recognized. In the summer of 1863, Vice-President Alexander H. Stephens carried a peace petition toward Washington, but got no farther than Newport News after learning the news from Gettysburg. Several other abortive missions and gestures followed, including the Hampton Roads Conference on February 3, 1865. Peace offensives on both sides of the picket lines marked the 1864 presidential election campaign in the North, but the reelected Lincoln seemed even harder in his determination to pursue the war to its necessary military climax. With warriors sustained on either side by two irreconcilable principles, Union versus Independence, Governor Joseph E. Brown of Georgia held the opinion that: "In a crisis like the present Statesmanship is even more important than Generalship. Generals can never stop a war, though it may last twenty years till one has been able to conquer the other. Statesmen terminate wars by negotiation."[94]

Verot probably would not have accepted Brown's defeatist plan to shatter the Confederacy into petty sovereignties as a price for gaining peace with terms, but he roundly seconded the need for a treaty, and he told the North: "By stopping the war at once, and making a treaty of peace with the South, you will take the only way that can promote your pecuniary interests. If you offer peace on reasonable and honorable terms, perhaps you could obtain free trade with the South, which will secure to you all the pecuniary advantages that the war robbed you of at first, and you would have a chance to send us again your calicoes, your knives, your soap, all your nick-knacks, and even your wooden nutmegs, if our people are willing to buy them."[95] Without peace, the North

---

[93] See Coulter, *Confederate States,* Chapter XXII, "Longings for Peace — and the End," 533–569.

[94] Quoted in *ibid.,* 539. Brown spoke these words in the Georgia House of Representatives on November 3, 1864.

[95] *Pacificator,* October 22, 1864.

would only realize, to the very letter, an old Irish legend:

> Once upon a time, in the city of Kilkenny, a grand fight occurred
> between two cats, in the sight of the whole population assembled.
> Such was the animosity, the rage, the despair of the two combatants,
> that they ate each other up to the tails. Two ignominious, worthless
> tails were the only sad remnants of this, the fiercest combat ever
> recorded in the history of the feline race.[96]

As to intervention by a foreign power, Verot probably concluded
by this date, late 1864, that there was little likelihood of it happening. He made no mention of that possibility in his "Address,"
where he might well have used it as a threat. Earlier, in March
of 1864, he had entertained the notion in a letter to Lynch, shortly
after the latter was named a commissioner to the Papal States.[97]
Verot did not think any good would come from Lynch's mission,
and told him so. Instead, he advised Lynch to see Napoleon and
implore him to interfere "in the name of humanity, civilization
& liberty." He also suggested Maximilian of Mexico as a likely
source of aid. But Napoleon was Lynch's best hope: he should
"ask for an audience with the Emperor & beseech him to have
pity on this poor distracted country once so prosperous & now
plunged in unspeakable sufferings, without any hope of liberation
unless some foreign interference supervene." (Lynch accepted this
advice, but he achieved no more success in Paris than he did in
Rome.) Another suggestion, made by Verot two years earlier, was
later entertained for a time in certain private quarters: namely,
the use of Catholic bishops, North and South, as peace commissioners. "I imagine," Verot had written, "that a Committee
of Catholic Bishops going to Washington under a flag of truce
might perhaps induce Lincoln & his cabinet to desist from the
ruinous course which they pursue."[98]

Early in 1865 the *Pacificator* ran a proposal by Father Lawrence
P. O'Connell, assistant pastor at Columbia, South Carolina, that a
grand peace party be established under Catholic auspices. "I verily
believe," he wrote, "that if both governments appointed half a
dozen Catholic Priests, and empowered them to decide this conflict, before one week they would settle the whole difficulty, and

---

96 *Ibid.*
97 ADC, Box 1864, Verot to Lynch, Savannah, March 22, 1864.
98 ADC, Box 1862, Verot to Lynch, Savannah, September 2, 1862.

give reasonable satisfaction to both parties."[99] A recently returned
Confederate officer in Athens, Georgia, replied to the proposal that,
though a Protestant, he was in favor of its adoption: "All other
bodies, civil, social, political and religious have been dissolved
but this one [Catholic Church]; and consequently it is the only
one which could inaugurate negotiations between the North and
the South."[100] The *Daily Constitutionalist,* for its part, commented
that the bishops would be better advised to deplete the federal
armies "by withdrawing from them all the Irish and Germans
of their faith. The attempt to subjugate us and the war would
end at once."[101] Neither proposal reached very far, much less
materialized. As for Verot, he made no contributions to the debate. Between him and Augusta, where his paper was edited,
communications by this date were nonexistent. A swath of trampled
soil intervened. General William Tecumseh Sherman had made
the coast. The bishop's writings were confined to his diary: "The
Yankees entered the city Wednesday, the 21st of December as
I was saying Mass. I heard their yells and hurrahs."[102] It was the
end of politics in Savannah.

Bishop Verot retired from the political arena as suddenly as
he had entered it four years before. He was ready now to make
the peace that he had urged, despite the fact that it was not the
kind of peace that he had wished for. There is nothing in his
letters or other writings after the fall of Savannah to suggest
that he was unwilling to forget the political warfare that had
engaged his attention so recently and so completely. When the
Cincinnati *Catholic Telegraph* attacked him for saying that federal
forces had burned Charleston and Columbia,[103] Verot let the
criticism pass in silence, saying to new Archbishop Martin John

---

[99] *Pacificator,* January 7, 1865; reprinted in Charleston *Daily Courier,* January
11, 1865, and *Constitutionalist,* January 11, 1865.

[100] *Constitutionalist,* January 14, 1865. The Protestant churches began to break
apart in 1845, and the schisms continued up to and during the war. The *Constitutionalist* editorialized: "The Christianity of the North excommunicated that of
the South with a holy horror; and the latter as haughtily defied the former.
Church after Church — Baptist, Methodist, Presbyterian (all save the Catholic)
split in two most accurately across the edge of the Mason and Dixon's line;"
April 20, 1865. The most thorough study of these schisms is in Stokes, *Church
and State,* II, 156–203.

[101] *Ibid.,* January 11, 1865.

[102] "Episcopal Acts," 163–164.

[103] December 13, 1865.

Spalding of Baltimore, "I feel very little inclined to enter into any controversy about this matter."[104] The only near political activity he allowed himself in later years on the issue of southern independence was to participate in ceremonies each April 26 commemorating the "Lost Cause" of the Confederacy. On one such occasion he spoke these final conciliatory thoughts on the Confederate dead: "The question of their duty at the outset of the strife, whether it was due to their native state or to the general government, does not enter in the question today. They did right, I will simply say, in fighting on the side where their consciences called them. They thought they were right, and gave their lives as the forfeit, and the purity of their motives cannot be questioned here."[105]

Neither did the Catholic Church as a whole question the motives of Verot, or of the other bishops of the land who had taken strong political positions, often squarely opposed, on the civil events recently endured. Relations among the bishops quickly picked up again where they had left off, amicably, quietly, with no sounds of reproach or of justification. In 1866, the bishops would assemble at Baltimore in plenary council, as though nothing had happened. But something, of course, had happened, and the American Church was a different church because of it. The long struggle against "Americanization" that Bishop Hughes had led was ended. Bishops, priests, and laity were now inexorably bound up with the nation, with her problems, social and economic, with her commonweal in general, with her destiny.[106] It would be thirty years before this rapproachement became intimate, in the days of John Ireland and James Gibbons, but things happen more slowly in peace than they do in war.

---

[104] AAB, 36-G-6, Verot to Spalding, Savannah, January 30, 1866. Archbishop Kenrick had died on July 6, 1863. Spalding was appointed to the metropolitan see from Louisville on May 23, 1864.   [105] Savannah *Republican,* April 27, 1868; *Examiner,* May 9, 1868; *Banner of the South,* May 2, 1868.

[106] "At the close of the conflict the two groups of native-born and second generation Irish immigrant groups had united to form a distinctive American Catholic cultural group . . . [and] the Catholic culture of the whole group became increasingly American." McAvoy, "Formation of the Catholic Minority," 30–31. Writing of the years after 1880, another historian hazards the opinion: "It might, indeed, be maintained that the Catholic Church was, during this period, one of the most effective of all agencies for democracy and Americanization." Henry Steele Commager, *The American Mind: An Interpretation of American Thought and Character Since the 1880's* (New Haven: Yale University, 1950), 143.

CHAPTER IV

THE LIVING AND THE DEAD

BISHOP VEROT'S DIARY during the closing years of the war, 1864 and 1865, is a straightforward record of his episcopal activities. From its pages we learn simply that the bishop traveled great distances by train, by horseback, or on foot to confer on Catholic soldiers and civilians the grace of the sacraments and the solace of his own personal words. The entries for these years were written during the darkest days of southern poverty and defeat, but there is nothing in the diary of self-congratulation for the assiduous performance of duty that stands out clearly from its pages, nor is there any expression of self-pity for hardships undergone and frustrations endured. Yet when the reader reflects on the desperate plight of the southern people at war during this period, and on the inconveniences, not to mention the hazards, of wartime travel, the diary begins to suggest much more than it says, and becomes plainly a record of spiritual valor.

Elsewhere we learn how Verot's heart went out to his suffering compatriots: "How often," he wrote, speaking of military conscription, "my heart has been torn by sorrow in seeing the father of a family snatched from his fireside and sometimes two or three of his sons with him, and forced to abandon a distressed wife and several young children incapable themselves of procuring the necessities of life."[1] Without any thought to himself, as one of his contemporaries wrote, the bishop identified himself completely with the best interests of his people. "He comforted them in their sorrows, alleviated their crosses, advocated their cause, and shed the light of religion far and wide over the land."[2] The fact that,

[1] *Annales*, XXXVII (September, 1865), 396.
[2] O'Connell, *Catholicity in the Carolinas and Georgia* (New York: Sadlier & Co., 1879), 541.

89

as the diary records, he ministered with equal energy to federal soldiers and prisoners confirmed the quality of his mercy, and demonstrated that it was not strained by the less important imperatives of political conviction. He was a fortunate bishop in that the same could be said for his priests, four of whom became ministering angels to the 30,000 diseased and famine-stricken Union prisoners at the notorious Andersonville prison camp, and thus wrote their names into one of the great stories of charity in the history of the American Church.

The first entry in Verot's diary for 1864 was dated January 25. On that date, General Sherman was already marching into the Confederate heartland, and had seized Vicksburg and Jackson, Mississippi. Within five months he would be in Georgia. Verot, however, recorded simply that he had given his usual retreat to the priests of his diocese, at Savannah. On February 1, he visited the Confederate warship *Georgia* and conferred the Sacrament of Confirmation on ten sailors. During the week following he confirmed ten sailors on board the warship *Savannah,* and visited various camps of soldiers about the city. In the second week of March, "I started for Dalton [Georgia] where the army of Tennessee [under General Joseph E. Johnston] was encamped; found there many Catholics and two Catholic Chaplains, Father [Anthony] Carius and Father [Emmeran] Bliemel.[3] I spent two weeks there in hearing confessions, preaching and administering confirmation. About 125 soldiers were confirmed and 150 received Holy Communion. I also confirmed a few Catholics of the place. I returned to Savannah for Palm Sunday and Holy Week." After Easter he left Savannah to administer Confirmation at Augusta, on April 3, and at Columbus, on April 10. "The next day I started for Florida down the Chatta[h]oochee [River] and preached in a meeting house to a pretty good audience; went to Quincy, where I found a few Catholics but could not say Mass for want of baggage, and arrived at Tallahassee for the third Sunday after Easter."

The next day, Verot left for the federal camps at Jacksonville, arriving there on April 21, two months after the federals suffered their worst defeat of the Florida campaign at nearby Olustee.[4]

[3] The citations from the diary for this chapter are from "Episcopal Acts," 160–166. For Fathers Carius and Bliemel, cf. Blied, *Catholics and the Civil War* (Milwaukee: The Author, 1945), 123.   [4] John E. Johns, *Florida During the Civil War* (Gainesville: University of Florida Press, 1963), 190–200.

"On Sunday, the 24th Ap[ril] I preached in [a] shanty converted into a church, and gave confirmation to a dozen of workmen and Yankee soldiers. The next day, 25th Ap[ril], started for St. Augustine by land in [a] buggy with Father [John Francis R.] Chambon, went to Mandarin and from there to Diego, where I confirmed 5 or 6 children; the next day at [the house of] James Mickler I confirmed half a dozen of persons, some colored. I arrived safely in St. Augustine for the end of April." Verot spent the month of May and the first week of June in the vicinity of St. Augustine, which was serving at this time as a Union rest camp. He left on June 5 and "after great difficulty passing the lines" reached the railhead at Lake City on the 11th, and preached there in the City Hall the next day. On June 14 he arrived back in Savannah. A few days later he was on the road again, this time to Augusta, "where I made some last arrangements for the publication of a new Catechism." (Cut off from the Catholic presses in Baltimore by the Union blockade of Confederate ports, Verot had to compose and publish his own catechism for the instruction of children and of adult converts. The completed catechism was soon in demand in other parts of the Confederacy as well. Bishop Elder of Natchez saw "some things to criticize, and many to admire in it." Verot also published an *ordo* for his clergy in 1862 and 1864.[5]) From Augusta, Verot went to Atlanta, intending to visit the Confederate troops, but "I found that it could not be done, as the soldiers were in the trenches. . . ." He left then for Columbus, Augusta, and, once again, Savannah, arriving home on July 10. He would remain at his see city until the 18th, when, at the call of one of his priests, he would leave for Andersonville, Georgia, and the most grisly sights of his life.

Verot's priests, meanwhile, were also caught up in the war. Four were serving in Florida: Fathers Edmund Aubril, C.P.M., Vicar-General of the Vicariate Apostolic and pastor of St. Augustine; John F. R. Chambon at Jacksonville and Mandarin; Charles A. Mailley at Tampa; and James O'Hara at Key West. Three

---

[5] AANO, Elder to Odin, New Orleans Papers (photostat), March 24, 1862; ADC, Verot to Lynch, January 8, 1862. Verot printed his 1862 *ordo* sometime before November, 1861, as he informed Archbishop Odin: "I believe that I told you that I had the *Ordo* of 1862 printed here, since it will be impossible to get it from Baltimore"; AANO, Verot to Odin, New Orleans Papers (photostat), November 21, 1861, in French.

Florida priests, William J. Hamilton, Henry Peter Clavreul, and Peter Dufau, had been transferred to Georgia early in the war. Father Hamilton had been pastor of Jacksonville's Church of the Immaculate Conception, burned and pillaged by federal troops in May of 1862. Verot brought him to Columbus shortly afterward, and later, in the summer of 1864, sent him to Macon. Father Clavreul, who had been recruited in France for the Florida missions by Verot in 1859, had started the war in Fernandina on Amelia Island at the northeast tip of the peninsula. "Fernandina was at that time a military camp," Clavreul remembered, "being the key of Florida. It was garrisoned by a force of 2000 men, recruits from all parts of the State, who, at the first appearance of the Federal gunboats [on March 2, 1862], abandoned the island to take refuge on the mainland. Two months later, finding myself unable to correspond with the Bishop, lately transferred from St. Augustine to the vacant see of Savannah, I left . . . for the episcopal city."[6] Thanks to the courtesy of General Horatio G. Wright, commanding the federal occupation force at Jacksonville, "I was . . . enabled to cross the lines; at the time skirmishing was rife between the contending armies, on the R.R. line between Jacksonville and Lake City."[7] Finally reaching Savannah, Clavreul was assigned by Verot to visit the hospitals and to minister to Confederate soldiers at nearby Thunderbolt battery and at the forts on the Savannah River.

In Georgia Verot had eight priests besides Fathers Hamilton, Clavreul, and Dufau. Four were stationed in Savannah at the Cathedral of St. John Baptist: Fathers Peter Whelan, John F. O'Neill, John F. O'Neill, Jr., and Charles Prendergast. Gregory Duggan and his assistant John Kirby were stationed at Augusta. Thomas O'Reilly was pastor of Immaculate Conception in Atlanta, and Michael Cullimore was at Columbus. Of this band, none was more intimately involved in the military action of the war than

---

[6] ASLA, "Very Rev. Henry Peter Clavreul's Diary." This is a later rendition by Clavreul of his original diary, as appears from his handwritten notations on the manuscript: "Copied verbatim from Diary" and "The following is taken from the Diary at the time."

[7] George Robbins, ed., *Diary of Rev. H. Clavreul* (Waterbury: The Connecticut Association of Ex-Prisoners of War, 1910), 16. This was a later and expanded rendering of an original diary kept at Andersonville prison camp. Clavreul produced this version in 1910, as recorded by him in ASLA, Clavreul aide memoire dated "St. Augustine, Florida, May 15, 1910." An earlier and shorter version in manuscript, dated "Mandarin, Florida, January 22, 1884," is in ASLA and is limited strictly to the Andersonville experience, described below.

Peter Whelan. Born in Wexford, Ireland, and ordained by Bishop England of Charleston in 1830, Father Whelan had spent the whole of his priesthood in the southern states, and shared his bishop's regional patriotism. Unlike Father Clavreul who was never on the battlefield as such, "and if I heard the roaring of a cannon in Fernandina, for instance, and at the taking of Fort McAllister, Savannah, I was always within the city limits,"[8] Peter Whelan was on the very battlements of Fort Pulaski on Cockspur Island outside Savannah in the spring of 1862 when the Yankees poured the fire of their unerring rifled cannons at the Confederate garrison. He had been sent by Verot to serve as chaplain to a company of Georgians known as the "Montgomery Guards," or as the Savannah *Republican* reported, "the Romish portion of the garrison," and he was by the same account, "a general favorite with the troops."[9] Fort Pulaski fell to the federals on April 11, 1862. The gallantry of the Savannah priest during the final days before surrender was recognized and widely acclaimed by those who served with him, including the fort commandant.[10] Whelan was taken prisoner and sent to Fort Lafayette, New York harbor. On July 23 following he was released on his parole as a priest and allowed to return to his post, "since the rebels do the same."[11] Bishop Verot assigned him on his return to be general chaplain to all the Confederate camps in Georgia. And it was in this new capacity as wartime circuit rider that Peter Whelan, in the summer of 1864, ended up among the horrendous scenes of Andersonville prison camp. It is from him and from Fathers Hamilton and Clavreul, and elsewhere from Bishop Verot himself, that we learn the story behind the lines of the bishop's next entry into his 1864 diary:

> I left Savannah July the 18th for Andersonville, where I had sent Father Whelan one month before and Father Clavreul a week before to attend to the Yankee prisoners to the number of thirty thousand,

[8] Robbins, ed., *Diary of Rev. H. Clavreul,* 17.

[9] Savannah *Republican,* June 23, 1862.

[10] Lilla Mills Howes, ed., "The Memoirs of Charles Olmstead," Part IV, *The Georgia Historical Quarterly,* XLIV (June, 1950), 189–190; F. D. Lee and L. J. Agnew, *Historical Record of the City of Savannah* (Savannah: J. H. Estill, 1869), 85; Savannah *Daily News and Herald,* July 22, 1868; Savannah *Morning News,* February 8, 1871.

[11] *O.R.,* II, 4, 268.

one-fifth perhaps being Catholics. I visited the Stockade and the hospital and administered the last Sacraments to some prisoners; the next day I went to Americus. . . . I then repaired to Macon. . . . The following day, Monday [the 25th], I went again to Andersonville to see yet better things by myself and bring supplies to the Missionaries.

Andersonville prison, or Camp Sumter as it was officially known, came into existence during the winter of 1863–1864.[12] Brigadier General John H. Winder, Superintendent of Military Prisons for the Confederacy, had decided to transfer the main body of Union prisoners who were being held in the exposed military territory of Virginia to an area removed from the immediate theater of war. Winder's agents chose a site on the South Western Railroad at a point one mile east of the railroad depot at Andersonville, in Sumter County, Georgia. Andersonville was in the middle of rolling hill country, 175 miles due west of Savannah. In November, 1863, Confederate soldiers, helped by a force of Negro slaves requisitioned from nearby plantations, began clearing pines from the sandy Georgia soil. The pines were cut into twenty-foot logs and planted five feet deep to form an almost impregnable double stockade around an inner prison area roughly 1540 feet long and 750 feet wide. Sentry boxes were erected along the top of the inner stockade. Eighteen feet in from the inner stockade wall was a deadline marked by poles and slats driven into the ground; prisoners stepping across the deadline would be immediately shot, On the west side workmen constructed two gates called the North Gate and the South Gate, each protected by a double stockade. Artillery pieces were placed at each corner of the outer stockade to prevent breakouts or riots. The only pleasant aspect of the prison as it neared completion was a stream of water, a branch of nearby Sweetwater Creek, which ran through the prison yard and divided it roughly in half.

This was the scene that greeted the first contingent of Union

---

[12] The best recent treatments of Andersonville are William B. Hesseltine, "Andersonville," *The Georgia Review*, III (Spring, 1949), 103–114; Hesseltine, *Civil War Prisons: A Study in War Psychology* (Columbus, Ohio: The Ohio State University Press, 1930), 60–63; Darrett B. Rutman, "The War Crimes and Trial of Henry Wirz," *Civil War History*, VI (June, 1960), 117–133. A novel based on extensive research has been published by MacKinlay Kantor, *Andersonville* (New York: World Publishing Company, 1955).

prisoners who arrived from Belle Island, Va., on February 15, 1864. Between that date and April of the year following, no less than 50,000 federal soldiers were incarcerated inside the narrow confines of this open pen, 33,000 at one time during July of 1864. The horror of the place is summed up in the grim statistics of death: between June 1 and October 31, 1864, a total of 10,187 prisoners died from disease or malnutrition; 2989 died under the broiling sun of August alone. After the war Union retribution would be visited upon the unfortunate Captain Henry Wirz, prison superintendent. Wirz was a native of Switzerland, a physician, a Catholic, and a prewar resident of Louisiana. Following a spectacular trial in Washington in August and September, 1865, at which two of Verot's priests, Fathers Hamilton and Whelan, testified, Wirz was found guilty of "war crimes" and executed. It is from the record of that trial and from Father Clavreul's wartime diary that we learn how Bishop Verot found out about the place.

Father Hamilton, who had had his church burned out from under him in Jacksonville, Florida, was serving in the spring of 1864 as pastor of the Church of the Assumption in Macon, Georgia. Andersonville, sixty-two miles to the southwest, was one of the missions attached to his parish. Accordingly, in May, 1864, as he recalled to the court during the Wirz trial, he visited Andersonville and discovered the nearby prison camp.[13] Captain Wirz provided the priest with a pass and personally escorted him to the entrance of the stockade. Hamilton looked around for three or four hours, then left. "The following week," he recounted, "I went and spent three days there among the prisoners, and then returned and wrote a report on the condition of the hospital and stockade to my bishop, in order that he might send the requisite number of priests to visit the prisoners there. . . ." The prosecuting attorney at Wirz's trial asked the priest:

Q. State to the court in what condition you found the stockade when you first visited it, and subsequently, and all the time while you were there.

A. The first time I visited the stockade I had only about three or four hours to spend there. I merely went to see what the condi-

---

[13] U. S. Congress, *Trial of Henry Wirz, Letter from the Secretary of War, Ad Interim . . . Transmitting a Summary of the Trial . . .*, 40th Congress, 2nd Session, 1867–1868, Executive Document 23, 8 (Washington, D. C.: Government Printing Office, 1868), 287 ff.

tion of the place was. My principal object was to find out, if possible, the number of Catholics who were prisoners there, in order
that we might induce the bishop to send a sufficient number of
priests. I did not pay much attention to what I saw or heard there
then. The following week I returned, and spent three days. I visited
the stockade and the hospital, discharging my duties as priest of
the Catholic church. On this, my second visit to the stockade, I
found, I think, about 23,000 prisoners there; at least the prisoners
themselves told me there were that number. I found the place extremely crowded, with a great deal of sickness and suffering among
the men. I was kept so busy administering the sacrament to the
dying that I had to curtail a great deal of the service that Catholic
priests administer to the dying, for the reason they were so numerous — they died so fast.

Father Hamilton went on to testify that "When I returned from
the stockade after my second visit to it, at the latter part of May
. . . I wrote to our bishop and told him that these men were dying
in large numbers; that there were many Catholics there, and that
they required the services of a priest, and he sent up Father
Whelan." Peter Whelan was in Savannah at the time Bishop
Verot dispatched him to Andersonville. He told the court during
the Wirz trial:

My office is that of a priest; I was in Andersonville from the
16th of June, 1864, till the 1st of October. The previous portion
of the year I was at Savannah, except for some time when I went
to attend Catholics in the Confederate camps.
Q. State how you happened to go to Andersonville, whom you
saw and met there, and all about your duties there.
A. Father Hamilton had visited the place in May, seen the
condition of the prisoners, and written to the bishop at Savannah
to send a priest there. He asked me to go and visit the prisoners.
According to his request I went; I stayed there until nearly the
1st of October, from, I may say, the 16th of June, 1864; I stayed
until the vast portion of the prisoners were removed to other points;
I would have stayed longer if the prisoners had been retained; my
duties were those of a Catholic priest — nothing more. I had no
commission from the government; I went there voluntarily, without
pay or remuneration, further than merely to receive rations.[14]

---

[14] *Ibid.*, 426–427. Jefferson Davis, President of the Confederacy, wrote in
1890: "A venerable and venerated priest, Father Wheelan [*sic*] of Savannah,
Ga., visited me in prison, and there told me that hearing of the great mortality

In July Bishop Verot detached Henry Peter Clavreul from his duties at the Cathedral of Savannah and sent him to assist Father Whelan. The bishop maintained the two priests there at his own personal expense.[15] Father Clavreul kept a diary, from which some years later he extracted two different narratives of his experiences at Andersonville.[16] He recorded that he remained at Andersonville from July 15 to August 20 when he was "taken sick with continued vomiting," and returned on September 24 to stay until October 6.

It was in July, 1864, that I left Savannah for Andersonville, being sent there to help the venerable Father Whelan, who had been ministering to the prisoners since March. Their number kept increasing owing to the advance of the Federals toward Georgia, being estimated at the time at thirty thousand. Father Whelan was already an old man, over sixty years of age. He assisted the prisoners not only by his ministrations as a priest, but also by material help, through his influence among the Catholics of Georgia. As for me, unknown and without influence [Clavreul had come up from Florida in 1862], I could only weep over the miseries I hourly witnessed. The comforts I brought them were the consolations of religion, and these, I may truly say, I gave with all the zeal and energy God's grace enabled me to impart.[17]

Bishop Verot himself left Savannah for Andersonville on July 18. Father Peter Dufau, his vicar-general, accompanied him. Father Clavreul's diary recorded their arrival under the date July 19: "It was about that time that Bp. Verot visited the stockade accompanied by Father Dufau. They remained two days, ministering during that time to the spiritual wants of the dying prisoners, confessing and anointing."[18] Verot was appalled at what he saw. Writing to France the next year he described the scene in vivid and moving language:

[The prisoners] were penned up inside an improvised enclosure

among the prisoners at Andersonville, he went there to console the sick, to shrive the dying, and to perform the offices for the dead"; "Andersonville and Other War Prisons," *The Confederate Veteran*, XV, (March, 1907), 112.

[15] NA, Union Provost Marshal's file, Verot to Secretary of War Edwin M. Stanton, Savannah, January 9, 1865.

[16] See footnote 7, above.

[17] Robbins, ed., *Diary of Rev. H. Clavreul*, 5.

[18] ASLA, 1884 ms. rendering of the original diary. Verot's diary records that he was at Andersonville on two separate occasions, four or five days apart; "Episcopal Acts," 160–161.

98 REBEL BISHOP

formed by trunks of trees sunk vertically into the ground. At various points along the top of this barrier, about five and a half yards high, were guard posts. The prisoners, more than thirty thousand of them, were packed together pell mell. Inside this bizarre prison they had to spend the hottest months of the year, June to September, without any kind of shelter to shade them from the tropical sun. Some of these unfortunates sought shelter by hanging their rags on the end of a stick. Lucky were those who had a wretched covering!

The diet was no better than the accommodations: the daily ration consisted of a little corn bread, where the bran was mixed with the flour, and several ounces of salt pork. But since most of the prisoners suffered from scurvy which affected their teeth, they were not able to take even this poor food. You can easily imagine the plaints and the murmurings of those poor devils; but there wasn't a thing that could be done about it. The Confederates maintained that they gave the same rations to the prisoners that they gave to their own soldiers; and it is certainly true that, owing to the blockade, they could not get any wheat bread. Nothing came of the propositions to exchange prisoners; this state of things continued for several months.

As the sicknesses mounted an appalling mortality quickly followed. Men became accustomed to heaping one on top of another, victims condemned to a death as horrible as it was premature. Informed of what was happening, I sent two priests to Andersonville, and I felt obliged to go there myself on two different occasions. These two priests [Fathers Whelan and Clavreul] spent all day in the camp hearing the confessions of the dying and administering extreme unction, for the Catholics there were numerous.[19] A number of Protestants and non-believers had the good fortune of conversion to our holy religion and received baptism. This was a new kind of ministry: we had to hear the confessions of the sick as they lay on the ground in the middle of the crowd; but the imminence of death did not leave time for human niceties.

What most revolted our human nature during the exercise of this ministry was the horrible stench that rose from this vast agglomeration of men packed together so closely. It truly took a superhuman effort to cross the thin stream of water that passed through the middle of the camp and served as the receptacle of all the filth.

The majority of those unhappy creatures were without clothes; many were entirely nude; it was a hideous sight. Yet it was useless to object. The Southern government could not clothe its own soldiers,

19 Perhaps one fifth of the total, or 6000 men, according to Verot's diary; "Episcopal Acts," 160.

so how could it have clothed its prisoners? The number of those who died was dreadful. Within the space of about two hours and without my advancing more than twenty paces into the enclosure, I personally confessed and anointed nine dying men, and I stopped only at the most urgent cases. I have to thank Divine Providence for having preserved the lives of the missionaries who devoted themselves to that harsh apostolate. One of them [Father Clavreul] did become sick there. The prisoners were extremely affected to see these two priests remaining constantly with them, and they often asked why no Protestant ministers came.[20]

The bare details related by Verot's priests at the Wirz trial describe the horror of the camp and adequately suggest the heroism of the priests whom the bishop stationed there. Father Hamilton, of course, went to the camp on his own initiative. His total stay of four days produced experiences that were indelibly etched on his mind at the time of the Wirz trial over a year later:

Q. Give the Court some idea of the condition of the stockade.

A. I found the stockade extremely filthy, the men all huddled together and covered with vermin. The best idea I can give the court of the condition of the place is, perhaps, this: I went in there with a white linen coat on, and I had not been in there more than ten minutes or a quarter of an hour, when a gentleman drew my attention to the condition of my coat. It was all covered over with vermin, and I had to take my coat off and leave it with one of the guards, and perform my duties in my shirt sleeves, the place was so filthy. . . . When I visited the stockade there was no shelter at all so far as I could see, except that some of the men who had their blankets there had put them up on little bits of roots that they had abstracted from the ground; but I could not see any tents or shelters of any other kind. . . . The heat was intolerable; there was no air at all in the stockade. The logs of which the stockade was composed were so close together that I could not feel any fresh air inside. . . .

Q. How did it affect the priests on duty there?

A. The priests who went there after me, while administering the sacrament to the dying, had to use an umbrella, the heat was so intense. Some of them broke down in consequence of their services there. . . . One of the priests from Savannah [Father Clavreul] came to Macon, where I reside, completely prostrated, and was

[20] *Annales,* XXXVII (September, 1865), 398–399. Translated from the French by the author.

sick at my house for several days. . . . I did not keep an account of the dying men I used to attend per day to administer the last sacrament, but judging from the hours I was engaged and what I know to be the length of the service, I suppose I must have attended from twenty to thirty every day. . . . I was kept so busily engaged in giving the sacrament to the dying men that I could not observe much; but of course I could not keep my eyes closed as to what I saw there. I saw a great many men perfectly naked, walking about through the stockade perfectly nude; they seemed to have lost all regard for delicacy, shame, morality, or anything else. I would frequently have to creep on my hands and knees into the holes that the men had burrowed into the ground and stretch myself out alongside of them to hear their confessions.[21]

Bishop Verot observed the same disintegration of morals and manner and attributed it to the continuous spectacle of death. The sights of Andersonville, he wrote, "when one encountered cadavers, it seemed, at almost every step, had the end of blunting all humane sentiment. The prisoners pitilessly refused the slightest service to their dying compatriots."[22] From Father Whelan the bishop heard how the prisoners on July 11 executed six of their fellow prisoners who had been accused of murder and theft within the compound, and he related this strange episode to his French readers as an example of the depravity existing there.[23] Five of the six condemned raiders were Catholic, and Father Whelan described the affair in greater detail to the Wirz trial court:

There was a court-martial of the prisoners held on these men and six of them were condemned. They were put in the stocks. I visited them the evening before they were hanged and gave them all the consolations of religion that it was possible for me to do. The next morning Captain Wirz came down to carry them to the stockade to be delivered to the prisoners there. I asked him to delay their execution for another day. He said to me that it was out of his power. They were prisoners who were plundering or robbing and using violence on other prisoners. . . . They were brought in by Captain Wirz with a company of soldiers. I cannot precisely give the words that he used, but I can give the substance of them. My feelings were engrossed by the condemned men and my attention

[21] U. S. Congress, *Trial of Henry Wirz,* 288–293. "Father Hamilton attended chiefly the Federal officers confined at Macon, he being stationed there with his congregation;" Savannah *Daily News and Herald,* June 4, 1866.

[22] *Annales,* XXXVII (September, 1865), 400.

[23] *Ibid.,* 400.

was turned to giving them all the consolation of religion before they passed off into eternity. Captain Wirz said something like this: "Boys, I have taken these men out and now I return them to you, having taken good care of them. I now commit them to you. You can do with them as you see fit." Then turning around to the condemned men he said, "May the Lord have mercy on your souls." The men were then placed on a platform of gallows. They begged of me to make an appeal to their comrades — an appeal to spare them from execution. I made it to their fellow-prisoners.[24]

One of the prisoners who stood by the gallows and listened to Father Whelan wrote afterward: "A Catholic priest who very frequently paid us a visit, begged hard that their lives might be spared; but finding he could not change the purpose of the men who were determined to carry out the sentence, he endeavored to get the doomed men to realize the awful position they were in."[25] After an abortive escape by one of the raiders, the miscreant prisoners were duly hanged, and their bodies buried in a separate portion of the graveyard. Whelan was asked by the Judge Advocate at Wirz's trial if the raiders were condemned because they were obviously criminals or because of the moral depravity of the prisoners as a whole. The priest answered, "Yes, there was great moral depravity in the prison before the raiders were hanged. I heard men complaining of it. There must have been great moral depravity in it when the prisoners themselves made application to have these men tried. I cannot say whether they had been guilty of any capital crime."[26]

Father Whelan described his general course of duties as "very onerous." They occupied the whole of his time, and his health was somewhat impaired as a consequence. He entered the stockade early each morning and remained until four or five o'clock. Often, because of the urgency of the calls made on him, "I had to shorten what is called the sacramentalia, and also the ceremony of baptism, and also that of extreme unction." On one occasion, struck by the mounting cases of malnutrition among the inmates, Whelan bought 10,000 bushels of wheat flour with $16,000 in Confederate

24 U. S. Congress, *Trial of Henry Wirz*, 428–429.

25 John W. Urban, *Battlefield and Prison Pen* (New York: Union Publishing Company, 1882), 332. Father Whelan's plea was also described by another prisoner, Robert H. Kellogg, *Life and Death in Rebel Prisons* (Hartford, Conn.: L. Stebbins, 1865), 171.

26 U. S. Congress, *Trial of Henry Wirz*, 429.

currency (equivalent to $500 in Union currency) borrowed from a Mr. Henry Horne of nearby Macon. "I gave the money to a gentleman in Americus of the name of Wynne, and he purchased the flour and sent it to Captain Wirz." Wirz promised the priest that he would have the flour cooked and distributed to the prisoners. Whelan could not say afterward if that was actually done; but Dr. John C. Bates, prison physician, testified at the trial that it was. Bates said that the bread was known popularly among the prisoners as "Father Whelan's bread."[27] Whelan told the Wirz court that the quality of the daily diet was so poor that many of the sick could not eat it:

> The prisoners looked, some of them, very emaciated — those who had scurvy — and diarrhoea followed from it. They were extremely emaciated, and there was a good deal of filth in the prison. I cannot tell you to how many dying persons I have administered spiritual aid. Perhaps it might have been fifteen hundred or two thousand. I think I would be safe in saying more than one thousand.[28]

Father Clavreul was present at the prison from July 15 to August 20, when he was taken sick, and again from September 24 to October 6. His diary kept at Andersonville opens with the names, ages, and nationalities of 1390 prisoners to whom he administered the Sacraments of Penance and Extreme Unction. His record of the condition of the camp and of the harsh life of a priest inside it duplicates with few exceptions the descriptions of Fathers Hamilton and Whelan. Clavreul says that the priests ate and slept in a wooden hut, 12 by 18 feet, a mile from the stockade, and that they subsisted on corn bread, cowpeas, and parched corn coffee. "After a restless night spent in our hut, on bunks, and a hurried breakfast, 5 o'clock found us every morning at the entrance of the stockade where we remained the whole

---

[27] *Ibid.,* 430, 662–663. After the war Father Whelan wrote to Union Secretary of War Edwin M. Stanton and asked for reimbursement of the funds he borrowed for purchase of the flour. Stanton's office replied that the priest would have to obtain vouchers, properly sworn to. Whelan sent back a blistering letter: "I have not the health, nor strength, nor money to run over Georgia to hunt up vouchers and bills of purchase. . . . Some worthless spy or detective is honored and rewarded, while the Catholic Priest, the true benefactor of the prisoners, is ignored, and perhaps cast off as if he were a noted swindler." Savannah *Daily News and Herald,* June 4, 1866.

[28] U. S. Congress, *Trial of Henry Wirz,* 431.

long day till sundown, with one hour of recess at midday."[29] Often, toward midday, he would walk back to the hut through the narrow aisle of a dismal room where the corpses of those who had died that day were laid out in four neat rows. For all the suffering that he saw, however, Clavreul could not blame the superintendent, Captain Wirz. "He was boorish, profane, although never, to my knowledge guilty of the acts of violence and cruelty that were afterward laid to his charge, being himself the sufferer of conditions he could in no way help." Bishop Verot also excused the conditions of the camp as unavoidable under the circumstances.[30] Whelan, too, refused to accuse Wirz directly of any personal responsibility, for which reason the Judge Advocate at Wirz's trial described the priest as less than candid.[31]

Father Clavreul recounted that despite —

sufferings which the pen cannot describe, I do not recall having heard either curses or imprecations on the part of the prisoners. They seemed to think themselves the victims of circumstances forced on the authorities at Washington, who, for fear that the war might be prolonged, would not listen to an exchange, no less than on the Confederates themselves. The crowded condition of the place in which they were confined, the food insufficient and loathesome, their clothing in rags, their exposure to the weather, the suffering which all this entailed, rarely elicited from them a word of anger. They seemed to look upon their misfortunes as a visitation from the Almighty. To this may be ascribed the success of our ministrations, not only with the Catholics, but with the men of the various denominations, and those who professed none. They saw, besides, that the two priests ever in their midst were the only clergymen who had volunteered to them their services.[32]

Two other priests served for brief periods at the prison, and deserve mention here. They were John F. Kirby, assistant pastor of St. Patrick's, Augusta, sent by Verot for a period of "several weeks," and Anselm Usannaz, S.J., from Spring Hill College, Mobile, Alabama, who attended the prisoners for an unspecified time.[33]

[29] Robbins, ed., *Diary of Rev. H. Clavreul*, 15.
[30] *Annales*, XXXVII (September, 1865), 398.
[31] Norton Parker Chipman, *Tragedy of Andersonville. Trial of Captain Henry Wirz, The Prison Keeper* (San Francisco: The Author, 1911), 198. Colonel (later General) Chipman was Judge Advocate of the military court that tried Wirz in August, September, 1865.
[32] Robbins, ed., *Diary of Rev. H. Clavreul*, 16.
[33] Savannah *Daily News and Herald*, June 4, 1866. Father Kirby was enfeebled

The fact that none but Catholic priests attended the unfortunate men at Andersonville was the subject of much complaint after the war by surviving prisoners. One prisoner wrote in his diary that "the churches of all denominations except one solitary Catholic priest, Father Hamilton, ignore us completely as they would dumb beasts."[34] A physician named Thomas H. Mann, at the time of his capture a private soldier in a Massachusetts volunteer regiment, recalled that "the only authorized representative of the Christian religion who possessed enough of it to visit the thirty thousand men in the prison pen was a Roman Catholic priest. . . ."[35] An Illinois cavalryman wrote: "The only minister who came into the stockade was a Catholic priest, middle aged, tall, slender, and unmistakably devout. . . . His unwearying devotion gained the admiration of all, no matter how little inclined one might be to view priestliness with general favor."[36] A foot soldier from Pennsylvania noted that the absence of other ministers was very strange, "situated as our prison was, in a State where several prominent Protestant churches were very strong," but he tells of one "rebel chaplain" who did enter the stockade on one occasion and conducted a short religious service.[37] Numerous other accounts made the same complaint.[38]

---

from his service during the 1854 yellow-fever epidemic in Savannah. Born in Ireland in 1821, he died at Baltimore in 1872. See O'Connell, *Carolinas and Georgia*, 234. Records kept at Spring Hill College say that Father Usannaz returned from Andersonville in 1864 *meritis aeque ac pediculis coopertus* — "covered with merits and with lice." He died at St. Charles College, Grand Coteau, Louisiana, according to the Province Catalog of the Dead. The author is indebted to Father Roy Vollenweider, S.J., for this information.

[34] Michael Dougherty, *Diary of a Civil War Hero, 1863–1865* (New York: Pyramid Books, 1960), 106. This entry is under the date "July 20, 1864," and so must refer to Whelan or Clavreul; Hamilton was not in the prison at that time. Other descriptions of the priest in question are on pp. 114, 115, 118, 119. The names of the priests were often crossed in these personal accounts.

[35] Thomas H. Mann, M.D., "A Yankee in Andersonville," *The Century Magazine*, XL, (July, 1890), 457.

[36] John McElroy, *Andersonville, A Story of Rebel Military Prisons* (Toledo, Ohio: D. R. Locke, 1879), 377. The priest was probably Father Whelan, who answered the physical description given.

[37] Urban, *Battlefield and Prison Pen*, 345. "A priest belonging to the Catholic church was almost daily among us, and worked faithfully among the sick and dying members of his own church. He had also always a kind word for all of us."

[38] James Madison Page, *The True Story of Andersonville. A Defense of Major*

Bishop Verot, for his part, was not surprised. The absence of ministers at Andersonville only confirmed what he had said about their northern counterparts in his sermon on abolitionism in 1861 — the ministers were motivated more by politics, he had said, than by their religion — and he commented now, somewhat unkindly, that it was the error of their doctrines that caused the ministers to lack "the force of charity demanded by such great needs."[39] To a correspondent in France he described how at the military hospital in nearby Macon a Protestant doctor was so impressed by the devoted care of the sick shown by Father Hamilton, and on the other hand so disenchanted with other ministers who never came to visit their coreligionists even when invited, that he presented himself to the bishop for reception into the Church. "The war has at least contributed to the progress of religion," Verot said, "by making known the true character of the Catholic priest. . . . The Catholic priests were the only ones who stayed by their posts."[40]

True as this may have been, Verot made his antithesis too sharp. Many ministers, faced with half-empty churches when the bugles first sounded, had taken up arms themselves and joined the male side of their congregations in the field. What of the ministers who remained? Some extenuation of their failure to attend the dying men of Andersonville may be argued from the fact that Protestant theology did not place the minister under the same imperatives as those that guided the Catholic priest. While the priest was obligated to confer certain sacraments on all those of his faith who were in danger of death, the Protestant minister's

---

Henry Wirz (New York: Neale Publishing Company, 1908), 66, 222; Kellogg, *Rebel Prisons,* 163, 171, 195; Chipman, *The Tragedy of Andersonville,* 197. ASLA, Robert B. McCully to Clavreul, New York City (n. d.): "I think it fitting to say that I am a Protestant and sorry to say that I never saw or heard of a protestant minister entering Andersonville"; C. A. Storke to Clavreul, Santa Barbara, California, June 16, 1910: "I am not a Catholic, and my whole life has been spent with those who are not Catholics but I have a thousand times called the attention of the protestant clergy to their entire neglect of the humanities at Andersonville."

[39] *Annales,* XXXVII (September, 1865), 399–400.

[40] *Ibid.,* 404. Certain Protestants, understandably, were sensitive on this point. The *Presbyterian* of Fayetteville, North Carolina, commented in 1869: "Many Priests, Sisters of Charity, etc. — who never permit their good deeds to be hid under a bushel — *were* kind to our sick and wounded soldiers; though what was

theology provided for no such sacraments, and his assistance to the dying was confined to counsel, Bible reading, and prayer. The layman held a more direct ministerial position in the Protestant religion than he did in the Catholic, and perhaps the ministers who remained in the churches at Andersonville, Macon, Americus, and other towns close by, were of the judgment that Bible-reading and prayer could be conducted as well by the prisoners as by themselves. The prisoners' accounts mention certain "praying bands" and Bible services that were directed by prisoners who had been lay elders back home. One account says that certain of the prisoners had even been ordained ministers before the war and if this was so, the Protestant sick and dying could not have been entirely denied the consolations of formal religion.[41]

Still it was true, as Father Whelan wrote to Secretary of War Edwin M. Stanton after the war, that the Catholic priest was the "true benefactor" of the prisoners at Andersonville.[42] Writing of one of the priests, a prisoner said that "the world should know more of a man whose services were so creditable to humanity and his church."[43] As long after the event as 1908, when Father Clavreul was spending the evening of his life as pastor of St. Joseph's Church in Mandarin, Florida, a correspondent in the North wrote him: "I have seen grown men weeping at the mention of your name. Can you not give them the happiness of grasping your hand before they pass away?"[44] Colonel Chipman, Wirz's prosecutor, said that "these noble men of God who braved disease and death in their holy calling will never be forgotten."[45] But forgotten they were, eventually. Under the spreading weight of war histories concerned with the more spectacular side of public slaughter, enamored of battles, and strategies, and colorful commanders, Bishop Verot and his

---

done by Protestants would outweigh ten-fold all that was done by these. But Roman Catholics know how to make the most of all they do in the way of charity and benevolence." Quoted in *Banner of the South*, January 9, 1869.

[41]Urban, *Battlefield and Prison Pen*, 338–342. Thomas H. Mann wrote that his personal Bible was so well read by others that "nothing remained of it to bring away." "A Yankee in Andersonville," 455.

[42] Savannah *Daily News and Herald*, June 4, 1866.

[43] McElroy, *Andersonville*, 377.

[44] ASLA, Monsignor William J. Slocum to Clavreul, Waterbury, Connecticut, July 20, 1908.

[45] *The Tragedy at Andersonville*, 198.

priests achieved at last the oblivion reserved to peacemakers, and the anonymity of true charity.

Following his two visits to Andersonville Verot spent the remainder of 1864 in constant travel through Georgia. His diary records that he was in and out of Savannah five times on trips that took him twice to Augusta, to Locust Grove, Athens, Washington, Milledgeville, Albany, Darien, Waynesville, Brunswick, and Thomasville. In between the towns on country roads he stopped at individual homes, which he identified simply as "Mrs. Brisbane's," "George Murray's," "John Dabignon's," etc. He heard confessions, baptized, and confirmed. He received large numbers into the Church — or back into the Church. He preached to farmers, to railroad workers, to soldiers, to Negroes, and to "tolerably large" audiences of "Crackers," as the old-line Protestant country people were called. In Albany he found the church being used as a military hospital. In Darien he found the Catholics so destitute they were living in slave quarters. In Savannah itself he spent nearly two months' time, off and on, attending the sick, "the priests being few in the city on account of the presence of two of them in the Stockade at Andersonville." Sometimes his itinerary was interrupted by "raids and rumors of raids."

And the biggest raid was yet to come, for, by November 16, Sherman had captured and burned Atlanta, and was marching toward Savannah with 60,000 men. As the federals spread across the land they put the torch to plantations, pillaged homes and stores, and appropriated everything of value in their path. Verot heard the news on about November 30, while in Wilcox County, 140 miles from Savannah and south of Sherman's line of march. He was visiting the family of Matthew McGovern, "the last of the rail roaders on the unfortunate Brisbane r.[ail] road."[46] Verot took

---

[46] Gangs of Irish laborers were imported to Georgia in the 1840's to grade the route of the Ocomulgee and Flint River Railroad projected to link the Georgia River stations near Macon and Albany. A. H. Brisbane was president of the company. When the company threatened to fold in 1841, Brisbane appealed for subsidies to the Catholic bishops of the country, on the argument that his Irish Catholic laborers were starving. The expedient brought cash contributions from Bishops England of Charleston and Hughes of New York. In 1843 the Irish labor force mutinied and beat Brisbane with stones and cudgels. Brisbane fled for his life. Some of the Irish remained to settle in Georgia. No rail was ever laid on the Ocomulgee and Flint River. See Ulrich Bonnell Phillips, *A History of Transportation in the Eastern Cotton Belt to 1860* (New York: The Columbia University Press, 1908), 273–275.

leave hurriedly after receiving McGovern's wife into the Church
and drove his horse and buggy to the nearest rail line at Naylor,
eighty miles to the southeast. There a Catholic named John O'Brien
led him to the railroad by torchlight and got him aboard the train
to Savannah, which Verot reached on Saturday, December 3, eighteen
days before Sherman. The bishop wrote:

> In Savannah we had . . . the forty hours Devotion, the cannon
> being roaring all the time. The Yankees entered the City Wednesday,
> 21st Dec. whilst I was saying Mass. I heard their yells and hurrahs:
> fortunately, nothing was injured in the church or in the house, al-
> though the cemetery fence was burnt. On Christmas day a collection
> was taken up for the orphans and the Catholics of Sherman's army
> gave about 400 dol[lars], which was a God-send, as there was no
> other money at the time than the Confederate money, which had
> become quite worthless. Soon after the fall of Savannah I paid a
> visit to Sherman and asked him a pass to cross the lines at any
> place, which he did with his own handwriting.[47]

On January 18, 1865, armed with Sherman's pass (for he intended to visit northwest Florida which was still in Confederate
hands) Verot obtained a horse and buggy and drove out of
Savannah "with great difficulty, the roads being very bad." The
diary records the same arduous travel detail as before — "went
across black swamp in a canoe with some danger"; "slept there
without mattress or blanket"; "preached also to soldiers in the
street"; "with immense difficulty reached Doctor town." But it
had never been this bad before. In many areas communications
were nonexistent. Food was in short supply. The defeated populace
was demoralized. Along the swath cut by Sherman's march to the
sea, desolation reigned on every side:

> I encountered at almost every step horses, cows, sheep, pigs, even
> dogs, lying dead on the road. On entering the houses, I was able to
> learn from the victims of this vandalism what it was they had had
> to suffer. Everything of value had been carried off, the furnishings
> broken up, the food eaten. At the approach of the Yankees some

---

[47] "Episcopal Acts," 163–164. Cf. NA, Verot to Stanton, January 9, 1865.
Verot wrote Stanton to ask for a pass. Stanton referred the request to Sherman,
as noted on the letter. To Stanton, Verot said, "Perhaps you will feel inclined
to grant this favor if I tell you that I have myself gone to Andersonville and
maintained there two of my priests at my own expense for several months in
behalf of the federal prisoners who were detained there."

St. Mary's College in Baltimore as it appeared about 1850

Bishop Augustin Verot
toward the end of his life.

Patrick Neison Lynch,
Third Bishop of
Charleston

Francis Patrick Kenrick,
Sixth Archbishop
of Baltimore

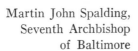

Martin John Spalding,
Seventh Archbishop
of Baltimore

Father Peter Whelan,
one of Bishop Verot's
closest associates

Father Henry Peter Clavreul,
another close associate
of Bishop Verot

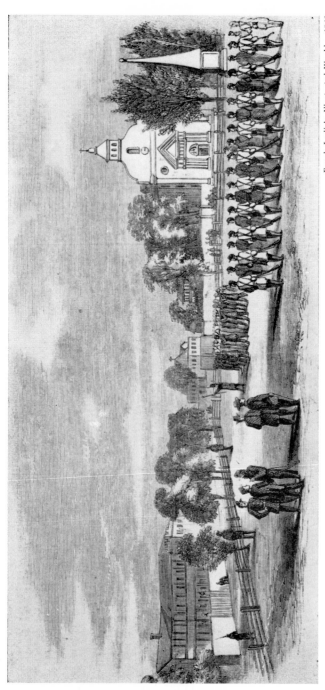

ST. AUGUSTINE DURING THE CIVIL WAR

Union occupation forces stand muster before the Catholic buildings of St. Augustine, Florida, shortly after their capture of the city in 1862. In the background are (right to left) the parish church, the parochial and episcopal residence, and the convent of the Sisters of Mercy.

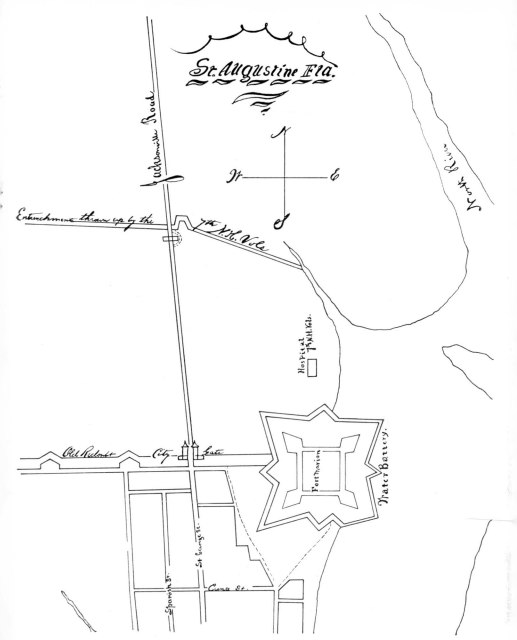

Text visible within the map:

St. Augustine Fla.

Jacksonville Road

N
W — E
S

North River

Entrenchment thrown up by the 7th N.H. Vols.

Hospital 7th N.H. Vols.

Old Redoubt — City — Gate

Fort Marion

Water Battery.

St. George St.

Spanish St.

Cuna St.

Courtesy of Jacksonville Free Public Library

NORTH ENTRENCHMENTS AT OCCUPIED ST. AUGUSTINE

Detail from Civil War map of St. Augustine shows Jacksonville Road (top) taken by Bishop Verot and Sisters of Mercy on eventful 1862 journey through the lines to Savannah. Verot was challenged and detained at the picket post, where legend reads: "Entrenchments thrown up by the 7th N[ew] H[ampshire] Vol[unteer]s."

ANDERSONVILLE PRISON IN THE SUMMER OF 1864

Frank Leslie's Illustrated Weekly, 1864

View from one of the two gates of the stockade shows sentry posts and "deadline" eighteen feet inside the inner wall. During July, 33,000 federal soldiers, "one-fifth perhaps being Catholics" Bishop Verot estimated, were confined inside this open pen,

BISHOP VEROT'S RESIDENCE IN SAVANNAH

Verot purchased this house for an episcopal residence at the close of the Civil War. It stood at the southwest corner of Perry and Drayton Streets. The handsome structure was demolished in this century.

RELICS OF BISHOP VEROT'S MISSIONARY TRAVELS

One of Verot's miters is shown with (left) his portable altar stone and carrying case, and (right) his crucifix, rosary, handkerchief, and eyeglass case.

Scene From Vatican Council I After a Sketch by Vespignani

families hid themselves in the woods or buried themselves in the swamps, waiting there two or three days until the enemy passed on. When they returned these poor people found their dwelling devastated, if it was not completely burned down, and hunger made them gather up grains of corn passed over by the horses. More than once I have had to ask hospitality in houses where not a single bed remained; I shared the lot of those unfortunate people in sleeping on the floor.[48]

Verot preached, baptized, and confirmed his way through southern Georgia, to the Florida border. In Florida he spent a short time visiting Tallahassee, Quincy, and Chattahoochee, and then returned to Georgia, arriving by stage the middle of February in Atlanta, "which was then in a state of desolation hard to describe." Thanks to Father Thomas O'Reilly, who had used his powers of persuasion on Union troops who burned the city on November 14, the Church of the Immaculate Conception and four nearby Protestant churches had been spared from the flames.[49] "I left some Confederate money with Father O'Reilly," Verot recorded, "and exhorted him to stay there patiently waiting for better times." After visiting six other towns in north Georgia, Verot bought a two-mule carriage and traveled back to Savannah, reaching the city on February 28 "after a tedious journey of nearly a week." He had taken care of the living — he did not know that soon again he would have to take care of the dead.

What can best be described as the "cemetery episode" began in the first week of March, 1865, when Verot discovered that federal troops were tearing up the Catholic cemetery outside Savannah. St. Vincent de Paul Cemetery, known popularly as Cathedral Cemetery, was located southeast of the city on Thunderbolt Road. Next to the cemetery Confederate engineers had erected Fort Brown with eleven field and siege guns, part of a formidable fieldworks system for the protection of Savannah against Sherman.[50] After the city fell, Union engineers laid out a more constricted defense line to protect the city against avenging rebel forces (if they existed). Captain Charles A. Suter, chief of engineers for the

---

[48] *Annales*, XXXVII (September, 1865), 396–397.

[49] "In Memoriam Father Thomas O'Reilly," *The Atlanta Historical Bulletin*, VIII, (October, 1945), 4–58.

[50] Charles C. Jones, Jr., *The Siege of Savannah* (Albany, N. Y.: Joel Munsel, 1874), 98–99.

military Department of the South, made an inspection of Fort Brown and decided that the new defense line should run directly across the cemetery, which occupied the summit and one side slope of a small hill nearby. Accordingly, troops were put to work demolishing a large section of the cemetery, and Catholic citizens of the city were advised to rescue their dead while they could.[51] Many persons did so, including the family of Mrs. Fanny Prendergast, and a group of Sisters of Mercy, who managed to bring out the remains of two bishops, Francis X. Gartland, first Bishop of Savannah, who died in the yellow-fever epidemic of 1854, and Edward Barron, formerly Vicar Apostolic to Africa, who had come to help Gartland in the epidemic and had died from the same cause. The bishops' pine coffins were reinterred temporarily in the convent garden of the Sisters of Mercy, along with the bodies of two priests and four sisters, also rescued from the advancing Union shovels.[52]

On March 9, Bishop Verot wrote a letter expressing his shock at the desecration of the cemetery to Major General Quincy A. Gillmore, commanding the Department of the South with head-quarters at Hilton Head, South Carolina.[53] Gillmore replied that he would soon be making a personal inspection of the cemetery area and he invited the bishop to accompany him. Verot, however, was unable to locate the general on the day appointed, and one day after the scheduled inspection, he learned that three hundred troops had been assigned to carry on the work already begun.[54] This news in hand, Verot determined to carry his protest to Secretary of War Stanton himself. It was one of the most blistering letters of his career.[55] Writing on March 22, Verot called the secretary's attention to the fact that Catholic cemeteries were consecrated ground, entitled to the same respect as churches to which they were appendages. He advised Stanton that there was a sentence of excommunication passed by the Church against

[51] NA, Record Group No. 107, Letters Received 1866, Captain Charles A. Suter to Colonel Woodford, Chief of Staff, Department of the South, Hilton Head, South Carolina, April 13, 1865.

[52] Martin S. J. Griffen, "History of the Church of Saint John the Evangelist, Philadelphia, From 1845 to 1853," RACH, XXI, (September, 1910), 135.

[53] O.R., XLVII, I, III, 203. Father Peter Whelan, back again in Savannah, had written a protest letter three days earlier; ibid., XLVII, I, II, 712.

[54] Ibid., XLVII, I, II, 967.

[55] Ibid.

those who usurped, invaded, and occupied church property. "Brutal force or infidel ideas may make light of such an ecclesiastical penalty but there is a power above which sides with the weak and defenceless [sic] and will act in due time, however obscure its operation may be." He pointed out that there was an abundance of ground on every side of the cemetery where fortifications might be erected, and that the Confederates had not found it necessary to desecrate revered ground, "although they had to defend the City against overpowering numbers." He concluded:

It is hard to see how such a military necessity should have arisen so suddenly, now that there is no opposing force at all, and that the Confederates, far from being able to attack, evacuate everywhere what they had.

I thought I could not do less than send my humble protest in behalf of the Catholic Church whose right and privileges I deem to be infringed by this proceeding; in behalf of an outraged community obliged now to carry away where they can the mouldering remains of their relatives and friends; in behalf of the Irish Catholic soldiers who are obliged to perform the work of hyenas, and in behalf of those who will have to stand in the midst of exhalations arising from opened and mutilated graves.

The letter nettled Stanton, who directed Major General James A. Hardie, his Inspector General (and a Catholic), to advise Verot that he did not appreciate "the disrespectful and unbecoming language of your letters towards the Govt. and its officers."[56] Nonetheless, Stanton directed General Gillmore to make a full investigation of the bishop's "bitter complaint," and "not to interfere with any cemetery or burial ground unless under an absolute necessity for the proper defense of the city, and in such case to see that the bodies are carefully removed and properly interred in a suitable place, and, if possible, under the charge of ecclesiastical authorities. . . ."[57] Verot meanwhile had made contact with Colonel Stewart L. Woodford, Gillmore's chief of staff, and had accompanied him on an inspection of the cemetery. There they found that the disinterment of bodies had been completed. Under Gillmore's orders Colonel Woodford then offered to put Verot in

[56] NA, Record Group No. 107, Letters Sent Vol. 58B, Hardie to Verot, Washington City, April 5, 1865 (copy).
[57] O.R., XLVII, I, III, 202, E. D. Townsend, Assistant Adjutant-General, to Gillmore, Steamer Arago, Hilton Head, S. C., April 13, 1865.

possession of another piece of ground nearby for burial use and to endorse favorably any application that Verot might wish to make for indemnity or damages.[58] Verot objected vigorously that he would accept no exchanges of any kind. "Here is my answer," he wrote Gillmore:

> The works ought to be stopped at once; the ground leveled as it was before; the walks marked out; the tombstones, railings, and ornaments of the graves restored as they were before; the fence around the cemetery put up again; the mortuary chapel, which was in progress of erection, built up again, and the expenses of the disinterring and interring the dead again defrayed to our Catholics.[59]

From Woodford, Verot learned that Gillmore was a Catholic, "a fact which I only suspected before,"[60] and he wrote again to Stanton to state that this discovery "gives me additional grief that the desecration of that cemetery should come from such hands. However," he went on, "I have often noticed that a certain class of Catholics, for fear of the reproach of partiality, will be the last to give the Church her dues."[61]

By April 13 General Gillmore was thoroughly exasperated by the recalcitrance of the rebel bishop, and he fired off two letters on that date to say so, one in answer to Stanton's directive, the other to Verot's immediate superior, Archbishop Spalding of Baltimore. To the War Department Gillmore wrote: "I fear that Bishop Verot's course in this matter, judging from the tenor of his conversation with my chief of staff, has been captious rather than charitable and that a feeling of hostility to the national cause has prompted him to embarrass my action."[62] To Archbishop Spalding he was equally blunt:

> I regret to be compelled to say frankly after careful reflection that I believe that Bishop Verot's course in this matter has been purposely vexatious and designed to stir up and perpetuate bad and disloyal feelings among the Catholic residents of Savannah against the National Government. I fear that he sympathizes so deeply with the rebellion and its adherents as to warp his judgment

---

[58] *O.R.*, XLVII, I, III, 203.

[59] *Ibid.*, 205.

[60] *Ibid.*

[61] NA, Record Group No. 7, Letters Received V–175 (146), 1865, Verot to Stanton, Savannah, April 6, 1865.

[62] *O.R.*, XLVII, I, III, 203.

and embitter his expression of opinions and protests. I feel it is due to myself to ask your attention to him and to respectfully request that you, as his spiritual superior, will advise him to confine his official remarks hereafter within more temperate and loyal limits.[63]

There is no record of Spalding's response, if any. The controversy was eventually resolved, however, without the intervention of extraneous parties — probably by the realization on Gillmore's part that he would not be able to move by any means short of divine the articulate and stubborn Bishop of Savannah. How the two men eventually got together there are no existing records to say; official War Department records show only that, on October 25 following, Verot was holding Secretary Stanton responsible for fulfillment of promises made him to restore the cemetery to its original condition.[64] Verot learned that he had won his fight when he went to Hilton Head on April 21 and met General Gillmore for the first time. "My letter to him and to Secretary Staunton [sic]," he recorded in his diary, "seems to have galled them and they promised to restore the cemetery to the former condition. I learned at Hilton Head the good effect my protest had produced and wrote a letter of apology to Gen. Gillmore, who seemed to be well pleased and invited me to dine with him and his staff at Hilton Head."[65] Gillmore placed his boat at Verot's disposal so that the bishop would have transportation back from Jacksonville and St. Augustine, both of which he visited in early May. On May 23, Verot wrote Stanton "to recall in all sincerity the objectionable language which the view of the desecrated cemetery wrung from my feelings at that time."[66] After several long delays, occasioned by the lack of both workers and funds, the War Department made good on its promise to restore the cemetery and

---

63 AAB, 34–B–16, Gillmore to Spalding, Hilton Head, S. C., April 13, 1865.

64 NA, Record Group No. 107, Letters Received, V–11, 1866, Major General Richard Delafield, Chief Engineer, U.S.A., to Stanton, Washington, May 26, 1866: "Oct. 25, 1865 Bishop Verot writes the Secretary of War reminding him of a previous correspondence in which a promise had been made that the cemetery would be restored to its former condition . . .;" and Verot to Stanton, Savannah, October 25, 1865.

65 "Episcopal Acts," 165–166.

66 NA, Record Group No. 107, Letters Received, V–237 (150), 1865, Verot to Stanton, Hilton Head, S. C., May 23, 1865.

return it to the Catholics of Savannah.[67] Verot began again construction of the mortuary chapel, and on December 23, 1866, he
solemnly reinterred the bodies that had been exhumed from the
wrecked graveyard in 1865. In the chapel together with the bodies
of Bishops Gartland and Barron, Verot placed the remains of
John Barry, second Bishop of Savannah, who had died in France
in 1859 and whose body Verot had brought home to Savannah
in 1866. It was, said the Savannah *Republican,* an "imposing ceremony."[68] The correspondent of the *Catholic Mirror* wrote back to
Baltimore: "The Bishop addressed a few words to the crowd,
explaining the ceremony of the reconciliation of the cemetery, and
the great respect due to the place where the bodies of Christians
are kept; and having thanked, in the name of the clergy and
people, those who had volunteered in levelling the breast works,
and those who had contributed to repair the sad vestiges of the
late war, the sun now fast sinking under the horizon, the procession
returned to the Cathedral."[69]

It was time to turn again from the dead to the living.

---

[67] NA, Record Group No. 107, Letters Received, V–11, 1866, Verot to Stanton,
Savannah, October 25, 1865; Brevet Lieutenant Colonel E. B. Carling to Lieutenant
Sam[u]el Rounds, Savannah, November 20, 1865; Verot to Stanton, Savannah,
February 7, 1866; Brevet Major General M. C. Meigs, Quartermaster-General, to
Stanton, Washington, February 23, 1866; Delafield to Stanton, Washington, May
26, 1866.
[68] December 24, 1866.
[69] January 5, 1867.

CHAPTER V

THE FREED NEGRO

IN WAR men perform acts that are remembered afterward as high drama because they were performed amid the smells of cordite or among the tents and colors of soldiery. The same acts in peacetime, lacking the surrounding excitement, might easily go unnoticed and unremembered. Human acts tend to be remembered by history in proportion to the excitement of the times in which they were committed or according to the influence that the acts bore upon others. By both measures Bishop Verot's accomplishments during the era of Reconstruction should hardly merit the historian's attention, and indeed hardly have. By comparison with what went before, the immediate postwar years in the South were admittedly dull (though not lacking in anger and aggravation). Bishop Verot's labor, like everyone else's, was slow and plodding. And what he accomplished for his Catholic people, and for the newly freed Negro populations, had very little influence on anyone except those directly affected. Besides that, it was largely a work of the spirit, and the spirit has never won much space in chronicles. Yet there is reason to say that Verot's actions during the years 1865–1870 were more noteworthy than what he had done in wartime, and that they deserve to mark for him a permanent place in the history of the Church and of the nation. Particularly is this true for Verot's leadership in education of the freed Negro — the first great social enterprise to occupy the interests of American Catholics.

At war's end in April, 1865, the bishop watched the peace settle like soot on a charred ruin. The flag of the Confederacy that he had hailed so spiritedly four years before was now furled forever, and its flagstaffs looked out upon a devastation equal to any that

115

western man had known in the century.[1] Worse than the physical destruction was the demoralization of the southern people. Throughout Georgia and Florida, the areas of his jurisdiction, Verot could see a general and spreading laxity of morals, a corruption of manners and a reaction from religious faith so severe it threatened to run into outright and universal skepticism. The Augusta *Constitutionalist,* seeing the same things, wrote: "A dreadful shipwreck has covered the face of foaming water with broken fragments, to which millions of half-drowned passengers are clinging."[2] Compounding the tragedy was the fact that four million of these passengers were Negroes, former slaves whose newfound liberties could only be exercised at the sanction of bayonets in the midst of a largely hostile population. Verot was convinced that the battle over the Negro's destiny must go no further. Political and sectional loyalties were now beside the point. If the peace was a forced peace, still it must be peace, and must be characterized by disinterested concern for the newly freed populations who stood at the divide between civilization and ruin. Now was the time for northerner and southerner alike to press for the material, educational, and moral advantage of a people whom the God of nations had commended, free of shackles, into their hands.

Religion had been one of the principal forces, along with humanitarianism and political theory, in producing the northern sentiment against slavery and the southern sentiment for it. Religion now had to serve with equal vigor in making the overthrow of that institution meaningful and beneficial. Verot had never seen any special virtue in the ties between religion and abolitionism. Nonetheless, now that the situation of the Negro was irrevocably altered, he was prepared to lay aside his proslavery doctrine as though it had never been true. While he would make scathing mention at least once again of the "hypocritical philanthropy" of abolitionism, from 1865 forward the bishop was, in fact, a model "abolitionist": he devoted himself to the welfare of the freedmen with a zeal that looked like the excitement of a man convinced that the sudden emancipation of four million men was an undiluted blessing. What reservations he maintained about the matter he successfully hid behind an outpouring of heartfelt concern for the

[1] For Verot's material losses, see Chapter VI.
[2] March 11, 1866.

freedman himself: some salutary religious effort must be made for him on the southern side, he said, and quickly.[3] One month after the fall of the last Confederate stronghold, Verot explained the challenge to the Society for the Propagation of the Faith in France:

> The abolition of slavery, which has played so large a political role in the war, and which is going to change radically the conditions of American industry, presents, in the moral and religious point of view, a question of the highest interest. We know that the Southern states contain four or five million colored persons. . . . Those Negroes were almost inapproachable: their masters were opposed to any communication with them; moreover, the forced labor to which they were subjected rendered it impossible for a priest to speak with them. . . .[4] The Catholic religion is eminently favorable for attracting and winning the admiration of the Negroes, because of the pomp, variety, and symbolism of its ceremonial ritual. Unhappily, we do not have enough clergy in these parts to give to the ritual its full magnificence; let us hope that this situation will improve.[5] For the present, we must make a beginning by establishing schools — a necessity. The [northern] Protestants have anticipated us here: they have opened free schools which the Negroes attend in great numbers. Masters and mistresses have come from the North to superintend these schools, and the high salaries paid the teachers will attract many more. The Bible Societies, which, as we know, are quite wealthy, provide amply for school expenses. We must, therefore, prepare for the contest . . . in procuring religious instruction for this simple and docile race. . . .[6]

[3] For similar expressions of concern on the southern side for the freedmen's moral and religious welfare immediately after the war, see the citations from the Alabama Baptist Convention, the Protestant Episcopal Church, and the Methodist Episcopal Church, South, in William Warren Sweet, *The Story of Religion in America* (New York: Harper, 1939), 472–473. Cf. Anson Philips Stokes, *Church and State in the United States* (New York: Harper, 1950), II, 247–258.

[4] Cf. C. G. Woodson, *The Education of the Negro Prior to 1861* (New York: G. P. Putnam's Sons, 1915), 183. Catholic priests "were denied access to the Negroes, in most southern communities, even when they volunteered to work as missionaries among the colored people."

[5] The Catholic liturgy impressed most of the southern bishops as a likely means of attracting the Negro. Typical of the later agreement with Verot's judgment on this score is the following from Bishop Lynch: "The ceremonies of the Church, the Processions, Novenas, etc. would satisfy the cravings of their still tropical nature for pomp and ceremony in a way that would draw many of them from the cold services of Protestant worship." ADC, Box 1865, Patrick N. Lynch to The President and Members of the Central Council of the Association of the Propagation of the Faith, Lyons, September 7, 1865.

[6] *Annales*, XXVI (September, 1865), 401–402. Verot to the Society, May 25,

In October Verot turned to more general considerations relating
to the Negro in a lengthy pastoral letter addressed to the people
of Georgia and Florida.[7] He reminded them of the new state of
the Negro that followed "after that long and sanguinary war which
has caused the blood of your sons to flow so profusely, and has
deluged the land in human gore, and converted it into a heap of
smoking ruins." All that carnage and destruction seems to have
produced nothing of worth, only shriveled, bitter fruit. All their
prayers for peace, he told his readers, seem to have gone for naught:
"the peace is not perhaps such a one as you desired." But men
are often blind in their petitions, "and we think we ask for bread,
when we really ask for poison." The fact is, the South was given
something of greater worth than that for which she asked.

> Peace has come to you, not with the perpetuation, but with the
> abolition of slavery. You have lost your servants. But let me ask
> you: had you complied faithfully with the obligation incumbent on
> you to give a truly Christian education and instruction to those
> servants . . . as it was your duty to do?[8] This obligation is now
> shifted from your hands into those of the servants themselves. Many
> will therefore find an enormous reduction in the account they will
> have to render to their God, at the bar of the divine justice. Is
> this not a just cause of joy and congratulation?

The average reader probably felt that Bishop Verot was stretch-
ing a great distance to find extenuating reasons for defeat at war
— and supernatural reasons at that. Nevertheless, even those
southerners whose faith was too shaken to admit of solace of this
order could find in the bishop's words a sound of hope, a sound
badly needed. To the Negro, too, Verot addressed hopeful words

1865. This apparently was the first written statement from a southern Catholic
calling attention to the moral and religious needs of the freedmen. In January,
1865, Bishop Lynch had written to Bishop Elder of Natchez, proposing the more
limited project of a Negro Catholic colony "of say 4000 or 5000 souls" at Sea
Island near Charleston. The colony never materialized. Archives of the Diocese
of Natchez, Lynch to William Henry Elder, January 10, 1865; cited in McMurry,
"Catholic Church during Reconstruction," 208. Lynch would later be one of the
chief southern advocates of the freedmen's welfare.

  [7] ADSA, Jubilee Pastoral of Right Rev. A. Verot, Bishop of Savannah and
Administrator Apostolic of Florida, October 4, 1865. Cf. *Catholic Mirror*, November 11, 1865.

  [8] The question recalls Verot's warning in the latter half of his 1861 sermon:
"This flagrant injustice against the souls of slaves would be the sure way to
render slavery an untenable and ruinous institution. . . ." Cf. above, Chapter II.

and a congratulatory message. They have acquired, he told them, an exemption from involuntary labor, and from the ties that bound them to masters. In effect, the national government has applied to them the provisions of the ancient Jewish jubilee, which restored to liberty all the Jews who had become slaves by sale. "This is for you a subject of heartful congratulations, and be it far from us to disturb you in the enjoyment of this boon." However, the Negroes should attend carefully to a few words of caution, lest through crime, immorality, or indolence they lose the precious benefits of true liberty.

> It is our duty to tell you that there is a slavery far worse than the one from which you have just emerged, which may hold you in bondage and from which you must free yourselves. It is the slavery of sin, the slavery of wicked and criminal passions, the slavery of bad habits and evil practices.

In vain would the freedmen imagine that they were free if they gave themselves over to practices that violated law and order, and the demands of their higher nature. It would be a sad mistake indeed if, contented with the liberty of the body, they gave their minds and souls to the ignominious slavery of error and crime. Verot reminded them, too, that "marriage is binding on the colored race as on the white race . . . and we hope that the strong arm of the law which has set you free will not leave you free to violate the decencies of civilized life." And while on the subject of civilization:

> We think it likewise our duty to remind you that labor, nay constant and serious labor is the lot of all men without any exception. . . . Freedom, far from exempting you from labor, has only thrown upon you the responsibility of supporting yourselves and your families by your earnest and persevering labor. Those who refuse to work would be obliged to resort to theft and dishonesty in order to live. This could not fail to bring upon them the severe chastisements of Divine and human justice. It would consign them to slavery worse than the former, and would make society grieve at having given them a privilege of which they were unworthy.[9]

Verot concluded hopefully that "these admonitions are scarcely

---

[9] Concern that the Negro would not, or did not, labor on his own free initiative was widespread among Catholic leaders, North and South. Archbishop Hughes had written during the war: "A recumbent posture, under a tropical

necessary for Catholic Negroes who, we trust, know sufficiently their duty upon these points. . . . Their number is unfortunately small." What precisely was the number of Catholic Negroes under his jurisdiction there are no extant records to say. By comparison with the total, however, the number of those who were Catholic must have been very small. Of the four million freedmen in the South as a whole Bishop Lynch estimated in 1867 that 150,000 were Catholics.[10] However, both Verot and Lynch were confident that the Church would win the Negroes to her civilizing influence: in Verot's words, "freeing from the thraldom of ignorance, sin and heresy the race that has lately been freed from the thraldom of men."[11]

In the spring and summer of 1866 preparations were afoot for a plenary, or national, council of all the American bishops, to be held at Baltimore in October. Verot learned of the forthcoming conclave while in Rome during a trip to Europe undertaken in

sun, is his [the Negro's] conception of Paradise." New York *Metropolitan Record,* May 10, 1862. The St. Augustine *Examiner* found the problem acute among Florida Negroes: e.g., March 9, 1867, April 20, 1867. One of Verot's missionaries noted in 1868 that Georgia's Negroes "don't want to work . . . they steal a great deal." Diary of Joseph Wissel, C.SS.R., cited in Andrew H. Skeabeck, "The Early Life of William H. Gross, C.SS.R., Fifth Bishop of Savannah, 1837–1885" (unpublished master's thesis, The Catholic University of America, 1949), 60. A recent authority describes a great part of the Negro population immediately after the war as lazy, self-indulgent, and improvident. Federal relief agencies encouraged the freedmen's idleness by dispensing rations to them. Contemporary observers saw "multitudes of Negroes loafing about, doing nothing." Henderson H. Donald, *The Negro Freedman* (New York: Henry Schuman, 1952), 171–176. However, the free Negro laborer before the war had acquitted himself well, despite discriminatory legislation and sometimes harsh treatment; see John Hope Franklin, *The Free Negro in North Carolina* (Chapel Hill, N. C.: University of North Carolina, 1943), 121–162. And by 1875 the postbellum free Negro had redeemed that reputation: "Indeed there was none who was willing to assert that free labor had not been a success"; Donald, *Negro Freedman,* 37, citing Edward King, *The Great South* (Hartford, 1875).

[10] Address at the Catholic Congress in Malines, Belgium, reported by the Paris *Monde,* September 9, 1867, and cited in the Cincinnati *Catholic Telegraph,* October 2, 1867. This figure compares with the estimate of 100,000 Negro Catholics at the time of emancipation in John T. Gillard, S.S.J., *Colored Catholics in the United States* (Baltimore: Josephite Press, 1941), 99.

[11] Jubilee Pastoral, October 4, 1865. Bishop Lynch stated at Malines in 1867 that "it is the Church's aim to enlighten and elevate these parias [*sic*] of American society. . . . A Protestant minister said of them, the blacks are like a fallow field, and will belong to whoever can secure them. Well, Messieurs, the Negroes will belong to the Church!" *Catholic Telegraph,* October 2, 1867.

June–August, 1865,[12] and wrote to Archbishop Odin in October of that year, saying that he would not be surprised if they met the following spring in Baltimore.[13] He would have been glad to learn, if he did not in fact know, that Archbishop Martin John Spalding of Baltimore thought that one of the most urgent duties facing such a council was discussion of the Negro problem. Spalding wrote to Archbishop John McCloskey of New York: "Four millions of these unfortunates are thrown on our Charity, and they silently but eloquently appeal to us for help."[14]

While Spalding and his fellow bishops were shaping their thoughts and proposals for this and other matters to come before the council, Verot thought it wise to place before the people of Georgia and Florida certain already well-shaped thoughts on the free Negro. A conciliar decree bearing on the dignity of Negroes would have slight effect if he could not first remove the prejudice against the race that existed among his Catholic people. Accordingly, on August 1, 1866, Verot wrote a pastoral letter that concentrated on this point. It was published in the Savannah *Daily News and Herald* under the heading: "Important Document . . . His Directions in Regard to Negroes and on Other Important Subjects."[15] The section on the Negroes attracted the attention of the *Catholic Mirror* and the New York *Times*, both of which reprinted it.[16] The content represented a new Catholic purpose in the South: "We may in truth say that the eyes of Catholic Europe are now turned toward this country to see what will be done for enlightening, civilizing and ennobling a race that has suddenly emerged from bondage to the enjoyment of civil rights and the blessings of liberty." Verot first described the enormity of the changes that had taken place:

---

[12] "Episcopal Acts," 166. Verot went abroad to secure funds and teachers for Negro schools; see below.

[13] AANO, Box 1865, Verot to Odin, Savannah, October 6, 1865.

[14] Archives of the Archdiocese of New York, McCloskey Papers, Spalding to McCloskey, Baltimore, October 9, 1865; cited in McMurray, "Church During Reconstruction," 197. Spalding's felicitous expression appears to have been lifted from a letter received by him from Bishop John Timon of Buffalo, written August 23, 1865, and cited in Peter Guilday, *A History of the Councils of Baltimore* (New York: Macmillan, 1932), 220. As ordinary of the oldest see, and by appointment from Rome, Spalding was apostolic delegate to the council, thus charged with preparing its agenda; see *ibid.*, 194–196.

[15] September 13, 1866.

[16] *Catholic Mirror*, September 1, 1866; New York *Times*, October 1, 1866.

These people have been kept hitherto in ignorance, in view of perhaps imaginary dangers, and an injudicious legislation prevailed forbidding, under the severest penalties known to the law, to instruct them in reading and writing, and the plain branches of education;[17] now that unreasonable severity was as detrimental to the country as it was unjust in itself, for in the late struggle, it extinguished the sympathies of Europe for the Southern States, and closed the bowels of compassion for them, although it was the general interest and perhaps the desire of the old world to cramp and divide a nation now become too powerful. This was indeed a great error suggested by cupidity and infidelity which had then unlimited and unrestricted sway over our land. This state of things has now ceased to exist, and if the abolition of slavery be the only permanent and irrevocable result of the war, as through a merciful Providence seems to be the case, we have no reason to feel sad at such a conclusion of the struggle. . . .

But, Verot continued, a sense of uprightness and of justice ought to suggest to everyone the propriety of giving to this race, so recently admitted to the boon of freedom, the full opportunity of obtaining instruction and knowledge, "which are the necessary appendages of the human mind." Statesmen, politicians, and philosophers in the southern states ought to recognize the necessity of providing this education to the colored race, "even setting aside all supernatural and Christian views."[18] It is a matter of satisfaction that the greatest and ablest men of the country have frankly and unequivocally confessed this conviction. For Verot's part, "we wish to do everything in our power to rescue from the bondage of . . . ignorance those who have been freed and delivered, from

17 Cf. Woodson, *Education of the Negro*, 8–9, 163–183. Reacting to the Nat Turner rebellion of 1831 in Virginia, the majority of the slaveholding states during the two decades following passed laws forbidding, to one extent or another, the education of Negroes, whether free or slave. The legislation in Georgia was particularly stringent; see 167. A great amount of clandestine instruction of the Negroes went on during this period, however, even some plain and open schooling; see, e.g., Franklin, *Free Negro in North Carolina*, 164–174.

18 During the two years following, many leading southern figures did recognize this need, and spoke out in its favor, including Governor James I. Orr of South Carolina, former Governor Andrew B. Moore of Alabama, Jabez L. M. Curry, former member of the Confederate Congress, and Episcopal Bishop Stephen Elliot of Georgia. See E. Merton Coulter, *The South During Reconstruction, 1865–1877* (Baton Rouge: Louisiana State University, 1947), 83; Henry Lee Swint, *The Northern Teacher in the South* (Nashville: Vanderbilt University, 1941), 121–122.

domestic and civil fetters"; and he promised to give his whole zeal to securing a happy conclusion to the greatest challenge ever to face Catholicism in the South.

His readers should not think, however, Verot cautioned, that in advocating this course he embraced the "hypocritical philanthropy" of abolitionism, that movement which deluged the land in blood because it forgot that "evil must not be done in order to obtain a good." He held the abolitionists, "not the people of the North at large," to be the unjust authors of all the evil means which led, inconsequently, to a good result. The abolition of slavery in Europe, which was the result of a gradual, centuries-long amelioration effected by Christianity, was a highly rational victory compared with that in which, during the rapid lapse of four years, "more than two millions of men have lost their lives in order to free four millions of them."[19] Yet, if Verot was still unwilling to grant any virtue to abolitionism, he did reverse himself on a point to which abolitionism had addressed itself, and on which he had curiously refused to speak in his 1861 sermon — the slave trade, as the concrete means by which southern masters gained title to their servants. Although on that earlier occasion Verot condemned this trade in the abstract, he studiously avoided stamping the sin upon the South. It was an omission that seriously weakened his proslavery argument because he failed to face up to one of the principal issues at question: namely, could the slaveholders claim any conceivable title to the men they held in bondage? Now, in 1866, Verot declared that "injudicious and unjust as was the means adopted to obtain this end [Negro freedom], we embrace the conclusion fully, sincerely, in good faith and irrevocably . . ."; and he gave the following as his reason:

African slavery seems to have commenced and to have been kept up by the cruel and evidently unjust proceedings of men to sell them to the tiger-hearted authors and abettors of the slave trade. . . . The title of former masters was very tottering and was nothing more than prescription, and the necessity of upholding the existing order of things and avoiding social convulsions. The late events have destroyed the last vestiges of that title, and consequently the former state of things can never be reinstated without violating all laws and all principles of justice.

[19] Verot erred in the number of deaths, now known to have slightly exceeded 600,000, or one out of four who fought.

Now that even practical justifications for the slave system had been removed, there was no other course remaining but to turn to the task of creating, from southern desire instead of under northern pressure, a new social order for the Negro. And in the performance of this task,

> We exhort all to put away all prejudice, all dislike, all antipathy, all bitterness against their former servants. Away with all feelings of bickerings, envy or jealousy which would only bespeak a narrow mind and the lack of noble and elevated feelings. The golden rule, *love thy neighbor as thy self,* must not admit of any exception.

Altogether, Verot had put together during the sixteen months following the war's end the most eloquent appeal for the Negro's welfare that had come from the Catholic Church in the South, and his presence at the plenary council in Baltimore was at least a partial representation of those four million "unfortunates" whom Archbishop Spalding had heard appealing for help. Forty-four bishops from every quarter of the country attended the council, which convened on October 7, 1866, and deliberated at its seventh session on the challenge presented by the freedmen. The fourth chapter of the *Acts and Decrees* issuing from the conclave urged the prelates and priests of the country to "devote to this work their efforts, their time, finally, if it be possible, their entire lives."[20] It left each bishop to decide for his diocese whether or not there should be separate churches for Negroes, but urged everywhere the foundation of religious communities of both sexes to open schools, orphanages, and other centers of ministration to the colored populations. That the bishops were in earnest can be seen from the language of their legislation: "And if, through neglect, this is not done, anyone who, unmindful of his duty, shall fail to provide the means of salvation to all seeking them, be they black or not, will merit the strongest condemnation."[21] The prelates expressed regret, however, that the problem had arisen in the way it had; for their own good it were better if the Negroes had been emancipated less precipitously:

---

[20] *Concilii Plenarii Baltimorensis II . . . Acta et Decreta,* Caput IV, #488 (Baltimore: John Murphy, 1868), 246. For a summary of the council as a whole, see Guilday, *Councils of Baltimore,* Chapter XVI, "The Second Plenary Council (1866)," 187–220.

[21] *Acta et Decreta,* Caput IV, #485, 245.

We would have wished that, in accordance with the action of the Catholic Church in past ages, in regard to the serfs in Europe, a more gradual system of emancipation could have been adopted, so that they might have been in some measure prepared to make a better use of their freedom than they are likely to do now. Still, the evils that must necessarily attend upon the sudden liberation of so large a multitude, with their peculiar dispositions and habits, only make the appeal to our Christian charity and zeal presented by their forlorn condition the more forcible and imperative.[22]

To Verot was given the task of writing, in the name of all the American bishops, to the Society for the Propagation of the Faith in France. He was directed to seek the Society's financial aid for the work that had to be done. His letter was a distillate of his earlier writings, but it added the ring of emotion to his oft-expressed fear that the Negro would fall into a state worse than the first. He concluded:

They may, no doubt, attend our instructions, but it is our duty to attract them by founding for them churches, schools and orphan asylums. The States in which these establishments are to be formed have been ruined by war. This is a powerful motive to stimulate your charity. We therefore propose to you these works for the poor blacks, who are so much abandoned, so much despised.[23]

Secular press comment in Baltimore was in general laudatory of the nature and of the aims of the plenary council. The *Gazette* praised the unity of purpose which marked the deliberations, so soon after "our late civil dissensions."[24] The *Sunday Telegram*, too, was glad that there was "no quarrel about churches North or churches South," and "though we differ in some particulars from the literal creed and ritual of the great Catholic Church, yet we cannot but admire the holy discipline that has subjected human passion and allayed or restrained the violence of human prejudice. . . ."[25] The *Sun* was particularly impressed by the attention given the Negro at the council, and hazarded the opinion that "the

---

[22] Peter Guilday, *The National Pastorals of the American Hierarchy, 1792–1919* (Washington, D. C.: National Catholic Welfare Conference, 1923), 221. In his 1861 sermon Verot had warned that "the sudden and abrupt manumission of slaves would be a misfortune of appalling magnitude, more so yet for the slave than for the master"; see above, Chapter II.

[23] *Catholic Mirror*, May 4, 1867.

[24] Quoted in *Catholic Mirror*, October 13, 1866.   [25] Quoted in *ibid*.

usages of that church which in the solemn ministrations of religion have allowed no distinction between master and slave . . . perhaps give it strong advantages at the outset for attracting the sympathies of the [Negroes]." The *Sun* went on to single out the Bishop of Savannah:

> A published letter some time since by Bishop Verot, who seems to be touched by that religious enthusiasm which led his fellow-countrymen and fellow-religionists, two centuries ago, to encounter all the hardships of savage life for the conversion of the Indians, indicated that the intellectual, moral and religious culture of the Southern negroes would engage the earnest attention of his church. In the pastoral of the plenary council this indication was realized. . . .[26]

At the close of the deliberations in Baltimore, Bishop Verot set out on a lengthy begging tour: "I went to Erie [Pennsylvania] to beg money for the burnt churches of my diocese and also to educate the colored people; went to the oil regions and collected about 900 dol. in the diocese of Erie; went to Buffalo, where I collected about 800 dol., and to Rochester, where I collected about 700, then returned after a begging tour of a little more than three weeks by the way of Cleveland, Columbus, Cincinnati, Louisville, Nashville, Atlanta, Columbus, and Macon. . . . Having returned to Savannah, I started with Father Alexander M. Delafosse for St. Augustine,"[27] where he set to work at once to enlarge the colored gallery in the parish church. A citywide fair netted him $350 for this purpose, and the local *Examiner* expressed its satisfaction that the white population, "setting aside all prejudices," gave its full support to the project. The paper added, somewhat smugly:

> We cheerfully congratulate the colored people for the success they have obtained, and this ought to go far to prove what some people in the North have so much difficulty to understand, that in the South are yet to be found the best of friends of the colored people who are willing to get their hands into their pockets and make sacrifices to come to their assistance.[28]

In the choice given him and other bishops by the council to provide separate or mixed facilities for the freedmen, Verot had

---

[26] Quoted in St. Augustine *Examiner,* January 26, 1867.
[27] "Episcopal Acts," 168–169.
[28] *Examiner,* January 5, 1867. Enlargement of the gallery was completed in June; *ibid.,* June 8, 1867.

chosen the latter. His judgment seems to have been borne out by the failure of a separate church for Negroes erected soon after in Charleston by Bishop Lynch.[29] Verot did, it is true, arrange for separate missions, or retreats, for the Negro as, for example, during the Redemptorist missions in Georgia and Florida conducted at his request in 1868 and 1869.[30] (The Redemptorist mission exclusively for Negroes at the Savannah cathedral on January 31, 1869, attracted "an immense concourse of people of all denominations."[31]) But for the most part, Verot chose to unite the congregations as far as that was possible. Symbolic of the integrating program he followed was the Palm Sunday procession in St. Augustine, April 6, 1868, which struck a correspondent of the New York *Metropolitan Record* as a ceremony "the like of which probably could not be seen in any other part of this continent." The congregation, colored with the whites, and escorted by federal occupation troops, marched through the streets of the city carrying palms. "The Priests, three in number, were escorted by about forty soldiers of the 7th U. S. Infantry as a guard of honor, and were followed by the colored members of the congregation. . . . The line contained about seven hundred persons, many being negroes. . . ."[32] The New York correspondent went on to comment:

> The negro population in St. Augustine is quite large, perhaps one-half, and the greater part are Catholics. . . . The wealthy non-Catholics of the city have made and are still making vigorous efforts to keep the negroes from joining the Catholic Church, but without much success. It is unquestionably true that Catholicism

[29] St. Peter's, dedicated January 12, 1868, the first Catholic church exclusively for Negroes in the deep South. In 1865 Bishop Lynch had written that "this would give us proper scope to adapt the preaching and instructions to their capacity, far more limited than that of the whites." ADC, Box 1865, Lynch to the President and Members of the . . . Propagation of the Faith, Lyons, September 7, 1865. St. Peter's did not prove the success Lynch had anticipated. In 1869 a correspondent of the *Freeman's Journal* found that the church had been taken over by the whites, with only a sprinkling of Negroes here and there: "I am convinced that this attempt at a Catholic church for the colored people is, thus far, a *signal failure*. This is also the conviction of all to whom I spoke on the subject." *Freeman's Journal,* September 11, 1869.

[30] See Skeabeck, "William H. Gross," 59–72; cf. Verot, "Episcopal Acts," 172; see below, Chapter VI.

[31] Diary of Joseph Wissel, C.SS.R., who gave the mission; cited in Skeabeck, "William H. Gross," 67.

[32] *Metropolitan Record,* quoted in the *Catholic Mirror,* May 30, 1868.

has made progress among the Southern negroes, since the war, and although the other sects spend a great deal more money in efforts to secure the colored people to their side, the Catholics keep ahead everywhere.[33]

There is no question that Verot felt himself to be in a contest with Protestants, particularly those from the North, who wished to wrestle for the freedman's soul. But it is equally obvious from his many words on the subject, that he cared less for the doctrinal battle than he did for the objective good of the persons concerned. The Catholic Church, he told the Negroes, "has no regard of persons, views in men not their origin, or their color, or their race, but only their virtues or their vices."[34] On this lone principle, irrespective of sectarian strife, Verot was ready to secure for the Negroes every advantage it was in his limited means to provide, including that of a good education.

Education of the Negro in Georgia following the close of the Civil War was not a program to which Georgians themselves were particularly attracted. Only a small minority believed that the freedmen should be equipped with knowledge befitting their new stature. The great majority thought education a waste of time for hewers of wood and drawers of water, and feared the loss of farm labor. As a result, Negro education was yielded into the hands of the Freedmen's Bureau (Federal Bureau of Refugees, Freedmen, and Abandoned Lands) and northern philanthropy, especially the American Missionary Society and the Freedmen's Union Commission, under whose combined auspices Negro schools were opened in all the principal cities in the fall of 1865. Until 1867, when Bishop Verot established Savannah's first school for Negroes under purely southern white sponsorship, northern government and church-related groups held almost exclusive control over the educational movement; during the year ending July, 1867, these groups had sixty teachers in the field and had expended altogether some $100,000.[35]

---

[33] *Ibid.*

[34] Address of Verot to the colored members of St. Augustine Parish upon the reorganization of the Society of St. Benedict the Moor for Negroes; *Examiner*, August 15, 1868.

[35] See Clara Mildred Thompson, *Reconstruction in Georgia, Economic, Social, Political, 1865–1872* (New York: Columbia University, 1915), 125, 340–341.

It should not be overlooked, however, that some Georgians had entered the field of Negro education prior to 1867, despite the general animus that existed against the work.[36] A white woman had opened a school at Dawson in 1861, and kept it going until 1868, with the support of the citizens of the town. During 1865 and 1866 ex-Confederate soldiers opened Negro schools in seven localities and managed to keep them alive for several years, until strong white opposition, breaking out as the 1868 presidential campaign approached, forced their abandonment. During that campaign there was violence at Marietta, Jonesboro, Columbus, Newton, and in many rural areas: Negro schools were burned, their supporters threatened, and "Yankee" teachers condemned in the round. White mobs seem to have treated southern teachers with more leniency than the northern, imported variety, who had come into the state out of religious and humanitarian interest, abolitionist experience, desire for money, reasons of health, or simple love of adventure. Georgians objected not so much to education of the Negro as to education of the Negro by the "Yankee teacher."[37] When Verot laid plans for a Negro school in Savannah, he did not have to worry about Yankee origins, although there was still some opposition to overcome. As for the Negroes themselves, they at first welcomed the schools established for them, attended the classes faithfully, and prized the white man's fetish that would win them wealth, power, and equality. By the early 1870's, however, their interest flagged, and many dropped out.[38]

Education of Florida's colored population began during the latter years of the Civil War when desultory instruction was given the 1044 Florida Negroes who served in the Union Army. In March, 1864, the Freedmen's Aid Society, a private association, established common schools for Negro children in St. Augustine, Fernandina, and Jacksonville. In 1865, additional schools were founded and supported, directly or indirectly, by the Freedmen's Bureau, the African Colonization Society, the American Freedmen's Union

---

[36] For an account of Georgian and southern initiative in this field, see Swint, *Northern Teacher*, 133–136; Coulter, *South During Reconstruction*, 84. There is no mention of any free southern desire to teach the freedmen at this period in Dorothy Orr, *A History of Education in Georgia* (Chapel Hill: University of North Carolina, 1950).

[37] Swint, *Northern Teacher*, 136.

[38] Donald, *Negro Freedman*, 100–101.

Commission (New York branch), the African Methodist Episcopal Church, and the African Civilization Society. By the close of 1865 there were ten schools in Florida enrolling 1918 Negro pupils, including two schools in St. Augustine with 250 students and four teachers.[39] In 1866, under the Presidential Plan of Reconstruction, Florida Governor David Selby Walker established a state system of common schools to be financed by tuition and by a tax of one dollar on each colored person between 21 and 51 years of age.[40] In 1867 many Florida planters expressed a desire to found schools for their free Negro laborers.[41] In all, the process of educating the freedmen got underway more smoothly in Florida than it did in Georgia. There were no Catholic schools for the colored either before or during the war, although some colored children may have been taught rudimentary subjects by the Sisters of Mercy, who had founded a school for white children at St. Augustine in 1859.[42]

Prior to 1865, the Catholic Church could point to no progress whatever in the education of the colored. Bishop England had opened a school for free Negroes at Charleston in 1835, but had been forced to abandon it under local pressure; Bishop Peter Richard Kenrick had to abandon, under similar pressure, a school for slave and free children started at St. Louis in 1844; Bishop William Henry Elder, of Natchez, experienced the same frustration in Mississippi. When Bishop Herbert Vaughn, of Salford, England, visited the southern states in 1871, he heard that "before the War it was unlawful not only to teach slaves, but even for coloured freemen to receive any education. During the slavery

---

[39] See Raphael O'Hara Lanier, "The History of Negro Education in Florida" (unpublished master's thesis, Stanford University, 1928, on microfilm at P. K. Yonge Library of Florida History, University of Florida), 12–25. Cf. Davis, *War and Reconstruction in Florida*, 385–390.

[40] For an account of these schools, see Nita K. Pyburn, *The History of the Development of a Single System of Education in Florida, 1822–1903* (Tallahassee, Fla.: Florida State University, 1954), 82.

[41] Swint, *Northern Teacher*, 127.

[42] See Sister M. Eulalia Herron, *The Sisters of Mercy in the United States, 1843–1928* (New York: Macmillan, 1929), 236: "Schools were opened immediately [in 1859] and special attention given to the colored children in whom Bishop Verot was particularly interested." The sisters were forced to close their school — there was only one, called St. Mary's Academy — in May, 1862 owing to the war. It reopened at Bishop Verot's request in September, 1866; see *Examiner*, October 27, 1866.

days the priest had no chance."[43] The Cincinnati *Catholic Telegraph*, which had supported emancipation and the Union, chided Bishop Verot with these facts when it learned, in June 1865, that the bishop was in Europe seeking money and teachers for Negro schools:

> The Right Rev. Bishop Verot, of Savannah, is in Europe, and we have seen in one of the papers his strong appeal for help to enable him to open schools for the negro population, represented by him to be in a very sad and demoralized condition. The bishop must feel a holy joy in the success of the North over the rebels, as he can educate the negroes now, which before the war, he dared not even attempt to do, except at the risk of his life.[44]

Verot left New York for Europe on June 10, 1865, aboard the *City of Baltimore*. After short stays in Paris, Rome (where "I had the great happiness of a private interview with Pius IX on Tuesday, July 11"), Marseilles, Lyons, and St. Pal de Mons, he went to his home village of Le Puy on July 5 to seek sisters from the Comgrégation de St. Joseph (Sisters of St. Joseph) whose motherhouse was situated there.[45] Verot represented to the superior general, Mother Léocadie Broc, the desperate situation of the Negro youth in Florida and Georgia, and asked that a group of sisters be sent to their aid. The superior, impressed, suggested that he ask for volunteers, and conducted the bishop to the novitiate for that purpose. Verot spoke to the assembled sisters and asked for eight of their number to come to St. Augustine and Savannah. Sixty volunteered. Pierre le Breton, Bishop of Le Puy, was absent at the time; upon his return, the superior received authorization to select the eight sisters from the number volunteering, and made plans to send them on as soon as convenient.[46] Before embarking at Brest for New York, Verot wrote to the superior: "I would not want to leave France without reminding you of the promises you made me at Puy. . . ." As a visible sign of his intent to hold the sisters to that promise, he sent along an English grammar and

---

43 John George Snead-Cox, *The Life of Cardinal Vaughn* (London: Herbert and Daniel, 1910), I, 171.

44 *Catholic Telegraph*, June 26, 1865.

45 "Episcopal Acts," 166.

46 The author is indebted for these details to Monsignor J. Faurie, vicar-general of the Diocese of Le Puy, who kindly transcribed the notes of this visit in ADP, and forwarded also transcripts of the correspondence that passed between Verot and Puy during the period 1865–1870. Translations are by the author.

dictionary.[47] In Georgia again, Verot wrote to Le Puy, expressing his pleasure at learning that the sisters were hard at work on the study of English, and underlining the challenge that faced them: "The Negroes who have gained freedom are found everywhere, and one sees them in every city in great numbers."[48] On February 21, 1866, he advised the sisters who were to come that they should depart not sooner than April, since "during wintertime the sea is very rough (even dangerous)." He had decided to have the sisters come to St. Augustine, "where I have a rather nice house in which they can stay and develop sufficient proficiency in English to give classes in the fall."[49]

> I want you to understand fully and clearly that it is for the Negroes and for them almost exclusively that I have arranged for the daughters of your Order to come into my diocese. I have five or six hundred thousand Negroes without any education or religion . . . for whom I wish to do something. Protestants from the North come here to set up schools for these unfortunate creatures. Why cannot we do the same with your sisters? . . . You should take second class aboard a French vessel (out of Brest); the price is 400 francs. You should try to get a discount. As for clothing, books and papers, take as much as you can: these things cost a lot over here, five times more than in France. You should write M. Cochin, rue St. Guillaume 25, Paris, who is president of an association for the aid of Negroes, so that he can assist the Sisters when they pass through Paris.[50]

On their arrival in St. Augustine,[51] the sisters were discovered to be still weak in English, as Verot wrote disapprovingly to Le Puy: "I had thought that they would know a little English; they must

---

[47] ADP, Verot to La Mère Léocadie Broc, Brest, August 25, 1865.

[48] *Ibid.*, Atlanta, November 18, 1865.   [49] *Ibid.*, Savannah, February 21, 1866.

[50] *Ibid.* On December 13, 1866, Verot wrote again: "Your Sisters will always have the distinctive mark of having been called to America for the express purpose of working with the Negroes." *Ibid.*, Savannah, December 13, 1866. Pierre-Suzanna-Augustin Cochin was author of the celebrated French antislavery tract, *L'Abolition de L'Esclavage* (Paris: Jacques Lecoffre, 1861), translated by Mary L. Booth and published in this country by Walker, Wise, and Company, Boston, 1863, 1864. During the 1860's he was a prominent member of Montalembert's Liberal Catholic movement and a close friend of Verot's Issy classmate, Lacordaire. Verot visited with Cochin at Paris in August, 1865; see ADC, Box 1865, Verot to Lynch, Paris, August 10, 1865.

[51] The sisters, eight in number (Marie Sidonie Rascle, superior, Marie Julie Roussel, Joséphine Déléage, Saint Pierre Borie, Clémence Freycenon, Marie-Joseph

learn. . . ."[52] After his return from the plenary council in Baltimore, which took place in October of that year, Verot took the
nuns under his personal instruction "so that they can get to work
as soon as possible."[53] The lessons must have proceeded at an
accelerated pace, for on February 9, 1867, less than two months
later, the local *Examiner* noted that "a school has been opened
for the colored children of the place under the superintendence
of the Sisters of St. Joseph." The paper judged that "it is right
to begin at the children, and the two races now necessarily in
presence of each other can but be benefitted by proper instruction
and education." As a free school, it "leaves no pretext to them
[Negroes] to remain in ignorance. . . ."[54] Six months later the
Examiner noticed "a good number of colored boys and colored
girls who had been prepared by the 'Sisters of St. Joseph,' and
showed by their way of acting that they had not frequented their
schools in vain."[55] The New York *Metropolitan Record* reviewed
the sisters' progress as of May, 1868, and made a small complaint:

> The Sisters of St. Joseph . . . are teaching the colored children,
> and have about sixty pupils. For this they receive no compensation
> whatever, except a little present occasionally, while some Northern
> ladies, engaged in the same calling, are liberally paid out of funds
> collected in the North. It is probably because the religion of the
> Sisters . . . and that of the managers of the Freedmen's Aid Societies
> are widely different that the Sisters are overlooked in the distribu-
> tion of the funds.[56]

More teachers arrived from Puy in 1867 and 1868, permitting
Verot to establish Negro schools in Savannah (1867), Jacksonville
(1868), and Fernandina (1870). Before his death in 1876 he would
have sisters and Negro schools in Palatka, Mandarin, and Key
West. The group that went to Savannah in April, 1867, numbered

Cortial, Marie Célenie Joubert, and Julie Clotilde Arsac), embarked on August
4, 1866, and arrived at St. Augustine toward the end of the same month. They
stayed several weeks at the convent of the Sisters of Mercy, then moved to their
own residence on Hospital Street. Toward the end of the year Father Peter Dufau
moved them again, to the former residence of the Christian Brothers on South
Charlotte Street, where they remained for the remainder of Verot's episcopate. See
"Notes" of Mother Marie Sidonie, in ASSJ.

[52] ADP, Verot to La Mère Léocadie Broc, Savannah, September 3, 1866.
[53] *Ibid.*, Savannah, December 13, 1866.
[54] *Examiner*, February 9, 1867.
[55] August 16, 1867, and August 24, 1867.
[56] *Metropolitan Record*, quoted in *Catholic Mirror*, May 30, 1868, and in
New Orleans *Morning Star*, May 31, 1868.

three sisters and two American novices. Verot announced their arrival to the congregation of the Cathedral of St. John the Baptist, and was greeted by a murmur of disapproval. Some Catholics joined other citizens of the city in protesting the presence and the purpose of the "Nigger Sisters." Despite the unpleasant welcome, the teachers began classes in a frame building within the cathedral grounds and received "about fifty Negro children, barefoot and covered with rags."[57] By August, Verot was gratified at the good already achieved in Savannah by their presence, "a good so solid that I am much reassured about prospects in that city."[58] Two years later the Savannah *Republican* discussed the outcome to date and noted the nonpolitical character of their work:

> The Sisters of St. Joseph are now teaching one hundred colored children, and are only prevented from teaching many more for the want of sufficient school house accommodations. They are quietly and unostentatiously accomplishing an immense amount of good amongst the colored people of this city. . . . They are not political emissaries sent here by some foreign influence to poison the minds of the colored people [educating] them to believe that the white [Southern] people are their natural enemies. . . .[59]

In 1870, John W. Alvord, General Superintendent of Education under the Freedmen's Bureau, reported to Bureau Commissioner General O. O. Howard that "the Catholics [in Savannah] have a school of sixty pupils, managed by the bishop and taught by the St. Joseph Sisters, an order in France trained especially for African missions. . . ."

> After looking in upon [this school], with very polite reception by the teacher, I called upon the acting bishop.[60] The call was a pleasant one. He complained, however, that your officers had refused to their church the aid given under the law to other parties. I promised, on his invitation, to examine the school more thoroughly, and if found to be teaching the elements of an English education would report in favor of its receiving such assistance.[61]

---

[57] ASSJ, "Early Days of the Sisters of St. Joseph in Florida," unpublished manuscript, 44.

[58] ADP, Verot to La Mère Léocadie Broc, St. Augustine, August 11, 1867.

[59] September 10, 1869.

[60] This was Father William Hamilton, left in charge as Administrator of Georgia and Florida during Bishop Verot's absence at the Vatican Council in Rome.

[61] Savannah *Morning News*, February 16, 1870; J. W. Alvord, *Letters from the*

The superintendent then related this curious incident:

> But knocking for admission next morning, the teacher held the door partly open and positively forbade my entrance — said *"the father* (after my call) had ordered her to do so." I was of course surprised, but parleyed pleasantly; told her that *"the father" had invited me to "visit the school whenever I wished!"* but in vain. She "presumed that the permission had been reconsidered." . . . I could only express my regrets, and on leaving sent my official card to "Father Hamilton," with the message that I was very sorry not to be able to see the school; that our Government made no distinction in religious denominations, and that if the school could *be reported on our blanks,* it would have most cheerfully granted the usual bureau aid. . . . This bishop should not complain of you hereafter.[62]

Upon Verot's return in October, 1870, from the Vatican Council, he was no longer Bishop of Savannah, but ordinary of the new see established at St. Augustine during his presence in Rome.[63] Henceforth his efforts for the Negroes would be concentrated in Florida. In taking possession of his new see, which was actually an old responsibility dating from 1858, he could also take satisfaction in the colored school system that he had started there. Other bishops in the South had not been so successful. Despite the injunction

---

South Relating to the Conditions of Freedmen (Washington, D. C.: Howard University, 1870), 13.

[62] *Ibid.* The author was not able to discover any Savannah Catholic reaction to this published letter; nor did he find any evidence that the school in question ever applied afterward for Bureau aid.

[63] To the superior at Le Puy, Verot wrote: "The Sisters in Savannah will always be at least virtually under my jurisdiction. For the bishop I have had named for Savannah [Ignatius Persico] is a good man who will always be in agreement with me, and will always do whatever I ask him." ADP, Verot to Madame la Supérieure, Rome, May 2, 1870. Bishop William H. Gross, who acceded to the See of Savannah on April 27, 1873, was less tractable, apparently, and less enamored of the sisters and their work; as appears from a letter draft in Latin in ADSA, Verot to Secretary of the Congregation of Propaganda (n.d.): "When the Diocese of St. Augustine was separated from the diocese of Savannah in 1870, there were Sisters of the Congregation of St. Joseph in both Savannah and St. Augustine whom I had brought over from France with the at least virtually expressed condition that they would retain their ties to the Superior General of the order in Puy. Bishop Gross does not understand this, and desires to have absolute jurisdiction over them. The Superior of the community in Savannah received an order last month from Bishop Gross to leave Savannah within 24 hours."

of the plenary council of 1866 to establish religious communities for the education of Negroes, the other prelates either failed to exercise the expected ambition in this regard, or else met resistance of such nature that their plans were not implemented as soon as Verot's. Some already existing religious orders who might have accomplished much good in the cause of Negro education shied away from the task for fear of alienating white patronage.[64] Archbishop Odin of New Orleans, though he tried mightily to follow the council's directive and his own wishes, was not able to open a Negro school until 1868 when the Religious of the Sacred Heart opened St. Joseph's School in St. Michael, Louisiana.[65] As late as 1889 resistance was so strong in Cloutierville, Louisiana, that in spite of the pleas of the sisters and of Bishop Antoine Durier of Natchitoches, the Negroes were forced out of a school established expressly for them and mulattoes.[66] Similar instances could be cited in almost every diocese of the South.[67] The only success story in these years was written in Florida and Georgia. Extant figures from 1879, three years after Verot's death, show the extent to which he succeeded in Florida alone: six schools were in operation: at St. Augustine, with 100 pupils; Jacksonville, 40 pupils; Fernandina, 83 pupils; Palatka, 14 pupils; Mandarin, 11 pupils; and Key West, for which no figures were given.[68] The number under instruction was small by comparison with the school systems sanctioned by the Freedmen's Bureau, the state, and private agencies endowed from the North. But given the small resources at his command and the shortness of accomplishment elsewhere in the Catholic South, Verot's Negro schools are deserving of history's notice.

When word reached Verot in November, 1868, that the Holy See had given solemn confirmation to the decrees of the Second

---

[64] See Ellis, *American Catholicism* (Chicago: University of Chicago Press, 1956), 99–100.

[65] Roger Baudier, *The Catholic Church in Louisiana* (New Orleans: A. W. Hyatt, 1939), 433.

[66] Ellis, *American Catholicism*, 100.

[67] *Ibid*. The plenary council's directive to found Negro orphanages fared no better. None was established in the South before the late 1870's.

[68] ADSA, MS table of school enrollment in the diocese dated December 4, 1879, at St. Augustine. None of these schools was integrated, and there is no record that Verot ever made an attempt to mix white and colored pupils.

Plenary Council, he took the occasion to reiterate his concern for the mass of colored people under his jurisdiction.

Alas! we should shed bitter tears when we reflect that we have in our Diocese a population of more than half a million souls of African origin who are . . . without the civilizing and soothing influence of Christianity. Wicked men and unprincipled demagogues, abusing their simplicity, their ignorance and credulity, have promised them rich spoils, coming either from the Government or from the estates of their former masters, and have thus made them dupes of their own malice and crafty rapacity. Immense gatherings of colored men, women and children coming for the distribution of the promised gifts have often been seen in our midst. What have these deluded creatures found in these meetings? Nothing but additional want and poverty, with new temptations to violence and theft, which can but bring misfortune and punishments on them. Oh! would that we could see such gatherings [for the Redemptorist missions later that winter], where they will learn industry, love of labor, obedience to God, submission to the laws of morality and religion! . . . They will have peace at home and peace with everybody, when the rights of everybody will be protected and respected. . . . In a country like ours, where there is such a vast extent of virgin soil imploring cultivation and with such a beautiful climate, free alike from the intolerable heat of summer and the killing blast of winter, and recalling to our imagination the Elysian fields of the Pagans, there is no room for want, distress, poverty, and suffering wherever there is industry, honesty, love of labor, and conscientious fidelity to duty.[69]

Such were the thoughts in Verot's mind when he addressed the other southern bishops at the Tenth Provincial Council of Baltimore, held in April, 1869. There Verot plainly took the lead among

---

[69] ADSA, Pastoral Letter, Savannah, November 11, 1868. Cf. Thomas Gamble, Jr., "A History of the City Government of Savannah, Ga., from 1790 to 1901, compiled from Official Records," *Mayor's Annual Report* (Savannah, 1900), 160: "After the war the newly freed slaves were in many instances in a deplorable condition, without means of a livelihood. . . . To render conditions in the city worse, hundreds of Negroes flocked in from the country, expecting to be supported by the general government, and were speedily reduced to a destitute state." Donald reports the same migrations to the towns in Alabama: the Negroes, once they started receiving rations from the Freedmen's Bureau, "thought that the government would support them and that they would not have to work. Conditions became very bad around the towns. . . . They were encouraged in this idleness by the agents who told them not to work because it was the duty of

his colleagues in proposing measures for the aid of the Negroes. With the seconding of Bishop Richard Whelan, of Wheeling, Verot proposed that the council require each bishop in the province to set to work at once on building schools, churches, and other facilities for the colored populations.[70] The motion was unanimously adopted,[71] and a decree was subsequently published.[72] Despite the decree, however, the Catholic response to emancipation continued to founder. Bishops had pleaded, both in conclave and singly, but everywhere, except in Georgia, Florida, and the Diocese of Charleston, precious few results answered the pleading.[73] Verot was the only bishop with a reputable school system, and perhaps part of the reason came from France with the teachers: he alone had teachers with no predispositions, South or North. Separate churches for the colored had not been proved effective in the pilot experiment at Charleston, and though the Negroes came willingly to missions and sermons, they left willingly, too, untouched, it appeared, by any firm commitment to Catholic Christianity.

What had gone wrong? Was it organization? A longtime student of the Reconstruction era appears to think so: the Catholics "for a time pondered seriously a special campaign to secure the freedmen. They had little success because in fact they made little effort. . . ."[74] The strongest reasons went deeper, however, and are suggested by the same historian's statement that "the Negro wanted more immediate access to God and a more friendly and emotional communion with Him than a Catholic priest could

their former masters to support them, and that they were due wages at least since January 1, 1863. They were also told to go to the towns and stay there until the matter was settled." *Negro Freedman,* 175.

[70] AAB, 39-A-N-1, 35–36.

[71] *Ibid.*

[72] AAB, 39-A-Q-1, 28: "Concilii Baltimorensis II Decretis inhaerentes, enixe in Domino omnes huius Provinciae Praesules hortamur, ut Negrorum intra eorum jurisdictionem degentium soluti omni modo provideant; nempe Missionibus pro iisdem constitutis, ecclesiis et scholis eorum usui, ubi haberi possint, specialiter destinatis, collectis etiam pro eorum spirituali bono in ditiotibus praesertim Provinciae Diocesibus erogatis."

[73] Examination of the correspondence and notes of Bishop Lynch in the ADC shows him to have had a consistent interest in the welfare of the Negro, and certain well-planned successes beyond the average performance of the southern bishops.

[74] Coulter, *South During Reconstruction,* 338.

offer."[75] Bishops Verot and Lynch had misjudged the Negro's liking for pomp and ceremonial; it was not nearly so strong as his liking for informal demonstrations of religious emotion. Bishop Elder complained that "their feelings have too much power and their reason too little";[76] and Jefferson Davis told visiting Bishop Vaughn in 1872 that while no one but the Catholic Church could supply the guidance and support the Negroes needed, the "field is not promising. . . . The Methodists and Baptists do much mischief among them; their religion is purely emotional."[77] In the *Catholic Directory* for 1877 Bishop Verot noted that "Northern fanatics, well salaried by their societies, have put up in many places meeting houses for them, where these simple, misguided people are drawn together by political excitement, inflamed harangues in the name of liberty, singing, shouting, clapping of hands, dancing, confused vociferations, and other indecorous exhibitions, which they fancifully call religious worship."[78] It is hard to tell if Verot wrote more in bitterness or in sorrow.

Of the northern denominations which came South to secure the Negro's allegiance, the northern Methodists made the most progress. The southern Methodists, too, gained adherents. But the Negro ambition was to have churches of their own, run by themselves, and for no extraneous political or social purposes. Thus the greatest number of them gravitated to the independent Negro churches, already existing in the North: the African Methodist Episcopal Church and the African Methodist Episcopal Zion Church, both of which sent emissaries south to reap the harvest.[79] Added

---

[75] *Ibid.* Cf. Donald, *Negro Freedman,* 125: "The Negroes liked to go directly to God himself and were quite unwilling to submit to priests claiming to stand between them and God. For this reason, the Catholic hierarchy had no success with them."

[76] Quoted in McMurray, "Church During Reconstruction," 222.

[77] Snead-Cox, *Cardinal Vaughn,* I, 174.

[78] "Diocese of St. Augustine," *Sadlier's Catholic Directory . . . for 1877.* Cf. the following: "I have sat many a night in the window of our house on the big plantation and listened to shouting, jumping, stamping, dancing, in a cabin over a mile distant; in the gray dawn, Negroes would come creeping back, exhausted, and unfit for duty." Myrta Lockett Avary, *Dixie after the War* (New York, 1906), quoted in Donald, *Negro Freedman,* 119. These emotional extravaganzas are treated extensively by Donald, 110–133, who finds in them some faint traces of a Catholicism once learned: " 'Lord, if you is busy tonight, and can't come down yourself,' one woman prayed, 'please send Mudder Mary wid her broom to sweep de chaff from our hearts' " (125).

[79] Coulter, *South During Reconstruction,* 338–339.

to the fact that the Catholic Church was not Negro-run, it also lost appeal from the fact that it had no place for the Negro preacher of no or little education. To train a Negro in reading and writing would take years; to train him in the difficult studies of Latin, philosophy, and theology would take an impossible length of time. Most bishops felt, too, that the character of the Negro was yet too unstable to accept the responsibility and the discipline, particularly the celibacy, of the priesthood.

Still another reason that may be adduced for the Church's failure to make significant headway among the freedmen was the strong opposition to the Catholic effort that came from Protestant quarters, both North and South. The American Missionary Association, supported in some places by funds from the Freedmen's Bureau, warned that Catholicism "was making extraordinary efforts to enshroud forever this class of the unfortunate race in Popish superstition and darkness."[80] In Virginia, Protestant missionaries condemned the efforts of the Church to proselytize the Negroes, and admonished the latter to having nothing to do with Roman Catholicism.[81] An extreme example was the charge, made in northern Presbyterian papers, that the Catholic Church was employing such means as the circulation of a letter allegedly written by Jesus Christ.[82]

Verot's official newspaper during these years, the *Banner of the South,* had to contend with similar criticism from Georgia Protestants. A weekly literary newspaper, the *Banner* began publication at Augusta on March 21, 1868, and continued until October 29, 1870, when it was purchased by an agricultural publishing house. Publishers were Leopold T. Blome and Patrick Walsh. The paper was printed in eight pages on the press of the Augusta *Chronicle and Sentinel* and enjoyed a circulation of about 6000. The editor

[80] Walter Lynwood Fleming, *Civil War and Reconstruction in Alabama* (New York: Macmillan, 1905), 646.

[81] See A. A. Taylor, "The Negro in the Reconstruction of Virginia," *Journal of Negro History,* XI (July, 1926), 429.

[82] See Oliver S. Heckman, "The Presbyterian Church in the United States of America in Southern Reconstruction, 1860–1880," *North Carolina Historical Review,* XX (July, 1943), 233. Verot could read in the Augusta *Daily Constitutionalist* that "the clergy of the North are not a power to be despised (August 25, 1865)," and "now that they have finished the slaveholders, they will take on the Catholics (March 10, 1866)."

was Father Abram J. Ryan, whose poem "The Conquered Banner," written in April, 1865, caused him to be known widely as the "Priest-Poet of the Confederacy." Bishop Verot gave permission for the paper to begin, as Ryan stated editorially in the issue of June 27, 1868, and conferred on it the title "official organ of the Bishop of Savannah."[83] Typical of the charges the *Banner* had to answer during these years was one from the *Methodist Advocate* of Atlanta, "not, so far as we can judge," the *Banner* said, "the organ of any Christian denomination, but of a political sect known as the Methodist Episcopal Church North." The Atlanta paper concentrated its fire on Verot's plan to open a Negro school in that city:

> Catholic education is to the mind what the Chinese shoe is to the foot — dwarfing and crippling, rather than developing and strengthening. . . . And this Church now proposes to educate the colored people! professes undying love to the rebellion and great interest in the education of the colored people at the same time! How wise, how sharp to be caught by either plea? Then, this school is for *colored* children! Every one acquainted with the facts knows that the Roman Catholics, as a people, are inveterate and bitter haters of the colored race. In the anti-draft riots in New York they hung colored men to lamp-posts in the city, burned an asylum for colored orphan children, and brutally murdered colored people in the streets, simply because they were colored, and because the war was likely to free them. Unless Rome had selfish interests in the case, it would not teach a colored man letters for a thousand years to come.[84]

Protestant opposition, the natural tendency of the Negro toward Negro-run evangelical groups, and lack of funds seem to be the special obstacles experienced by Bishop Verot. Of these, the lack of funds engaged his attention the most. On begging tours in the

[83] See microfilm holdings at the University of Georgia. See also Eugene P. Willging and Herta Hatzfeld, "Catholic Serials of the Nineteenth Century in Georgia," Part X, *RACH*, LXX (September, December, 1959), 113–114. Hereafter cited as *Banner*.

[84] Quoted in *Banner*, April 17, 1869. In 1868 Richard S. Rust, secretary of the Freedmen's Aid Society of the Methodist Episcopal Church, warned of the "peril from Romanists" who were "working to proselyte the freedmen." The evangelical churches, he said, should provide Negro schools as soon as possible, lest the freedmen attend schools of the Romanists, "whose instructions [would] disqualify them from becoming loyal citizens or intelligent Christians." Quoted in Swint, *Northern Teacher*, 164.

North, and in correspondence directly after the Civil War,[85] Verot
emphasized that he could not bring Catholic civilization to the
Negro unless he had sufficient financial resources. The extent of
his penury as late as 1872 can be imagined from his talk to
students of St. Mary's Seminary in Baltimore: "The Diocese of
St. Augustine . . . is very poor, the poorest indeed of all the
devastated regions of the South; money cannot be found there
even to keep in repair the few churches that exist, much less for
the new churches that ought to be built for the accommodation
not only of the Catholic whites, but also of the colored people. . . ."[86] In 1876, shortly before he died, the bishop noted sadly
that outside the few cities where he had schools, "the Church
has not made any gain among the colored population."[87] "The
limited number of the clergy and their yet more limited resources
are the causes of this momentary sterility."[88] Had he lived longer,
Verot would have discovered that the sterility he described was
somewhat more than momentary. By 1879 his sisters, brought
from France "for the express purpose of working with the Negroes,"
were teaching many more white than Negro pupils, 407 to 248.[89]
The years following did nothing to stem this reversal of purpose,
as the sisters turned more and more to the instruction of the
whites. The civil atmosphere was not such as to persuade them
otherwise. In 1916 one of their number, Sister Mary Thomasine,
would be arrested and jailed for violating a 1913 state law forbidding white teachers to "teach negroes in a negro school."[90]
Although subsequently acquitted on the grounds that the law did
not apply to private schools, the nun would hear an opinion that
showed only too clearly what sentiments were back in power:
"To say that such teaching would have a tendency to promote
social equality among the races . . . is to insult the superior

---

[85] See, e.g., AAB, Verot to Spalding: 36-S-4, March 15, 1865; 39-B-G-23,
October 13, 1865; 39-B-B-24, February 27, 1866.

[86] *Catholic Mirror,* May 25, 1872.

[87] *Sadlier's Catholic Directory . . . for 1877,* 56.

[88] *Ibid.*

[89] ADSA, manuscript table of white and colored school enrollment in the
diocese, dated December 4, 1879, at St. Augustine.

[90] See *Compiled General Laws of Florida,* 1927, Section 8112, Chapter 6490,
Acts, 1913.

race."[91] The pastoral effort was no more effective or lasting than the educational; in this domain Verot saw the Negroes slipping away almost from the start. In 1873 a visiting correspondent of the Brooklyn *Catholic Review* observed that among the Negroes of Florida the Church's progress was neither rapid nor significant, and that the colored Catholics were gifted with an "uncertain perseverance":

> That which has been accomplished has been almost wholly done by the local and humble forces of the resident Catholics themselves. . . .
> [The Negroes] are influenced by numbers and by the tie of race. Thus where Catholics predominate, particularly among themselves, they will readily attend the Catholic Church; but where Catholics are in the minority their conversion is difficult and their perseverance uncertain. The shouting and singing "gatherings" of their own race . . . have a great attraction for them, and have drawn away not a few weak-minded Catholics.[92]

In St. Augustine "where the blacks are almost wholly Catholic," the correspondent reported, the Negroes were markedly more faithful than they were elsewhere in Florida. "Despite the 'attractions' of a Methodist and Baptist gathering, the latter lately organized there [St. Augustine] by some Georgia negroes, the colored residents have remained, with rare exceptions, wholly attached to the faith." However, did the same correspondent return to St. Augustine at the turn of the century, he found that the exceptions had become less rare. One of Bishop Verot's acquaintances, Father Jeremiah J. O'Connell of Columbia, South Carolina, described what happened to the bishop's Negroes:

> They are naturally a sensual race of people and their former condition of servitude aggravated the fatal propensity. Piety and the obligations of the married state they cannot realize, with rare exceptions . . . and [they] frequently fall away. If Catholicity

---

[91] Opinion of Circuit Court Judge George Cooper Gibbs, May 20, 1916. See court file in the suit, "Ex Parte Sister Mary Thomasine," Docket No. 3, p. 44, Law no. 778, Circuit Court, St. John's County, St. Augustine, Florida.

[92] Brooklyn *Catholic Review*, April 10, 1873. How "uncertain" was known in 1923, when it was estimated that in Florida "there were more Catholics of the colored race before the Civil War than there are now." See Benedict Roth, ed., *Churches of the Diocese,* Part 2, 25. The results nationally may be measured by the fact that in 1956 there were only 483,671 colored Catholics in the United States out of a Negro population of 16,000,000. See Ellis, *American Catholicism,* 101 and n.

were a system of singing, sensational preaching, and vociferous prayer, and limited to external observances, they would join the Church in thousands. Since their emancipation they are opposed to mingling with white people. . . . Though nominally attached to some sect, they know no religion, and have none, and are in some localities lapsing into fetishism. Their natural assemblies are boisterous demonstrations or clandestine political gatherings. They were demoralized by political adventures and tricksters who made use of their votes for plundering the impoverished country. Thus deluded, their condition is in many instances worse than at any former period of their existence. They are indolent and improvident. If they can procure food, they will make no further effort to improve their condition. . . . They merit our deepest commiseration. Their sins and ignorance are a misfortune rather than a cause of condemnation, and the deep-rooted evils of the system from which they have emerged.[93]

In the long run Bishop Verot failed. His failures, however, should not obscure the fact that he took the part of the Negro with a vigor and eloquence unmatched in the southern Church. If, as has been written,[94] Catholic purposes failed because few bishops devoted much effort to the colored, Bishop Verot unquestionably deserves exception. It would be difficult to find a southerner of any persuasion, religious or political, who interested himself as deeply in the moral, intellectual, and material welfare of the freedmen — in the necessity, as Verot said, of "enlightening, civilizing, and ennobling a race that has suddenly emerged from bondage to the enjoyment of civil rights and the blessings of liberty."[95] Bishop Verot had set the pace for the first great social enterprise to engage American Catholicism. The last analysis would tabulate more failures than successes. But readers of his 1861 sermon would know that it was the latter half of it that counted.

93 O'Connell, *Carolinas and Georgia,* 421–423.
94 Coulter, *South During Reconstruction,* 338.
95 Pastoral Letter, August 1, 1866.

CHAPTER VI

RECONSTRUCTING THE CHURCH

THE RECONSTRUCTION ERA in American history does not fall among the more cherished recollections of the southern people. Where "reconstruction" was carried out with particular zeal by the federally assigned military governments, the defeated populace inclined to view the program more as a wrecking than as a building operation. Southerners became convinced that any real reconstruction of their economic and civic life would have to be done by themselves, on their own initiative. Many stories of fortitude and self-sacrifice resulted.

In Georgia and Florida the Reconstruction years deserve to be remembered by Catholics as a time when their Church rebounded with amazing strength from one of the greatest setbacks that ever befell her in this land. Within the short space of years from 1865 to 1870 Bishop Verot lifted the Church out of the catastrophe that had wrecked his churches and demoralized his subjects, to a position of health and strength superior to that which existed before the war. Georgia, which had ten churches and chapels, seven schools, and about 8000 Catholics in 1861, by the end of the decade had nine churches (six standing buildings), thirty chapels and stations, eleven schools, and a Catholic population of about 20,000.[1] Florida, which was erected into a separate diocese in 1870, showed even more remarkable progress. Prewar figures showed the state with six churches and chapels, four schools, only three priests, and a Catholic population numbering perhaps 3000.[2] By the end of the decade the new Diocese of St. Augustine had nine-

---

[1] *Metropolitan Catholic Almanac . . . 1861,* 74–75; *Sadlier's Catholic Directory . . . for 1871* (New York: D. and J. Sadlier Co., 1871), 275–278.

[2] *Metropolitan Catholic Almanac . . . 1860,* 85–86; St. Augustine *Examiner,* August 18, 1860.

teen churches and chapels, seven schools, twelve priests, and about
10,000 Catholics.[3] Still further improvement showed in both Georgia
and Florida during the 1870's. Out of what Verot called the "heap
of smoking ruins"[4] he succeeded in bringing forth a Church of
renewed vigor and promise. Quite rightly, a noted European historian has recently singled out the prelate responsible for this
success as "one of the great artisans of Southern 'reconstruction.' "[5]
The outlook was certainly grim when Verot began in 1865.
Four of his churches lay in ruins. One, at St. John's Bar (Mayport)
at the mouth of the St. John's River in Florida, had been torn
apart by pillaging Union soldiers, who carried away the sacred
vessels, and ended their foray by parading about in the priests'
vestments. Another church, at St. Mary's, Georgia, had been
burned to the ground.[6] The church at Dalton, Georgia, had been
burned by Union soldiers after the war under the plea that the
church had been used as a smallpox hospital; Verot's claim for
damages to this church made to the War Department in September,
1866, was unsuccessful.[7] The incident most galling to Verot was
the sacking and burning of Immaculate Conception Church in
Jacksonville by Union troops in 1863. Both church and rectory
were destroyed. "The officers of the Government," Verot wrote
in the 1866 *Catholic Almanac*, "regretting this sad occurrence,
have given boards to put up a temporary shelter to assemble the
Catholics of the place. They are unable to rebuild the church
and the house. . . ."[8] To benefactors in France Verot complained,
probably in error, that the commander of the regiment that committed this act "was a former Methodist minister, who could not
resist the wicked satisfaction of destroying a Catholic church."[9]
True or not, Verot plainly took his own kind of satisfaction from
the incident: fourteen years later he would still be incensed over
this act of "recklessness and bigotry."[10]
More immediately serious than these material losses was the

[3] *Sadlier's Catholic Directory . . . for 1872*, 284–288.
[4] Jubilee Pastoral, October 4, 1865.
[5] Roger Aubert, *Le Pontificat de Pie IX*. Histoire de l'Eglise, Vol. 21, Fliche et
Martin, eds. (Paris: Bloud et Gay, 1952), 433.
[6] *Annales*, XXXVII (September, 1865), 404.
[7] "Episcopal Acts," 168.
[8] *Sadlier's Catholic Almanac . . . for 1866*, 94.
[9] *Annales*, XXXVII (September, 1865), 404.
[10] *Sadlier's Catholic Directory . . . for 1876*, 304.

appalling poverty of his Catholic people. Verot informed Archbishop Spalding that "the circumstances arising from this change of flag" were producing extreme hardships on his people, and that relief must be had as quickly as possible. Those families who lived in the area of Georgia devastated by Sherman's troops were particularly hard-pressed: "I have seen with my own eyes the distressing conditions of those families. The last blade of fodder and the last grain of corn have been taken away from them, and they are left to the mercy of the elements to perish from want." In Savannah the Sisters of Mercy with forty-five young girls under their care were "on the brink of starvation." Conditions at the male orphanage were no better. Provisions could be found in Savannah "but there is no money on hand to buy them with, the Confederate money having no value, & the cotton which the people had, having been taken away from them."[11] In Florida the Catholic people were so desperate that, without help, many would have to abandon their homes and flee elsewhere lest they die of hunger.[12] When Archbishop Spalding sent $1,200 in October following, and another $800 in February, 1866, Verot gratefully responded: "Your people have done indeed a noble thing in behalf of the South. May it be returned to them a thousand fold!"[13]

His chief task in the beginning, and practically his only alternative until financial assistance began arriving from the north and from the Society for the Propagation of the Faith in France, was to comfort and console. Through the medium of his only natural resources, his words, he endeavored to assuage grief and to mitigate hardship. He drew what blessings he could from the "Lost Cause." He asked former slaveholders to find "joy and congratulation" in the fact that they no longer had to render an accounting for the treatment of their slaves before the bar of divine justice. He appealed to Catholics to reflect upon the basic Christian scale of values: "The war has left you poor, distressed, and reduced to beggary. Be not dismayed: this state of things so untoward in the eyes of the world is full of hope, of consolation, and of spiritual treasures in the eyes of faith and religion. Worldly prosperity is not always a blessing. . . . It makes

---

[11] AAB, 36-G-4, Verot to Spalding, Savannah, March 15, 1865.

[12] *Annales*, XXXVII (September, 1865), 405.

[13] AAB, 39-B-G-24, Verot to Spalding, Savannah, February 27, 1866.

men live and die as if there was no reality but this earth, and
no other world beyond the grave."[14]

There were other religious consolations. Although the Church
had come out of the war poorer in material resources, she was
much richer in reputation and esteem. The people of the South
"have heard the preaching of our missionaries; they have seen
them in the hospitals and in the camps; they have witnessed
their zeal and their devoutness. A good number of *crackers* have
seen our priests and our Sisters of Charity for the first time in
their lives, in the towns and in the camps where conscription
called them, and they could not but carry away a very favorable
impression of what they saw with their own eyes."[15] Catholics
could also take pride in the fact that the southern bishops had
become known far and wide for their firm southern patriotism, and
for their willingness to support what they judged to be the legitimate aspirations of their people. Yet not the least consolation
was the Catholic's assurance of belonging primarily to a supra-
human society that could not be divided even by the deepest of
human differences. Alone among the churches, Catholicity had
not been rent asunder by the war; and almost alone among them
after the war, she continued on in perfect unity, as evidenced by
the solemn and amicable council of her bishops at Baltimore in
October of 1866. Verot told his people:

> The war which converted the country, formerly so peaceable and
> prosperous into a vast battlefield, where hundreds of thousands have
> found an untimely grave, has placed in a clearer light the divine
> origin and the divine mission of the Catholic Church. The civil
> society was convulsed in our midst, and for a moment seemed to
> be doomed to perish. Not so with the religious society in communion
> with the See of Rome. The kingdom of Christ is not of this world,
> and hence the political strife that agitated, disrupted and upheaved
> the country, did not affect the union of the members of the Catholic
> Church. The same union between the Churches which existed be-
> fore the war, existed also during, and after the war, so that when
> the political parties laid down their arms, there was no need of a
> reconciliation between the different parts of the Catholic Church in
> the country, because there had been no disruption of union.[16]

---

[14] Jubilee Pastoral, October 4, 1865.
[15] *Annales*, XXXVII (September, 1865), 403.
[16] Pastoral Letter, August 1, 1866.

Bishop Verot was constantly on the road during these years, preaching, organizing, repairing churches, and erecting new ones. Between 1865 and 1870 he made seven extended trips through Georgia and an equal number of journeys through the mission fields of Florida. His diary is checkered with short notices of rebuilding and repair: "I started for St. Augustine and . . . made a contract for the quarrying of cochina [coquina, or shell rock] and sent 40 squares to Jacksonville. . . . On the mission to visit Mandarin, Jacksonville, St. John's Bar and Fernandina, staying about a week in each place and giving Confirmation and ordering repairs and improvements rendered necessary by the war. . . . In [Macon] I found the workmen busy at restoring the old Presbyterian Church so as to convert it into a very decent Catholic church. . . . I started for Tallahassee, visiting on the way Lake City, where I took measures for repairing the house belonging to the Church and putting up a little chapel. . . . Bought back the church lot of old Fernandina, which had been lost during the war, and gave orders for a little chapel in the old Town. . . . Went to Middleburg where I saw the church fallen to the ground and could find no carpenter to put it up. . . . Went immediately to Macon, where I found much disorder and confusion in the financial state of the church; published and printed notice of what had been done and exhorted the people to finish the church. . . . The new church of Brunswick was blessed and placed under the invocation of St. Francis Xavier. . . . I laid the cornerstone of the new church in Atlanta on September 1st, 1869."[17] By 1866 funds were coming in again to the Georgia and Florida missions from the Society for the Propagation of the Faith in France, and it was largely through this assistance that Verot was able to get his construction work under way. To complete his projects, Verot had to go on begging tours through the north. He came back with $2,400 from New York and Pennsylvania in December, 1866, and $1,500 from Rhode Island and Connecticut in May of the following year.[18] As economic conditions began slowly to improve in the South, his own people were able to contribute moderate amounts to the work of building and repair.

It was not administration alone that caused the bishop to under-

---

17 "Episcopal Acts," 166–173.
18 *Ibid.*, 169.

take his fourteen journeys into the mission country of Georgia and Florida during the years 1865–1870. There were also confirmations to confer, retreats to hold, and sermons to preach. And there was circuit-riding missionary work to be done. Verot never excused himself from the ordinary labor of the priest in the field. Father Clavreul remembered him during this period:

> . . . The Bishop, who frequently visited the missions through Florida and Georgia, took me several times with him. At St. Augustine and Savannah I had seen him officiate, heard him preach, and every time was vividly impressed with the dignity he showed in the exercise of the pontifical functions. In the missions I saw the same zeal, the same constant efforts to impart to the members of the family he visited the knowledge and love for our holy Faith.[19]

On one such missionary trip undertaken in the fall of 1865 Verot sought out the Catholic inmates confined at the federal prison of Fort Jefferson on the island of Dry Tortugas at the southernmost tip of Florida. He spent a day and a half among them, offering Mass, hearing confessions, and preaching in the open air. One of the prisoners has left an account of the visit — Dr. Samuel A. Mudd, the physician who had set the fractured leg of John Wilkes Booth, and as a consequence found himself implicated in the assassination of Abraham Lincoln. Mudd had been in chains at Fort Jefferson for five months by the time that Verot arrived together with Father James O'Hara of Key West on December 28. Mudd related their encounter in a letter to his wife:

> On the morning of the 28th Bishop Verot, of Savannah, and the Rev. Father O'Hara arrived here about 6 o'clock to see me; my chains being taken off, I dressed in my best, and was soon ushered into their presence with my *usual* guard of honor. I found them preparing to say mass, and had the happy fortune of being present during the divine service.
>
> After service I had a short conversation with Bishop Verot and Rev. Wm. [should be James] O'Hara. . . . In the evening I had the pleasure of listening to a very learned and practical lecture from the Bishop. After the discourse, I repaired to my quarters, took my usual supper, said my beads, and enjoyed for a time a promenade up and down my gloomy quarters, when a rap at the door was heard, and my name called. On going to the door, I found

---

[19] ASLA, "Clavreul's Diary."

our most pious and venerable Bishop had called to bid me good-by; he intended leaving in the morning. I had given the subject of confession my attentive thought during the day, and remarked to the Bishop that I regretted I was not allowed the privilege of confession that evening; he said then, if I desired, he had the permission already accepted, and I had the satisfaction and happiness to confess to the Bishop.[20]

The next morning Mudd assisted again at Verot's Mass. "After Mass I bid [sic] the good and pious old man good-by and received his blessing," Mudd told his wife. "I have not the language at my command, my darling, to express the joy and delight I received on the occasion of this unexpected visit." To his sister the next day Mudd wrote that the bishop was "a most saintly man, plain and unassuming as an old fiddlestick."[21]

It was increasingly evident that the bishop needed helpers. Despite his own willingness, even desire, to work on the missions, the work at hand could not, of course, be done by himself. Nor could it be done by the few priests he had to assist him. Florida, especially, needed priests and sisters. In May of 1866 Father O'Hara abruptly disappeared from Key West, for reasons unknown, thus leaving the state with four resident priests. As for the missions, how thin the ranks were is casually indicated in a January, 1866, entry in Father Clavreul's diary:

> In the beginning of January, 1866, Bishop Verot . . . arrived at Jacksonville from Savannah. My first words were to ask to work on the Florida missions, which was my purpose when I left France, September, 1860, at his request. The Bishop at once divided between us, both Father [John F. R.] Chambon and myself, the immense field which for some time had been attended by Father Chambon alone. He retained charge of Jacksonville with Mandarin, Sampson, Diego [Palm Valley] and the other missions east of the St. Johns [River]. As to myself, with headquarters also in Jacksonville, I had to attend to all the missions west of the St. Johns River [from the Georgia border to the southern keys — practically the whole of Florida!].[22]

On his trip to France in the summer of 1865 — Verot had had

---

[20] Nettie Mudd, ed., *The Life of Dr. Samuel A. Mudd* (Saginaw, Mich.: Richard D. Mudd, M.D., 1962), 154–155.

[21] *Ibid.*, 158.

[22] ASLA, "Clavreul's Diary."

to argue hard to convince Archbishop Spalding it was worth the expense[23] — the bishop had found Sisters of St. Joseph to teach his Negroes and another priest for St. Augustine, Alexander M. Delafosse. Later, through intermediaries, he recruited several more priests from France, Italy, and Canada.[24] To Spalding, Verot wrote asking that the archbishop send "some of your infirm or disabled priests" to spend the winter at St. Augustine and to assist there in offering Mass and in hearing confessions. "Before the war," Verot told him, "we used to have in St. Augustine sometimes a number of priests unfit for duty in the North, but who could yet be very useful in Florida which is the true home of consumptive persons."[25] Verot apparently received a number of priests for temporary help by this means, for his diary and correspondence occasionally record a strange name at St. Augustine or Jacksonville during the latter 1860's. Year by year he was able to add to his roster of priests, until by 1870 he had eleven priests on full-time assignments.

Yet, even with the gradual increase, he was not able to stay abreast of the needs. The Church in Georgia, with its somewhat larger company of priests, was similarly hard-pressed. What were the problems? For one thing, the Catholic populations in both states were growing apace, thanks to conversions (among both Negroes and whites) and to immigration from the North. For another, Catholics, like the rest of the people of the defeated South, had a morale problem: and ever since the war's ignominious close, this low morale had tended to manifest itself in an increasing popular indifference to religion. Verot thought that it was time to meet this latter problem head on. What was needed, he thought, was an intensive moral regeneration. He decided to bring in Redemptorist missionaries in the hope that they would be able to build a fire under his own people, and perhaps even cause the beginning of a moral reawakening in the South as a whole.

The Congregation of the Most Holy Redeemer, founded by St. Alphonsus Maria Liguori at Scala, Italy, in 1732, enjoyed a handsome reputation in the United States for its revival-type apostolate. From the American motherhouse of the Congregation at Ilchester,

23 "Episcopal Acts," 166.
24 "Episcopal Acts," 172.
25 AAB, 39-B-G-24, Verot to Spalding, Savannah, October 13, 1865.

Maryland, Redemptorists, as priests of the Congregation were called, went out to various parts of the country to give short missions, or retreats, in parish churches and mission chapels. They were noted for the apologetical bent of their preaching and for their ability to evoke visions of the horrors of hell: in Savannah one of the missionaries would record, laconically, "Many faintings throughout the church."[26] This was just what Verot thought was needed to shake up his indifferent Catholics. He sent a call for four Redemptorists in the fall of 1867, and on November 27 wrote a pastoral letter to his people announcing that the band would arrive in January of the approaching year.[27] During their three months' stay in Georgia and Florida, Verot hoped, his people would find "the refreshing dew and the fertilizing showers of Divine help and celestial influences" to draw them away from their tepidity and desolation. He asked them to attend punctually and steadily all the exercises of the mission when it came to their church, setting aside all reasons, all pretexts, and all objections to the contrary:

> Not only do we beg of you personally to come to the Mission, but we beg of you in the charity of Christ to bring to the Mission all those over whom you have some influence — your relatives, friends and acquaintances. Alas! among them there are perhaps many who for years have slept the heavy sleep of death; they are, perhaps, immersed in business about merchandise and money, forgetting the only business of man, which is to serve God and save his soul. They are advancing every day towards an unfathomable precipice, with their eyes shut; each step brings them nearer to the yawning abyss.

The four Redemptorists arrived on January 16, 1868: Fathers Joseph Wissel, Nicholas Jaeckel, Timothy Enright, and William H. Gross. Wissel was the veteran of the group. Gross was but five years ordained and the most talented of the three younger priests. He had been a student at St. Charles Seminary in Baltimore when Verot was pastor of nearby Ellicott City, and he remembered

---

[26] Diary of Father Joseph Wissel, February 5, 1868, quoted in Skeabeck, "William H. Gross, C.SS.R.," 61.

[27] "Pastoral Letter for the Approaching Mission, 1868," printed in Joseph Wuest, C.SS.R., ed., *Annales provinciae Americanae congregationis S.S. Redemptoris* (Ilchester, Maryland, and Boston, Massachusetts: n.p., 1923), V, Part II, 75–79.

Verot well. Only five years later he would be one of Verot's successors as fifth Bishop of Savannah. From Wissel's diary kept during the mission and from Gross's letters to his superiors in Ilchester, we obtain suggestions of the physical condition of Verot's diocese and vicariate, and of the religious state of his people three years after the war. Wissel traveled separately to Savannah by train, passing through Atlanta. He recorded:

> Jan. 14 . . . Passed many old fortifications, entrenchments, grave-yards, — reminiscences of the war. Also shattered buildings, Atlanta that was destroyed by Sherman is built up again. The Rail r[oad] is all new.
> Jan. 15 . . . Everywhere are traces of Sherman's devastation. The negroes look abandoned. . . . They steal a good deal.
> Jan. 16 . . . We saw Savannah today. What a quiet place. Nice houses not finished and abandoned. — So also prot[estant] churches. . . . [There are] swamps about here. This is a sickly place.[28]

When Gross arrived, he was also struck by the desolate appearance of Savannah:

> The city . . . looked extremely sad and gloomy. The large heaps of burnt and demolished buildings, other splendid residences half finished and now going to decay, the deep green mould cast by the damp climate upon all edifices, and the crepe-like moss hanging in long streams from the numerous trees along the streets, give to Savannah a sepulchral appearance and gloom unparalleled. It is no doubt extremely unhealthy.[29]

Verot prepared a schedule that would take the four missionaries, either in pairs or all together, to the major centers of Catholic population in the two states. He named Wissel as vicar-general of the Diocese of Savannah and of the Vicariate of Florida. In his diary, the bishop recorded the missionaries' progress. He thankfully recorded that the first two missions given at Savannah "produced much good."[30] Father Gross also thought that the first efforts held much promise:

> We began our campaign by a mission in the Cathedral — if the wrecked building deserves such an appellation — and we had one

---

[28] Wissel Diary, quoted in Skeabeck, "William H. Gross, C.SS.R.," 60.

[29] Gross to William Wayrick, C.SS.R., Jacksonville, Florida, February 16, 1868, printed in Wuest, ed., *Annales . . . S.S. Redemptoris,* V, Part II, 85.

[30] "Episcopal Acts," 171.

in St. Patrick's Church, Savannah. We had altogether about four thousand confessions. We had the best attendance, and I found all my hopes and expectations as to missions now in the South abundantly realized. Not only are the Catholics just ripe for missionary labors, but the Protestants also. We had from 25 to 30 converts in St. Patrick's alone — the number received during the Cathedral mission I neglected to find out, but it also was considerable.[31]

Much the same degree of success was recorded at each subsequent place the mission was given: Jacksonville and St. Augustine in Florida, then Augusta, Macon, Columbus, and Atlanta in Georgia.[32] In Jacksonville, where the mission was given in the makeshift board church erected by Union occupation troops, Fathers Gross and Enright were impressed by the active, cheerful character of the people. "Our mission was a perfect jubilee," Gross wrote. "The Protestants even attended in such glee that balls and parties were deferred until after the Mission. . . ."[33] Wissel noted in his diary: "Jacksonville all in a glow about the mission. Great things done here."[34] In St. Augustine the daily *Examiner* found much to praise in Fathers Wissel and Jaeckel who were attracting extraordinary crowds at the old Spanish church. It hoped "that our City will long remember the present occurrence, and that the Mission will banish many vices from our midst, and will give a tone of morality, honesty and industry that will be more creditable to our City than the empty privilege of being the Oldest City in the Country."[35] In Georgia the missionaries occasionally ran into stiff opposition from Protestant ministers, but they nevertheless continued to draw large crowds.[36] Bishop Verot was convinced by the time the missions ended at Atlanta on Palm Sunday that they had done more good for the religious life of his people than anything he had promoted before. The number of Catholics who had come back to the practice of their faith, the number of converts who had come into the Church, and the number of Protestants who had been favorably affected by the preaching of the Redemptorist band, were unexpectedly greater than what he had

---

31 Gross to Wayrick, Wuest, ed., *Annales . . . S.S. Redemptoris,* V, II, 85.
32 "Episcopal Acts," 171.
33 Quoted in Skeabeck, "William H. Gross, C.SS.R.," 62.
34 Entry of February 27, quoted in *ibid.,* 62, n. 25.
35 February 22, 1868.
36 Skeabeck, "William H. Gross, C.SS.R.," 62–64.

envisioned when he scraped together the funds out of his meager resources to support this three months' adventure. In a second pastoral letter addressed to his people on April 5, the day of the mission's closing at Atlanta, Verot said that he "cannot enumerate the solid and substantial good that has been accomplished by the Mission." But he tried, and poured his praise not only upon the missionaries, but also upon his eager, receptive subjects:

> Their ministrations have been everywhere crowned with success from the moment they opened the Mission in the Cathedral of Savannah, till they closed it in Atlanta. Everywhere the Catholic population and a large number of those who did not belong to the household of the faith, have rallied around their pulpit, an anxious crowd of penitents have literally besieged their confessional, leaving them scarcely any moment for the refection of their bodies and the rest of their exhausted brains. In the Cathedral of Savannah, in the new Church of St. Patrick in our city, in the time-honored Spanish Church of St. Augustine, in the extemporaneous church or shanty of Jacksonville, over the ruins of the church burnt during the war (the Jacksonville church was burnt by the Federal troops), in the edifice of Augusta, in the new church of Macon, and the humble sanctuaries of Columbus and Atlanta, the same consoling scenes have been witnessed over and over again, of anxious multitudes pressing around the Missionaries to listen to the word of grace which fell from their lips, and drink freely of this fountain of religious instructions and emotions. It was truly the voice of God through his humble and frail organ. The voice of man is only empty sound: the voice of God penetrates the heart and makes the heart embrace a new life. *"The voice of God,"* says the Prophet, *"in power; the voice of God in magnificence; the voice of God breaketh the Cedars, yea the Lord shall break the Cedars of Libanus."* Ps. 28.

The fruits of the mission, Verot said, were not so bright perhaps in the eyes of men. But even the most prolific of spiritual advantages are often unseen entirely by men, "hoodwinked men," who are prisoners of carnal desire or of pride or of arrogance. Yet the spiritual principles preached by the missionaries would inevitably have their manifest effects in public society, beginning with domestic society, the family:

> The domestic society is the element of that other larger society, the State and the Church. If the elements and constituent parts be

good, the building will indeed be solid and prosperous. If the elements be bad, nothing can be expected but confusion, strife, disorder and total ruin. Our young men have been exhorted and directed to avoid the snares which the evil one lays before their feet, and to realize by their examples and virtues the bright hopes which religion and the country repose in them.[37]

Verot invited the Redemptorists to return the next year, and they agreed to do so. In January, 1869, an enlarged band of seven missionaries began a circuit that took them to twenty-two churches in Georgia and Florida communities, large and small, in eight weeks. Over 1500 people attended the mission at Augusta, a major Catholic center, but two missionaries gave the same three-day mission to the fifteen Catholic families in Americus, Georgia. Bishop Verot recorded "a special mission week given to the colored people in Savannah and in St. Augustine, Jacksonville and Columbus,"[38] which was one of the first such programs offered to Negroes in the South. Everywhere the Redemptorists enjoyed the same success as before. In 1870 a final Redemptorist campaign took two missionaries on a restricted mission to Key West and Dry Tortugas Island.[39] In all, during nine months of work in three years' time, the missionaries could account for thousands of regained Catholics and several hundred conversions. No great moral reawakening in the southern states resulted in the train of their labors, and perhaps would not have resulted even had the missionaries been doubled or tripled in number. But commendable progress had been made, among Protestants as well as Catholics, and Bishop Verot was satisfied that he had used his resources well. In 1869 and 1870 he continued his program to bring more helping hands into Georgia and Florida. In Providence, Rhode Island, he obtained three more Sisters of Mercy for St. Mary's Academy in St. Augustine. In Montreal, Canada, he found five Sisters of the Holy Names of Jesus and Mary to open a new convent and school at Key West. He also obtained two priests from Genoa, Italy, and another from Besançon, France. Overall, the outlook by 1870 was brightening.[40]

---

[37] "Pastoral Letter for the Conclusion of the Mission," Savannah, April 5, 1868, printed in the St. Augustine *Examiner*, April 11, 1868.

[38] "Episcopal Acts," 172.

[39] New Orleans *Morning Star*, March 14, 1869.

[40] "Episcopal Acts," 171–172.

On a broader scale during the immediate postwar years 1865–1870 the Bishop of Savannah and Vicar Apostolic of Florida was engaged in promulgating the *Syllabus of Errors* of Pope Pius IX, in urging the erection of Florida as a separate diocese, and in promoting a healthy order in the temporal affairs of the Church.

The *Syllabus of Errors*, issued by Pius IX in 1864, was a list of eighty propositions current in European liberal thought that the Pontiff judged to be in grievous error. Religious and civil society were threatened, Pius IX declared, by such spreading doctrines as "separation of Church and State," "freedom of the press," and "equality of religions before the law." The *Syllabus* was actually no more than a series of restatements in abstract form of responses to concrete problems and challenges already published earlier in various papal documents. Still, it caused a great excitement in Europe when it appeared.[41] In this country the *Syllabus* was not widely circularized until after the war, and even then its impact was blunted by the preoccupation of both bishops and faithful with problems more immediate and less theoretical.[42] The impression made here was not striking for the additional reason that American Catholics were scarcely affected by the ideological chasms then opening up in Europe.

Many of the doctrines condemned in the *Syllabus* were already long-established features of American society. As Bishop Verot explained in his first postwar pastoral, "Many of these errors and false theories suppose a political and religious organization of the States of Europe, differing altogether from what exists on our side of the Atlantic."[43] A European in origin, he could sympathize with the pope's rebuke to what Verot called the "mean tortuous reptiles" of Europe who have "endeavored to vomit upon the world their deadly poison, in the shape of pernicious doctrines and theories, and insert their venomous fangs into the hearts of incautious Christians"; but he would not bring the same passion and language to bear on these doctrines and theories in the forms in which they had already been realized and were being daily practiced, in one degree or another, by his fellow Americans. Although he

<hr>

[41] See Aubert, *Pie IX* (Paris: Bloud et Gay, 1952), 245–260.

[42] Cross, *Liberal Catholicism* (Cambridge, Mass.: Harvard University Press, 1958), finds that some American Catholics were divided on the *Syllabus* in the 1870's and 1880's (72).

[43] Jubilee Pastoral, October 4, 1865.

shared the pope's censure of religious indifferentism, for example, and asserted that this was one condemned proposition that circulated more in the United States than perhaps in any other country, he did not go on from this ground to propose that the state owed the Catholic Church special respect and protection, since "the Government of America ought not to make any discrimination, this being one of the articles of the Federal Constitution." Similarly, he hedged on his condemnation of freedom of the press, which he conceded was one of the "cherished ideas of this Republic" and a "favorite dream of the country." Verot stated simply that there must be some judicious limit to what could be printed or publicly spoken:

> Even in our Government where this liberty seems to be a fundamental dogma, the Press had lately to be muzzled, and the practical votaries of that liberty of the Press were cast into dungeons. Indeed nothing can be more evident than the fact that the Press and the Stump can become most powerful engines of evil. Allow the Press and fanatics to publish, and to proclaim "that all property is common, and that no one has a right to be richer than his neighbor," as Communists and Agrarians say, or "that a man can marry several wives," as the Mormons say and practice; or "that it is allowable and praiseworthy to kill a tyrant by one's own authority," as some fanatics and Republican zealots have asserted, and these doctrines will bear their sad fruits of havoc and destruction; they will sap the basis of morality, social order and society itself.

These comments, written in 1865, were the only ones that Verot addressed to his people on the subject of the *Syllabus*. During the five years following he appears to have grown even more reluctant to promulgate ideological anathemas. His people had struggles to wage and principles to oppose, but the arena in which American Catholics fought was not the lecture hall or salon: it was the more pedestrian arena of the marketplace, city hall, school, and newspaper, where, even if people knew nothing about rationalism or pantheism, their intense American feeling for liberty, combined fitfully with long-standing prejudice against Rome, would cause them to react adversely if they heard Catholics condemning those "isms." By 1870 Verot would be so convinced of the futility of dealing with Americans on negative terms, he would argue before the bishops at the Vatican Council in Rome that "if we are saddled

with the obligation of promulgating the *Syllabus,* then that will
be a sign of widespread conflagration, and all our churches will be
burned."[44] The statement would be a clear exaggeration of the
facts, but it would show that Verot had made up his mind on the
question occupying the attention of many American bishops,
whether it was better at this stage for the Church to continue
attacking or to begin to conciliate her American critics. By 1870
Verot would have seen too much goodwill manifested by individual
Protestants and nonbelievers toward the Church, during the Redemptorist missions and during his other efforts in this period to
secure material advantage for the Church,[45] ever to think again that
the Church's proper response to the American scene was mere and
intransigent opposition. He would have more to say on the subject
during the debates at the Vatican Council.

Florida's Catholic population was growing at a rapid pace during
the years 1865–1870. The 3000 Catholics found in the state at the
end of the war increased to about 10,000 in 1870. Verot probably
did not foresee this degree of growth when, in 1866, he proposed
to Archbishop Spalding that Florida be erected into a separate
diocese with St. Augustine as see. The vast mission territory of
Florida needed a separate jurisdiction, he felt, despite the small
number of Catholics at that time. He told Spalding that the new
diocese, if erected, should include the section of Florida west of the
Apalachicola River that then belonged (and still belongs) to the
Diocese of Mobile. As for his proposed see:

> St. Augustine has many titles to the honor of being an episcopal
> city. It is the oldest City of the United States; the population is
> almost exclusively Catholic; Pope St. Pius V nearly three hundred
> **years ago addressed a brief to Melendez** [Pedro Menéndez de
> Avilés] the founder and governor of St. Augustine, and there are
> more antiquities & precious reminiscences in St. Augustine than
> in any other church of the United States. There is also a num-
> ber of houses, lots & lands in St. Augustine belonging to the
> Church. The only reason I know against the expediency of raising
> St. Augustine to an Episcopal See is that the City is not populous
> having only two thousand inhabitants, & that Florida is exceedingly
> poor; if not assisted by the French Propagation of Faith, it could
> scarcely support one priest: things however may improve.[46]

---

[44] See Chapter VIII.

[45] See next chapter.

[46] AAB, 39-G-7, Verot to Spalding, St. Augustine, May 24, 1866.

Spalding decided to wait on the improvement. By 1869 Florida's situation had improved markedly, and in Baltimore on April 26 of that year, at 10:30 in the morning, during the Tenth Provincial Council, Bishop Verot described that improvement to the assembled bishops of the province. Bishops Whelan of Wheeling and Lynch of Charleston moved that the new diocese be created. The resulting vote was unanimous in favor. Whelan proposed that Jacksonville be made the see because of its growing importance as a port and general transportation center. The other bishops, however, joined Verot in choosing St. Augustine. Two days later a letter draft to Rome requesting the new see was read and approved.[47] Rome would write back on February 25, 1870, during the course of the Vatican Council, and approve the petition.[48]

Other organizational matters occupied Verot's attention during these years, and he held diocesan synods in every year but 1867 to deal with them. At the close of the synod of 1868 he treated the outstanding problems in a lengthy pastoral letter "on the Temporalities of the Church,"[49] which included directions on lay trusteeism, pew rent, support and salary of the clergy, collections, debts, the support of infirm and superannuated clergymen, etc. It was a master plan of organization that must have taken him long months to prepare. Most space was devoted to what Verot called "the mode of representing congregations or churches in their temporalities," which was, in effect, a condemnation of the lay-trustee system that had been common among Catholic churches in the South prior to the war. During the 1868 synod, Verot recorded in his diary, "I told the Rev. gentlemen . . . that there was no church in Georgia under the Trustee system. The last church, namely, that of Locust Grove, having passed to me the property."[50] To insure that the trustee system would not be invoked again, Verot excoriated it in his postsynodal letter as opposed to the very nature of the Church, which was monarchical by divine institution. True, he granted, there had to be some means of representing the individual churches so that they could build, make repairs, sue and be sued, and contract

47 AAB, 39-A-N-1, 19, 29.

48 AAB, 39-A-Q-1, Sacred Congregation of the Propagation of the Faith to Spalding, Rome, February 25, 1870.

49 ASLA, "Pastoral Letter on the Temporalities of the Church in the Diocese of Savannah," Savannah, May 7, 1868.

50 "Episcopal Acts," 171.

debts. But "the mode is not by Lay-trustees, although this plan borrowed from our separated brethren has existed for a time in some places of the Diocese."

> The Protestant system of trusteeism in this country had, to some extent, crept into the Catholic Church, and after a hard struggle and long fight, the right of controlling the property of the Church has been everywhere given up by Lay-men at the request of the various councils of the Church, which have shown how intolerable an evil it was, that men should hold the keys of a Church and keep it locked against the Pastor appointed by the Bishop [as happened in St. Augustine in 1830], or open it for one in opposition to the Bishop, and under the anathemas of the Church.

In place of lay trustees Verot decreed that he, as bishop, would act as sole owner in trust of all ecclesiastical property. However, because "the Bishops have been instructed by our Lord to determine nothing, particularly in matters of importance, without consulting and asking the advise [sic] of their inferiors," Verot announced that on all questions related to construction of a new church or school or to extraordinary repairs to an existing building, he would call together all the male members of a congregation to represent the membership in the determination of what ought to be done. He also worked out a compromise trustee formula for the assumption of debts and expenses for which he did not want to assume personal responsibility: "On such occasions a building committee may be appointed, with authority to purchase and contract debts in order to erect a Church, or school-house, or such building as may be needed. But such a committee acts on its own responsibility and risk; for it would be simply ridiculous for them to buy and contract debts and then send the bills to the Bishop or to anybody else." Verot concluded his remarks with the prayer from the Mass of the Third Sunday after Pentecost, *Sic transeamus per bona temporalia ut non amittamus aeterna:* "may we pass through temporal goods here below, so as not to lose those that are eternal in the next world. Amen." The pastoral was then directed to be read in all the churches of Georgia and Florida, one half of it on each of the two consecutive Sundays following its reception. It was the first and the last pastoral that Verot wrote on purely administrative affairs.

Everywhere across the country during these postwar years the

Catholic Church was enjoying an increase in numbers and influence. She had come out of the war with an enhanced reputation among Americans north and south for her unity and for her charities. Increasingly, it became hard for doctrinaire Protestants to attack her, and the *Presbyterian* of Fayetteville, North Carolina, complained that "The shrewdness with which the Roman Catholic Church became all things to all men during the late war is now also an element of influence with many of our people."[51] In 1867 the *Catholic Mirror* of Baltimore was exulting in italics that *"The Catholic Church has become a power in the land."*[52] The total Catholic population of the country increased from 3,103,000 in 1860 to 4,504,000 in 1870: 620,000 from natural increase, 741,000 from immigration, and 40,000 from conversions (conversions among soldiers in the war had been mostly deathbed conversions). During the same period the number of priests increased from 2235 to 3780.[53] While the Church was not actually a "power in the land," her voice was being heard more often and more respectfully than ever before, and many people, Catholic and non-Catholic alike, could agree with the *Presbyterian Banner* of Pittsburgh that "Surely this is not a circumstance to be regarded with indifference."[54]

In the South, Catholics still formed a negligible minority of the total population, but here, too, there had been consoling growth. Although a number of parishes in Georgia were still beholden to the Society for the Propagation of the Faith in France for very survival, and only two of Verot's churches in Florida were self-supporting, at St. Augustine and Jacksonville,[55] the bishop could take heart from the steady progress made by his poverty-ridden priests and people — a showing quite out of proportion to their numbers and resources. In a period of extreme hardship his people had built new churches over the blackened ruins of war, had repaired churches damaged by looting, had opened new institutions including schools unsupported by taxation, and had proved their fidelity as well as their generosity by hanging on to the Faith in difficult times. It was an accomplishment for which Verot took no

---

[51] Editorial quoted in *Banner of the South,* January 9, 1869.
[52] January 5, 1867.
[53] Shaughnessy, *Has the Immigrant Kept the Faith?* (New York: Macmillan, 1925), 153, Table XXVI.
[54] Editorial quoted in the St. Augustine *Examiner,* July 20, 1867.
[55] Brooklyn *Catholic Review,* April 10, 1873.

credit himself. "If Catholicity has become deeply rooted in our country," he wrote to the Society for the Propagation of the Faith in France on behalf of the Tenth Provincial Council of Baltimore in 1869, "if it has found here a rapid and wonderful growth, we owe it, in great part, to the co-operation of your wonderful Work."[56] Certainly he could not have done what he did without assistance from France. Again, without the devoted response of his priests and people, his leadership would have gone for naught. Still, it was Verot who obtained that assistance, who did the leading, who rode the circuit himself to see that the work was done. In both the first and last instance it was Verot who made it possible for Abram J. Ryan to wax eloquent in the *Banner of the South:* in Georgia, Ryan exclaimed, "Our Church is on the march." The poet-editor described the Church as the "angel of peace" who "lays her soft and gentle hand upon the war-furrowed brow of the trampled South." He pointed with pride to the increase in conversions: "Thanks to the zeal of our venerated Bishop and his Clergy, the Church is rapidly gaining ground in Georgia. We venture to say that, in proportion to the population, no more converts to the Church are made in any State of the so-called Union, than we have had during the last year in Georgia."[57] In January, 1869, the *Banner* was running prominently placed excerpts from the speeches of Father Isaac Hecker, liberal Paulist editor of *The Catholic World,* who believed that "This great Republic is destined in the providence of God to become a great Catholic country! (Applause.)"[58] The *Banner* had every right to share Hecker's optimism: at the turn of the year 1869, when these sentiments were expressed, Verot was only five months away from consummating one of the most notable alliances of Church and State in the history of American Catholic education.

---

[56] Verot to the Society, May 2, 1869; *Catholic Mirror,* July 3, 1869.
[57] January 23, 1869.
[58] January 23, 30, 1869.

CHAPTER VII

THE CATHOLIC PUBLIC SCHOOL

THE CATHOLIC CHURCH in the United States has always been closely associated with the education of youth. Bishop Verot's Vicariate of Florida could claim precedence in the field: a school begun under Catholic auspices at St. Augustine in 1606 antedated by more than a quarter century the educational foundations in later English and Dutch colonies; and a free, or public, school founded by the Church at St. Augustine in 1787 was probably the first of its kind within the present limits of the United States.[1] But education had been a close concern of all the other Christian denominations, too, especially during the colonial and early national periods. One remembers that most of "the framers of the law, the makers of States, the up-builders of this American Union" were products of denominational schools.[2] Most late eighteenth-century schools, from primary grades through college, were under church or private auspices, and public funds were appropriated to their support without any hesitation on doctrinal grounds.[3] Nor did the Revolution cause any break in the religious aim and administration of education. Church and private schools were regularly supported by the

---

[1] The 1606 school was begun by Franciscan friars; see Rev. Maynard Geiger, O.F.M., *The Franciscan Conquest of Florida (1573–1618)* (Washington, D. C.: The Catholic University of America, 1937), 201, and J. A. Burns, *The Principles, Origin and Establishment of the Catholic School System in the United States* (New York: Benziger Brothers, 1912), 145. The free school at St. Augustine was started by Father Thomas Hassett, Irish-born *vicario* of the Spanish-Minorcan parish; see Joseph B. Lockey, "Public Education in Spanish St. Augustine," *Florida Historical Society Quarterly*, XV (September, 1937), 147–168.

[2] Herbert Baxter Adams, *The Church and Popular Education*, Johns Hopkins University Studies in Historical and Political Science, Series XVIII, Nos. 8–9 (Baltimore: Johns Hopkins, 1900), 12.

[3] Samuel W. Brown, *The Secularization of American Education,* Teachers College Contributions to Education, No. 49 (New York: Columbia University, 1926), 5 ff.

states during the early national period, as far as 1820 at least.[4] "Free," "common," or "public" schools without denominational connections were beginning to appear during these years, but proportionate state support for church and private schools actually increased within the same period.[5] Protestant groups received the great majority of these grants, but some Catholic schools benefited, too.[6] The outstanding Catholic example was in Lowell, Massachusetts, where, for a period of sixteen years (1835–1851), two Catholic schools were supported out of common school funds, and were comprised within the public system.[7]

This long and almost exclusive tradition of public support for church-affiliated schools, which American Catholics held in high regard, began to weaken in the 1820's. There were several reasons for the change. Firm belief in traditional Christian doctrine was declining. The swelling populations caused by immigration seemed to demand more efficient, therefore more centralized, administration of the educational process. Under the growing spell of Rousseau, the emphasis in educational theory began to fall on the more worldly purposes of individual self-improvement, social betterment, civic duty, and ethical training. And, most important reason of all, the rise of Jacksonian democracy caused men to press for a broader, more inclusive base to education, together with guarantees for free and equal access to its benefits.[8] As a consequence, the nonsectarian, common, free schools came increasingly to the fore, and public support of religious foundations faded in proportion. Church and private schools continued to be the main educative agency in the middle and southern states for a longer period, but

---

[4] Richard Gobel, *Public Funds for Church and Private Schools* (Washington, D. C.: The Catholic University of America Press, 1937), 20–30, 147–180.

[5] *Ibid.*, 36–38.

[6] Owing to this aid and to assistance received from foreign missionary associations in Lyons, Munich, and Vienna, Catholic schools enjoyed steady growth and expansion between 1808 and 1840 when there were about 200 parish schools functioning: J. A. Burns, *The Growth and Development of the Catholic School System in the United States* (New York: Benziger Brothers, 1912), 19.

[7] Gobel, *Public Funds*, 322–323.

[8] For a recent summary of events and influences which led to the "revolution in American education" during this period, see Russell Blaine Nye, *The Cultural Life of the New Nation, 1776–1830* (New York: Harper & Brothers, 1960), Chapter VII, "The Training of Free Minds," 150–171. Cf. Merle Curti, *The Social Ideas of American Educators* (New York: Scribners, 1935), Chapter II, "New Conflicts and a New Solution, 1800–1860," 50–101.

they, too, would yield to the new order after the Civil War.[9] Between 1820 and 1865, and largely through the efforts of the rationalist and humanitarian Horace Mann, the state-supported secular, public school gained ascendancy in American education.[10]

To the Protestant churches the development posed no terrors: the attitude of the teachers, the Protestant-tinged textbooks, the daily Bible reading, and the democratic character of the schools did no violence to Protestant minds. To the Catholic Church, however, the new order posed a threat of some magnitude. In the view of its bishops the plea of "nonsectarianism" was specious, made to cover up a take-over by the Protestants of the full resources of the state. To safeguard their religious interests the bishops called for the establishment of more parochial schools, even though this meant, in their view, a double taxation for education. Parochial schools were urged with increasing fervor at the First Provincial Council of Baltimore (1829), at the First and Second Plenary Councils (1852, 1866), and at the Third Plenary Council (1884), which made the parochial school mandatory.[11] Except, perhaps, for the rivalries that erupted between the immigrant national groups in the Church,[12] the Catholic bishops experienced no more vexing problem during the period 1820–1900 than what they universally called "The School Question." Bishop Verot had as much anxiety about the matter as any of his fellow prelates. But he also had a solution.

Verot was not the first with a solution. Bishop Hughes in New York had several of them, including a plan to obtain a proportionate share of state funds. Hughes made a vigorous campaign to that end in 1840, but met nativist opposition somewhat more vigorous. A

[9] William A. Maddox, *The Free School Idea in Virginia*, Teachers College Contributions to Education, No. 93 (New York: Columbia University, 1918), 10; Edgar W. Knight, *Public Education in the South* (Boston: Ginn and Company, 1922), 275.

[10] See William Kailer Dunn, *What Happened to Religious Education? The Decline of Religious Teaching in the Public Elementary School, 1776–1861* (Baltimore: Johns Hopkins Press, 1958); Howard Mumford Jones, "Horace Mann's Crusade," in Daniel Aaron, ed., *America in Crisis* (New York: Alfred A. Knopf, 1952), Chapter V, 91–109; Curti, *American Educators*, 101–139; Sidney L. Jackson, *America's Struggle for Free Schools* (Washington, D. C.: American Council on Public Affairs, 1941).

[11] See Guilday, *Councils of Baltimore, passim.* Hughes of New York announced in 1850 that "the time has come when it will be necessary to build the schoolhouse first, and the church afterward"; quoted in Cross, *Liberal Catholicism*, 137.

[12] See Ellis, *American Catholicism* (Chicago: University of Chicago Press, 1956), 46–52.

fierce debate on the issue occupied New York politics for two years following, and Hughes had finally to concede defeat. In 1841 and 1842, Hughes was also busy on a strategy being used by Francis Patrick Kenrick, then Bishop of Philadelphia, to break the monopoly of Protestant bodies over the growing school systems. Three days of destructive riots in 1844 grew out of Kenrick's efforts in Philadelphia. Hughes narrowly missed the same consequences in New York in the same year.[13] He did succeed in promoting passage through the state legislature of the Maclay Bill of April, 1842, which took the public schools out of the hands of the Protestant-dominated Public School Society, and placed them under state direction, but it was a hollow victory: the Maclay Bill forbade state aid to any religious schools in the city; nativist resistance hardened as the result of Hughes's action;[14] and the public schools in New York and elsewhere began to move away from a Christian orientation to one increasingly more secular. Catholics at the date of this writing who are scandalized by the secular character of public education might well ponder the actions of their coreligionists who, following the example of Hughes, spent the next fifty years attacking the reading of the Protestant Bible in public school classrooms.[15]

By the year the guns began at Fort Sumter, American public opinion was firmly grounded on the notion that the Catholic Church's intransigence on the school issue was proof of its foreign

[13] These events are graphically described in Billington, *The Protestant Crusade* (New York: Macmillan, 1938), Chapter IX, "The Philadelphia Riots," 220–237; see also the important chapter, "The Catholic Church Blunders, 1850–1854," 289–322, for some of the later developments and effects. Hugh J. Nolan, *The Most Reverend Francis Patrick Kenrick, Third Bishop of Philadelphia, 1830–1851* (Washington, D. C.: The Catholic University of America Press, 1948) has a detailed account in his chapter, "The Native American Riots of 1844," 288–342. For Hughes's school plan, see Henry J. Browne, "Public Support of Catholic Education in New York, 1825–1842: Some New Aspects," *CHR*, XXXIX (April, 1953), 1–27; and Sister Marie Leonore Fell, S.C., "Bishop Hughes and the Common School Controversy" (unpublished master's thesis, The Catholic University of America, 1936).

[14] Billington, *Crusade,* 158.

[15] For examples of Catholic opposition to the King James Bible in public schools, see Daniel F. Reilly, *The School Controversy* (Washington, D. C.: The Catholic University of America, 1943), Chapter I, "The Background of the Controversy," 1–39. Cf. Cross, *Liberal Catholicism,* 135: as late as 1890 conservative Bishop Bernard J. McQuaid was denouncing public schools in Rochester as "crypto-Protestant," thereby causing religious teaching to be dropped altogether from the public school curriculum.

character and of its opposition to republican ideals and to the American way of life. That canard would die hard, especially as it occurred to most of the Catholic prelates of the time (among whom the Irish predominated) that, if the common school was Americanism, so much the worse for Americanism. In 1858, Martin John Spalding, then Bishop of Louisville, made a few conciliatory gestures, and tried to approach the problem from a detached position: "The great question of the day for us Americans is, undoubtedly, that of Common School Education."[16] But Protestants were not listening; so far as they were concerned the question had been answered. Neither were Catholics for their part listening to Orestes Brownson, who warned them that their present state of mind "would denationalize the American Catholic and tend to keep Catholics a foreign colony in the United States. . . ."[17] Nor did even Isaac Hecker attend to Brownson's words on this point. Hecker, who shares with Brownson the accolade of one recent historian of having done more than anyone else to domesticate the Catholic faith in America, was more mindful of the distinction between Protestant ideals and American ideals.[18] To the latter Hecker gave unstinting adherence and devotion; but Protestantism was a different thing altogether.[19] Bishop Verot seems to have made the same distinction, and it is time now to examine his peculiar situation in Georgia.

Savannah was the first city in Georgia to establish a public school system, in March, 1866.[20] During its first year of operation,

[16] "Common Schools," *Brownson's Quarterly Review*, Series III, I (January, 1858), 70–102.

[17] "Public and Parochial Schools," *Brownson's Quarterly Review*, Series IV, III (September, 1859), 330.

[18] See Gabriel, *American Democratic Thought* (New York: Ronald Press, 1956), Chapter V, "Democracy and Catholicism in the Middle Period," 54–69.

[19] "The great American delusion, taught Hecker, is the belief that democracy springs from Protestantism. . . . Democracy, tied to Protestantism, is bound to a dying system. Hecker sought to relieve the democratic faith of the burden of the death it bore." *Ibid.*, 67. Cf. Hecker's address on the school issue in the *Banner*, May 1, 1869.

[20] "Our school system was the first to be organized in the State of Georgia . . . March 31, 1866." 51st and 52nd Annual Reports of the Public Schools of Savannah (Savannah, 1917), 9. Cf. copy of "Act to establish a permanent Board of Education for the City of Savannah . . . approved March 21st, 1866," in "Proceedings of [City] Council, December 9, 1868," in ASCH. In December, 1866, this act was amended to extend authority over Chatham County as well; Thompson, *Reconstruction in Georgia* (New York: Columbia University Press, 1915), 123.

520 white pupils were enrolled in three schools, Chatham Academy, Massie, and Bernard Street.[21] The system grew steadily until in 1870 there were seven schools in the city, instructing 1754 pupils.[22] Burned-out Atlanta did not have a public school system until 1870,[23] and the state was equally slow in executing a school law, largely because the poverty resulting from the war precluded the imposition of extra taxes. The Georgia legislature passed a school bill on a close vote, 62 to 58, as early as November 26, 1866, but amended it to postpone execution until January 1, 1868, when it thought financial resources would be adequate. No general state-supported system was actually established, however, until 1873, and then by the plan of the reconstruction legislature of 1870.[24]

Prior to the war, in 1858, the Georgia legislature had passed a measure supporting the establishment of "poor" schools, also called "free" schools, to be administered by the various counties. The nucleus for a free school organization in Chatham County had been provided in 1842 through a $5,000 gift from Peter Massie, of Glynn County. In 1854 two lots were set aside by the city council for educational purposes, and a Massie Common School was completed in 1856. The teachers received their support from the Savannah city payroll. The city established another similar school in 1857. In accordance with the 1858 state law, the county established a Board of School Commissioners, which operated the two school units at city expense through 1863, when wartime difficulties intervened.[25] It was this pioneer school system that Verot discovered upon his accession to the See of Savannah in 1861. He also found a Catholic free school operating under the auspices of St. John the

---

[21] Thompson, *op. cit.,* 338.

[22] "Minutes of the Board of Education, 1866–1880," p. 378, ASBE; cf. F. D. Lee and L. J. Agnew, *Historical Record of the City of Savannah* (Savannah: J. H. Estill, 1869), 155: "The public school system of Savannah is equal to any, and superior to many others, in the United States. About one thousand pupils are instructed in the public schools." Lee and Agnew list for this year five primary, grammar and intermediate schools, and two high schools, one boys' and one girls'. This list compares with Board of Education records, ASBE, "Minutes," p. 378, and contradicts the figure of twenty public schools in Savannah in 1870 given in Thompson, *op. cit.,* 338.

[23] Thompson, *op. cit.,* 338.

[24] *Ibid.,* 121–122.

[25] See Orr, *Education in Georgia* (Chapel Hill: University of North Carolina, 1950), 175–176. This is the most detailed recent account of the subject.

Baptist Cathedral.[26] One year later, faced with financial losses in the operation of the parish school, Verot decided to ask for a share in the public school fund. Accordingly, in March, 1862, he made the first unsuccessful move in what would be an eight-year contest with Chatham County and the city of Savannah. The moment is recorded in the following minutes of the school commissioners:

Savannah, March 27th, 1862. The School Comrs. for the county met this day at the house of the secretary. Present A. Parker, Chm., G. P. Harrison, Wm. Morrel, S. J. Dupon & J. Stoddard. . . . This meeting was called to take into consideration an application for assistance to the Catholic Schools [should be in the singular] of the City, made by the Bishop of Savannah. His letter, as well as the reply which the Chairman was instructed to make, are as follows [Verot's letter missing] : — To Rt. Revd. Augustin Verot, Bishop of Savh xxx That this board was appointed by the Inferior Court of Chatham County for the purpose of establishing Schools, *selecting teachers,* and superintending generally the public schools both in the City and county. That our schools are open to all classes of children, without regard to their religious opinions. We do not feel at liberty to change our usual and accustomed course in such matters; nor that we have any right to do so, without the authority and direction of the Legislature of the State. The small modicum to which the County is entitled, has all been appropriated for the current year. We fully appreciate and understand the pecuniary embarrassments of the present time; and we cordially throw open the doors of our schools to all of your parish, who may be deprived of their accustomed education, owing to the small means at your command. That such a necessity may, by any possibility, exist, we deprecate; and trust that it may be avoided.[27]

---

[26] The prior history of Catholic education in Savannah may be summarized briefly as follows: In 1833 Irish immigrants supported a small school opened by Father Jeremiah F. O'Neill, who cared for the parish from Charleston, South Carolina. An English classical school began in the church vestry in 1835, under William Carmody. There is a meager, and doubtful, record of an academy opened this same year by a Mr. Phelan, from Ireland. In 1845, Patrick McCormick, sexton, taught a small school for boys. And in 1860, O'Neill, then pastor of St. John's, began Cathedral School, a combination school and boys' orphanage. This was the school that Verot inherited. See Rev. E. D. Mitchell, "Catholic Schools in Savannah," Savannah *Morning News,* September 19, 1936; Haygood S. Bowden, *Two Hundred Years of Education* (Richmond: Dietz Printing Company, 1932), 196.

[27] ASBE, "Minutes of the School Commissioners [of] the County of Chatham." March 27, 1862.

Verot probably found little to argue with in this reply, especially since the county schools were having difficulties of their own, equally extreme: in 1864 they had to charge tuition to stay alive; the next year they were being operated by occupying federal troops under General Gillmore. After the establishment of a full-scale public school system in 1866, however, the bishop rose to battle again. He was not deterred by the fact that his fellow prelates at the plenary council of 1866 had decided not to press for public aid to parochial schools.[28] In his 1862 effort, judging from the reply made to him, Verot had asked for an outright share in the distribution of public funds. He would use that strategem again. But in November, 1867, he conceived another plan, and laid it before the board of education.[29] Since, "with our views of religion and education," he could not conscientiously send Catholic children to public schools, he had been forced to continue his parochial school, despite the "double burden" which that entailed. Equity demanded some form of accommodation. But "instead of asking for a separate portion of the educational fund, which we think we might justly claim, we propose that you receive our schools under your management and supervision. . . ." He then proposed the following conditions as a basis for agreement:

1. The Catholic schools shall be under the control and subject to the rules and regulations of the Board of Education.

2. The Catholic schools shall have a representation in the Board of Education consisting of three members, one of whom shall be a Catholic Priest.

3. The teachers of the Catholic schools shall be nominated by the representatives of these schools in the Board of Education, subject to the approval of the Board.

4. The catechism of the Catholic Church may be taught in these schools, and the selection of histories, reading books, and such other textbooks as may touch on religion, shall be left to the Catholic representatives in the Board.

During the previous year of 1866, Verot continued, the Cathedral School educated about 700 pupils, boys and girls, at an expense of about $7,000. Since the financial burden was becoming increasingly

---

[28] Again in 1869, at the Tenth Provincial Council of Baltimore, the bishops of Verot's province declined to seek state support in any form for Catholic schools. See AAB, 39-A-N-1, p. 39, notes of the fifth Congregatio Privata, no. 3.

[29] ASBE, Minutes, November 8, 1867.

irksome, he appealed to the board "as liberal and enlightened men" to acknowledge the justice of the claim. "Under such a just and liberal union, we can all work together harmoniously, and *unitedly support a system of public schools which will be an object of pride to our entire community.*"[30]

The importance of this communication will be clear to the reader familiar with Catholic opinion of the public school system in the period after the Civil War. It was immediately prior to the war, it will be recalled, that the lines hardened between Catholic and general public opinion on the school issue. Between that time and the day in 1890 when the liberal-minded Archbishop John Ireland, of St. Paul, addressed the National Education Association at St. Paul, Minnesota, no American prelate announced himself as favoring the public school systems as such, nor as even recognizing the right of the state to teach or to exercise authority over the educational process.[31] James Cardinal Gibbons, Ireland's great friend and champion, stoutly defended the latter's thesis that the public schools had a right to exist, and that the state functioned quite properly in compelling the nation's youth to receive at least the rudiments of a secular education. The Ireland-Gibbons position caused a great excitement among American Catholics in the period 1890–1893, and opponents sent a copy of Ireland's N.E.A. address to Rome, where it caused yet another excitement, finally stilled by Gibbons' persuasive letters to the Roman Curia.[32]

---

[30] Author's emphasis.

[31] Ireland addressed the N.E.A. in July, 1890, saying of the state school: "It is our pride and glory. The Republic of the United States has solemnly affirmed its resolve that within its borders no clouds of ignorance shall settle upon the minds of the children of its people. . . . The Free School of America! Withered be the hand raised in sign of its destruction!" Ireland, *Church and Modern Society,* 202. See Reilly, *School Controversy,* 106: until Ireland's address and the publication of Thomas Joseph Bouquillon's famous speculative tract supporting him (*Education: To Whom Does It Belong?* Baltimore, 1891), "It is probably safe to say that from the time the school question in any of its many phases began to trouble Catholics of the United States, no one of any standing among them had publicly taught the right of the State to educate." Cross, *Liberal Catholicism,* who relies on Reilly for this period, states that Bouquillon's tract "more explicitly acknowledged the prerogatives of the state than any other American Catholic had yet done (142)," but he does not cite any earlier episcopal announcements or writings that allude to the right even indirectly; cf. his Chapter VII, "The Question of the Schools," 130–145.

[32] See Gibbons' letter to Pope Leo XIII, December 30, 1890, translated from the French and quoted in Reilly, *School Controversy,* Appendix C, 242–247.

Ireland's flamboyant manner and grandiloquent language brought
to full stage a liberalizing movement that had in fact been proceeding for twenty-five years within the American hierarchy — a
movement which very few people at the time seem to have noticed
until its force was suddenly thrust upon them in 1890. No one seems
to have been aware that in Savannah as much as twenty-three years
before, a blunt-speaking prelate, as candid and forceful as Ireland
himself, was laying the groundwork for a Catholic public school
system, and urging the advisability of allying the Church with the
public schools in a "just and liberal union." Bishop Verot, stung
by Savannah's initial refusal of his plan, would later balk at his
generous treatment of the public schools (and then reaffirm his
faith in the end); but he was apparently the first prelate in the
land to recognize, even implicitly, the right of the state to educate. He was also, apparently, the first postwar prelate to conceive
and to realize the Catholic public school, which Ireland and Gibbons
embraced warmly a score of years later.

On the evening of November 19, 1867, eight members of the
Savannah board of education met at the home of their chairman,
Richard D. Arnold, M.D., and gave their approval, one member
dissenting, to the draft of a reply to Bishop Verot.[33] The letter,
in effect, advised the bishop that if he was having trouble maintaining his school, he ought to avail himself of the opportunities
provided by the public schools: "The Board regrets that any persons in the community should decline to accept [these] opportunities," but somewhat later in the reply suggested that it was not
overly regretful: "Your application acknowledges that you have
been compelled, under your separate system . . . to rent school
houses and employ teachers for the instruction of a large number
of children, at a great expense. Should we assent to your proposal,
we would be obliged to assume these additional burdens. . . . The
funds at our command do not warrant our entering into any
engagements for increased expenditure." As for the question of

Gibbons wrote: "The Americans are proud of their schools, which they regard
as the glory of the country. . . . To attack them is, in their eyes, to attack the
nation itself, and it would be absolutely useless to try to change their views on
this subject. . . ."
[33] ASBE, Minutes, November 19, 1867.

taxes and the revenue distributed from them, the board members laid down a principle that has since, from other cases, become classical:

Nor can they recognize any right in individuals or associations to claim any proportionate part of the public educational fund on account of a voluntary refusal, from peculiar religious motives, to partake of its benefits. As well might the Board acknowledge a similar right in all who from personal reasons should prefer to send their children to *private schools*, or not to send them to school at all!

The board took particular exception to Verot's suggestion that three Catholics, including a priest, be added to their number. "No member of this board holds his seat in any similar capacity, nor is any sect or faith specially represented in it." (Two of the members present for approval of the draft were Protestant ministers, Rev. S. Landrum and Rev. A. M. Wynn.) On this point the board concluded that Verot's proposal was impractical, and "calculated to produce rather discord than harmony in their operations." Furthermore, the board did not desire, and did not feel authorized, to mix into public education the doctrine or tenets of any particular creed. "Teachings upon subjects of religion concern, according to the Constitution of the United States, the *consciences of individuals,* rather than the arrangement of public corporations or institutions." In conclusion, the board felt that to grant Verot's application would mean destruction of the unity of the public school system; it would mean the creation of not one inner jurisdiction but many, "by producing an indefinite number of separate denominational schools under the nominal but powerless control of a body intended to be general, comprehensive, conservative and practical in its operation."

In all, the letter was a well-reasoned reply to Verot's proposal and must have appeared both plausible and compelling to any citizen who accepted its premises — which Verot did not. One year later, after increased hardships in maintaining the Cathedral school, Verot decided to go over the head of the board to the city council. He also decided to change his strategy and revert to the plan of 1862. During the month of November, 1868, he composed and circulated a petition to which 374 Catholic householders, mostly Irish

in name, affixed their signatures.[34] The petition was presented to
the city council on December 9, and read as follows:

> We, undersigned Catholics, residing in the City of Savannah, lay
> before your honorable body an humble and respectful petition,
> which we trust will not be set aside. Forming a large portion of the
> population of the City, as appears from the report of interments
> in Laurel Grove and Cathedral Cemetery,[35] we have organized
> Schools, which are in the highest sense poor Schools and free
> Schools, and the Scholars are so numerous that the public Schools
> supported by the City could not physically accommodate them. We
> have done so because we believe it is far the better plan to teach
> children the elements of literature and science under the influence
> and shelter of the religion which they profess, as has always been
> done in times past, and we would consider it an infringement of
> the true liberty of conscience, if we were obliged to subject our
> children to the influence of a religion which they do not profess,
> or of no religion at all. We, therefore, submit to your honorable
> body to consider whether it is proper to make us pay taxes for
> Schools which we do not patronize, and whether it would not be
> better in accordance with equity and genuine liberty to divide the
> fund allotted for free Schools, in the proportion of the free Scholars
> found in each School.

With this statement and the Board of Education's reply of the
year before, one hears the distant battle sounds of a contest still
being waged. Indeed, it would be hard to say that the arguments
advanced in the Church-State school controversy at the date of this
writing have changed in any essential character from the arguments
advanced in the engagement at Savannah in 1867–1868. Each side
would have more to say in elaboration, however. The council —
to Verot's dismay — referred the Catholic petition to the Board of
Education for review, and received the reply that "after much
general conversation on the petition," there was nothing in the
principles of their earlier decision which they desired to alter or

[34] This petition, with its signatures, was found in the ASCH. It has since been
transferred, with the city council's permission, to the Archives of the Diocese of
Savannah.

[35] Lee and Agnew, *City of Savannah,* estimated in 1869 that the Catholic
population was 8500 out of a total of 45,000: 5000 in the Cathedral parish, and
3500 in St. Patrick's parish founded by Verot in 1863; 181. In 1868 Verot organized a second parochial school in the rear of St. Patrick's Church, near the
Central Railroad depot.

retract.[36] The board did, however, touch upon the possibility that the city council might wish to act on the matter in a fashion different from the convictions of the board, in which case the board "will be compelled to ask from the City Council an appropriation of at least twenty thousand dollars for the ensuing year." The board also took the occasion to point out an error in Verot's petition: "The public schools are not 'supported by the city.' The City has contributed to their support, from time to time, by generous gratuities, but the Board of Education is an independent body corporate, created by the Legislature of Georgia. . . ." As a parting shot, it warned that such a program as Verot proposed would mean eventually that every known religion in Savannah, from Hebrew through Swedenborgian, would have a right to clamor for separate educational facilities. Such a scheme would dissolve "the whole grand plan of public education into the primary elements of separate, private, or denominational and strictly Sectarian Schools."

Verot was incensed when he learned that the council had referred his petition to the board, and said so in a lengthy and critical letter which the council received on March 3, 1869.[37] The letter reveals that Verot's liberality had its limits, and that, while he was willing to seek an accommodation with the powers of secular education, he was not pleased with the kind of responses he was getting. He should not have expected any more than he received, of course, given the distance public school philosophy had traveled by that date. And there must have been, in addition, genuine doubt in the minds of board and council members as to the correctness of his reasoning and the propriety of his aims. The assumption of Catholic school responsibilities by a public body was a matter freighted with too many unknowns — and several really stark possibilities to a Protestant mind — to expect from the competent civic authorities any display of supererogation. Bishop Verot was a fighter, however: he had fought the Civil War; concurrently with this campaign he was fighting in the corner of the Negro; one year later, he would be the so-called *enfant terrible* of the Vatican Council. Not surprisingly, therefore, he rejoindered strongly to his third refusal in six years. In so doing, he changed the style of his attack (for the

---

[36] ASBE, Minutes, December 12, 1868.
[37] ASCH, Verot to the Honorable Mayor & City Council of Savannah, n.d. but marked "In Council Mch 3rd, 1869."

third time), reverting to his 1867 conception of the Catholic public school. If a major struggle was in the offing, he would fight it out on those lines. But first — about the board of education:

> We think it our privilege and even our duty here to state that the Board of Education has little, if any, jurisdiction in this matter, for it was appointed by a legislature considered by some of dubious authority,[38] and particularly it was appointed without any participation or even knowledge of the inhabitants of the City of Savannah, especially without the concurrence of the parties interested in the distribution of the educational fund, namely the heads of poor families, whom the laws of Georgia wished to assist in giving an elementary education to their children. That board was thus irregularly appointed against the spirit and the letter of the laws of Georgia and it was made *permanent* against all Republican Customs and traditions, so that the Board claims the privilege of disposing *forever* of the public educational fund, without any mode of redress if some parties think themselves injured by its operations.

Verot then proposed, again directly to the city council, his own views on how the matter should be settled. He has conceived a settlement, he wrote, that would be creditable to the council, in keeping with the spirit of the existing laws of Georgia, and conformable to the practice of the most enlightened governments of the new and old world. In stating his plan he denied any wish to see the public system fragmented into denominational schools, as the board had warned would happen.

> This plan is to recognize the Catholic Schools of this City as a collateral branch of the public schools maintained and supported at the public expense. The public schools already existing meet with the desires and approbation of the various religious denominations of the City; none of them have, so far as our knowledge extends, taken exception to them; we would be sorry to disturb

[38] "An Act to establish a permanent Board of Education for the City of Savannah . . ." March 26, 1866, Charles J. Jenkins, governor. The Act is reproduced in ASCH, Minutes, December 9, 1868. Possibly Verot's criticism of the authority of the 1866 legislature was based on reasons cited in Coulter, *South During Reconstruction* (Baton Rouge: Louisiana State University, 1947), "The new [President] Johnson organizations [of 1866] were a little less than normal state governments, so considered by the armies of occupation and by Johnson himself, and utterly repudiated by Congress. The army . . . was omnipresent, ready to impose its will against the states, disallowing their laws and interfering with their courts"; 36–37.

them in the enjoyment of the privileges they possess, and they do
not desire or ask any subdivision of the schools. But this separate
organization is imperiously demanded with regard to Catholics, and
the motives upon which this separation is required rest upon the
liberty of conscience, the bill of rights, and the imprescriptible and
inalienable privileges of parents to educate their children in a manner which will not be at variance with their religious convictions.
. . . The coloured children likewise whom we have undertaken to
educate at great expense, which has almost become unbearable, will,
under the parental care of the Sisters of St. Joseph, have their part
in the gratuity of the City, and will, it is hoped, increase the
number of orderly and industrious inhabitants of the city.

The bishop then listed a number of precedents to support his
plan which he found to be operating, in one form or another, in
Canada, France, Prussia, and other areas under "enlightened liberal
influence."[39] Under the council's own "enlightened appreciation"
and "true liberality" he fully expected that some justice would be
done to the Catholic children who, forming nearly one half of the
poor class "which the State of Georgia wished to assist in a special
manner," could not physically be accommodated in the already overflowing public classrooms. If the council follows his plea, "you will
inaugurate in Savannah an honorable policy which will be a noble
example of liberality to other places, and will maintain peace and
harmony on a point which may otherwise easily engender feuds and
discords."

During the three months that followed the last refusal of aid for
Verot, and before the above letter was laid before the council, the
bishop's newspaper, *Banner of the South,* had opened up its big guns
in strategic support. From Augusta, Abram J. Ryan's gifted pen
laid down a weekly salvo, beginning with a point-by-point refutation of the board of education's replies of 1867 and 1868.[40] Ryan's
articles objected particularly to the board's defense of its schools
as not denominational or sectarian, and cited one of the textbooks
currently in use at Savannah, Wilson's *Outlines of History.* "Many

---

[39] Cf. the Catholic liberal Isaac Hecker speaking in New York two months
later: "Catholic Austria does this [allots public funds to parochial schools] for
Protestants; Catholic France does this for Protestants; Protestant Prussia does
this for Catholics; Protestant England does this for Catholics — shame on Americans, who pretend to be lovers of fair play, not to give to Catholics what Austria
and France give to Protestants (applause)." *Banner,* May 1, 1869.

[40] *Banner,* December 28, 1868; January 9, 1869.

of its pages," Ryan wrote, "insult the faith of the Catholic. Its
religious spirit is *Protestant* . . . and still, with sublime non-
chalance, you assert that there is nothing *sectarian* in your School
system." As for the principle that the board laid down with regard
to taxation and the distribution of its benefits, Ryan seems at first
to have been hard-pressed for an answer, saying only that it was
offered as "an accepted axiom" when, in fact, its truth had not yet
been proved. A week later, more sure of his thoughts, Ryan said
that exclusion of Catholics from the tax fund benefits was discrimination, and in violation of the rights inherent in the American
philosophy of taxation.[41]

The New York *Freeman's Journal* leaped into the fray toward
the end of January, condemning the "very unfortunate piece of
bigotry at Savannah, Ga." where city authorities, "impregnated
with the direct form of New England Puritanism, are running the
Yankee Machine known as Public Schools," and refusing to give
attention to the appeal of local Catholics.[42] Nor were Protestant
quarters inactive: the Southern Methodist organ, *Christian Advocate,* delivered a lengthy attack on the "Fathers" in Savannah under
the title "Catholic Priests at War with the City Schools."[43] Among
other things, it said: "It has been a year since one of these 'Fathers'
said that he was 'glad the negroes were in power, for it would
break up the public schools.' It seems, now, that he only uttered
in advance the sentiment of the Catholic organ [*Banner*]." In
February, Bishop Verot probably received Hecker's *Catholic World*
issue of that month, in which the latter quoted with satisfaction
an editorial in *The American Educational Monthly:* "We are quite
sure that if the Catholics were the majority in the United States,
and were to attempt such an injustice [as that involved in the school
question] our Protestant brethren would cry out against it, and
appeal to the wise and liberal examples of Prussia and England,
France and Austria!"[44] Hecker himself would complain a short
time later: "You have got us down now . . . if you keep up this
injustice until we get the power — we have got to have it, it is

[41] *Banner,* January 15, 1869. Cf. Hecker, speaking later in New York: "All
we ask is, if we give a certain amount of the taxes that go for education, we
should have also the right to say how that taxation should be distributed
(applause)." *Banner,* May 1, 1869.

[42] Quoted in *Banner,* January 30, 1869.

[43] Quoted in *New Orleans Morning Star,* January 31, 1869.

[44] Quoted in *The Catholic World,* VIII (February, 1869), 695.

coming — then you know it is natural for men to take revenge. Now we do not wish to do this. Treat us fairly, and when our turn comes we will treat you fairly."[45]

Whatever the merits of the arguments on either side, by the end of June, Bishop Verot had reason to believe that by fighting hard he had appreciably strengthened his position. It must have been a great satisfaction to him to learn that on June 23, 1869 the board of education reported to the city that it was "manifest that the question now before the Council is one of great social and practical importance," and that "with a true spirit of liberality and concession, we must believe that it is a practicable thing for the citizens of Savannah to harmonize and cooperate in the great and noble work of educating the children of our city."[46] It was the first breakthrough.

The statement of June 23, announcing a reversal of the board for education policy, was accompanied by a detailed ten-point "Plan for placing the Catholic Schools under the control of the Board of Education." Some of the provisions bear resemblance to Verot's 1867 plan, although nothing is said in them about Catholic representation on the board.[47] In sum, it emphasized the board's intention to maintain a strict control over the Catholic buildings and their management; over the curriculum and textbooks "except books on History which may be such as are commonly used in Catholic Schools"; and over the qualifications of the teachers, among whom "Catholic teachers shall be preferred." On August 3, Verot submitted a counterplan of five points.[48] Not unexpectedly, these points suggested further concessions to the Catholic character of the schools. The first four points repeated word for word Verot's original petition in 1867, adding only, in the fifth point, a provision for closing the schools on Catholic holy days (which the board had suggested in its own proposition). Verot even closed

---

[45] Quoted in *Banner*, May 1, 1869.

[46] ASBE, Minutes, June 23, 1869.

[47] One of the members on the board by this date was a Catholic, J. B. Read, M.D.

[48] ASCH, Verot to Dr. J. J. Waring, Chairman of the Committee on Education [of the City Council], August 3, 1869. Signed by Verot and Father William Hamilton, president of the "Catholic Free School Association, St. Johns Parish," also by eight parishioners connected with the Association.

with the same words he had used in 1867, hoping that "we can all . . . unitedly support a system of public schools which will be an object of pride to our entire community."

Taking both plans under advisement, the city council placed the matter in the hands of a four-man committee, which conferred with the board and with Bishop Verot and his supporters. On August 18, 1869, it reported to the council in the form of majority and minority reports. The minority of one, James J. Waring, recommended "that the Council accept in good faith this last preposition from Bishop Verot," but added that such acceptance would mean petitioning the Legislature for amendment of the 1866 act establishing the board of education. With this point and with Waring's belief that three Catholics should be admitted to membership on the board, the majority report disagreed. The three gentlemen who formed the majority, William Hunter, Edward C. Anderson, and E. A. Soullord, expressed their settled conviction that simple division of the educational fund according to religious denominations would work "a great evil" on the public school system; they suggested furthermore that Catholic representation on the board, as desired by Verot, would be "impolitic," tending to divide that body's purposes. Nonetheless, the majority were not unwilling to grant the basic justice in the bishop's petition and advised some form of compromise between the two propositions submitted as being the most likely means of settling this long-discussed "bone of contention." For its part, the majority report felt the board's draft to be "as generous as the basis upon which the Educational Board rests will permit," and it desired to "urge it upon our Roman Catholic friends." But it called for arbitration: "Your Committee think now they have arrived at a point where both parties, the Board of Education and the Petitioners, cannot fail to understand each other fully, and as the difficulties are so nearly solved, they now propose to leave the matter with the respective parties in interest, seeing no reason why they may not agree, and recommending that an amicable adjustment at an early date be consummated. . . ."

In substance, both reports were favorable to Verot's idea; they differed only in the means proposed to implement it. The basic unanimity of the Council was reflected in its final decision, made a week later on the resolution of Alderman William H. Burroughs:

Resolved, That the Council adopt the majority report of the committee on education, and that the same be referred to the Board of Education, with the recommendation from Council that the children of our Roman Catholic fellow-citizens be received under the charge of the public school system at the earliest day practicable, and with the further recommendation that as vacancies occur in the Board of Public Education such vacancies be filled so that all classes of our community now entitled to be educated under the charter of the Board of Education may be fairly and indiscriminately represented in said Board of Education.[49]

The major victory had been won, and Verot could relax. He appointed Father William Hamilton as his personal negotiator to adjust existing secondary disagreements between himself and the board, and, in October, sailed to Europe for the Vatican Council. The lengthy and detailed arbitration which ensued can be studied in the minutes of the board. The two parties reached a conclusion in the spring of 1870 after a long effort on Hamilton's part to improve the plan in the Church's favor.[50] Hamilton eventually accepted a plan in which all the provisions of the two earlier propositions were incorporated save that one requiring admission of three Catholics, including a priest, to membership on the board. On the evening of May 17, 1870, the board adopted a report urging immediate action on the agreement.[51] A further motion was offered by Solomon Cohen, member of the board, and unanimously adopted by that body: "Resolved 'that the Secretary forward to the Revd. Father Hamilton a copy of the report made and adopted this evening, and request him to inform the superintendent the earliest day when the teachers of the Catholic Schools will be ready for examination.'" The Catholic Public school was under way. The plan behind it read as follows:

1. The Catholic schools shall be received under the control of the Board of Education.
2. Catholic teachers shall be preferred for these schools, when such as are qualified can be obtained.

[51] ASBE, Minutes, May 17, 1870.
[50] "The delay to consummate the union which at one time threatened to result in entire failure, was caused by a misunderstanding between the negotiating parties." ASBE, Report of W. H. Baker, Superintendent of Schools, printed in Minutes, September, 1870.
[51] ASBE, Minutes, May 17, 1870.

3. The text-books used in these schools shall be the same as are used in the other Public schools, except books on history, which may be such as are commonly used in Catholic schools.

4. These schools shall be opened with reading the Scripture and the Lord's Prayer. Such versions of Scripture may be used as the teacher may prefer.

5. The school buildings shall be under the control of the Board of Education.

6. The Trustees[52] of the Catholic school building shall have the power to withdraw them from the Board of Education at the end of any school year, whenever they are dissatisfied with the arrangements, provided that they shall give three months' notice of such withdrawal.

7. In the case of such withdrawal the Board of Education may remove all apparatus, books, movable fixtures, and furniture which they may have furnished for these schools.

8. The Board of Education shall have full control of the discipline, instruction, and general management of these schools, the same as of the other schools under their care, including also the length of sessions, the arrangement of school, courses of study, work and duties, and all the interests of the schools.

9. The teachers of these schools will be expected to attend the meetings of the Normal class the same as teachers of the other Public schools. They will give respectful attention to the suggestions and instructions of the Superintendent, and are expected to exert themselves to carry out his views in the management and instruction of their schools.

10. The holidays shall be such as are usually given in Catholic schools.[53]

Preparations immediately got under way for opening Cathedral School and St. Patrick's School on a public school basis in July of the same year. The teachers of the two schools were examined

[52] Hamilton, mindful of the lay-trustee controversy that had racked the American Church before the war, had attempted unsuccessfully to persuade the board to change this wording. ASBE, Minutes, May 17, 1870.

[53] ASBE, Report of W. H. Baker, Superintendent of Schools, printed in Minutes, August 14, 1871. One stipulation in the agreement was not published in the plan itself, but later was alluded to in Baker's report, *ibid.* "On the other hand, it was agreed and distinctly understood between the two parties that religion was not to be taught in the schools during the hours which, by the rules of the Board, are set apart for proper school work. After the work of the session is completed, there could be no objection to the rooms being used for religious purposes. . . ."

and found to be adequately educated, though inexperienced.[54] Considerable repairs were needed to place the Catholic buildings on a similar footing with the rest of the system. Textbooks, blackboards, and other necessary schoolroom appurtenances were also in poor condition or lacking altogether. The desks in use were heavy and clumsy and the benches were without backs. "To require children to use these seats for four or five hours a day would not only be uncomfortable, but really injurious," decided Superintendent William H. Baker; however, he continued, "when these facilities are provided, there is every reason to believe these schools will rank with the foremost in the system."[55] Twenty-five hundred dollars was expended on these needs during the first year.[56] In September, according to the reports of the principals, 811 pupils enrolled in the two schools. The board promptly assigned fourteen additional teachers, bringing the total number of teachers in the system to forty-three, and the total number of pupils to 2438 as compared with 1754 pupils the year before. Superintendent Baker reported in the same month that "the position I occupy has enabled me to ascertain the views of all parties in the community and it gives me pleasure to report that the end attained has received almost universal approbation." He thought it useful to add: "There was no compromise of principle on either side. If mutual concessions were made, they were only such concessions as honorable men are ever ready to make to accomplish a great and good end." Because there were a few citizens who were under the impression that "honest principle had been yielded on one side or the other," he hoped that his statement would disabuse their minds of that thought. Mayor John Screven was also pleased at the outcome: "The result of this settlement is a uniform and inexclusive system under which all children in the community may enjoy the advantages of this great public beneficence."[57]

When Ignatius Persico, Verot's successor to the See of Savannah, arrived in October, 1870, he announced his pleasure to the board members, saying "the plan is unique."[58] In April of the year following, Persico took part in the board's examinations of the stu-

[54] ASBE, Minutes, June 7, 1870.
[55] ASBE, W. H. Baker, "Report," in Minutes, September, 1870.
[56] Ibid.
[57] Quoted in Gamble, Mayor's Report, 284.
[58] Quoted in ASBE, W. H. Baker, "Report," in Minutes, August 14, 1871.

dents of Cathedral and St. Patrick's Public Schools. "The Bishop
said he was familiar with the school systems which prevail in
the British colonies, in England, and America, and that the system
adopted by Savannah is superior to them all which had been
brought to his notice."[59] News of the plan seems to have filtered
very slowly to the North, where it did not come to the attention
of the Catholic papers until 1873. In February of that year the
Brooklyn *Catholic Review* announced the plan, and said that it
"reflects the greatest credit upon the liberal spirit and justice of
the Board of Education . . . and ought on every ground, in this
country of equal rights, to be copied in every city of the land."[60]
Later the paper editorialized that in the long-contested school
question, "Savannah has taken the initiative in the adoption of
a just and equitable system."[61] The Boston *Pilot* agreed: "The
City of Savannah, Georgia, is, so far as we know, the only one
wherein Catholics receive pay for conducting schools for Catholic
children. . . ."[62] The *Pilot* was gratified to learn, from the superintendent's report of 1872, that "the system . . . has proved most
satisfactory to all concerned, and has not been jarred by the
slightest discord,"[63] and it communicated the news to "unthinking
people" who warned of "the harm that is to come to the cause
of popular education from allowing Catholic schools to participate
in the school fund."[64] A letter writer from Savannah told the
Pilot that "Bishop Verot, as a matter of course, was exceedingly
anxious for its [the plan's] success, and did all in his power toward
it."[65] The letter continued:

> . . . Several places have already followed our liberal example, and
> Savannah justly lays claim to being both the originator and pioneer
> of a system of general education that meets all issues, disposes all
> controversies, suits all classes, allays all prejudices, and promotes
> feelings of love and friendship. . . . To [Verot and the "protestant
> liberality" of Mayor Screven, the Council and the Board] it is that
> not only the Catholics of Savannah, but of the entire United States

[59] Savannah *Daily Republican,* April 25, 1871.
[60] *Catholic Review,* February 21, 1873.
[61] Quoted in Boston *Pilot,* May 24, 1873.
[62] *Pilot,* February 15, 1873.
[63] ASBE, W. H. Baker, "Report," printed in Minutes, August, 1872.
[64] *Pilot,* February 15, 1873.
[65] *Ibid.,* June 2, 1873.

are indebted for a school system that is as simple as it is effective, and is so rapidly gaining in public favor that several cities have adopted it.

Of the "several cities" to which the letter refers, the writer may have had in mind the example of Macon, Georgia, where in 1873 Mount de Sales Academy, operated by the Sisters of Mercy, was integrated on the Savannah plan into the Macon and Bibb County Public School System.[66] St. Mary's Academy in Augusta became a unit of the local public school system, also along Savannah lines, but not until much later, in 1890.[67] Catholics in Atlanta were unsuccessful in their efforts to secure a school accommodation.[68] And a similar attempt failed in St. Augustine, Florida, where Bishop Verot hoped to reproduce his Savannah triumph. Under the bishop's prodding, "the Catholics of St. Augustine" petitioned the state legislature in 1875 "to apportion moneys in the different schools in proportion to the average attendance of the pupils." The petitioners "ask only what is done now in Savannah, what is done in Canada and in Prussia, where there are Catholic Schools and Protestant Schools authorized by law."[69] The legislature refused to act, however, and the plan failed of passage.

The *Pilot* letter writer may also have heard of the accommodation worked out in 1873 at Poughkeepsie, New York, between Father Patrick F. McSweeney, head of St. Peter's Parochial School, and the local board of education. Under the Poughkeepsie Plan, approved by Archbishop McCloskey, the board elected to rent the parochial school building and its furnishings during the school hours at the nominal sum of one dollar per year, otherwise to run the school along lines similar to the Savannah Plan.[70] There does not seem to have been any causal connection, however, be-

---

[66] See Sister Mary Felicitas Powers, R.S.M., "A History of Catholic Education in Georgia" (unpublished master's thesis, The Catholic University of America, 1952), 54.

[67] *Ibid.*, 41.

[68] Robert H. Hollingsworth, "Education and Reconstruction in Georgia," *Georgia Historical Quarterly*, XIX (October, 1936), 238. See Philadelphia *Telegraph*, September 7, 1883: "The Catholics of Atlanta several years ago sought similar privileges, but were opposed by Senator [Joseph E.] Brown and Congressman Nathaniel Hammond, members of the Board of Education."

[69] *Freeman's Journal*, January 22, 1876.

[70] See the Poughkeepsie Plan in Reilly, *School Controversy*, 75.

tween it and the Savannah compromise. The Poughkeepsie Plan would last until 1899, when certain local citizens brought a charge of sectarian favoritism against the board of education.[71] Before the end, its general features would spread to other municipalities,[72] and it would achieve a certain notoriety as a precedent for similar plans inaugurated under Archbishop Ireland at Faribault and Still-water, Minnesota, in 1891, at the height of the controversy surrounding that prelate. Under Ireland's arrangement, made one year after his N.E.A. address and popularly called the Faribault Plan, Catholic school buildings were rented to the city under the same general terms as those secured earlier at Poughkeepsie.[73] It is worth noting that in neither place did the prelates in authority, McCloskey or Ireland, achieve quite the full and formal integration into the public school system that characterized the Catholic public schools of Savannah. The integration was intimate enough, however, to cause a storm of controversy when Ireland's rhetorical flourishes first brought the notice of American Catholics to what had been going on in the country since Verot's breakthrough in Savannah.[74]

Conservative Catholics, both clerical and lay, had not previously viewed the mounting movement of school compromises with any special alarm. But Ireland was committed to a number of causes, e.g., the Knights of Labor, The Catholic University of America, Negroes, and secret societies, that bore the brand of a liberalism that many Catholics sensed as inimical to the Church's best interests; and when he put into practice at Faribault and Still-water everything that he had said in the abstract before the N.E.A., the tocsin sounded.[75] Conservative prelates like Michael Corrigan,

---

[71] For the circumstances which brought the Poughkeepsie Plan to a close, see Gobel, *Public Funds,* 493–494.

[72] Reilly, *School Controversy,* lists the various plans initiated between the Savannah Plan and the Ireland controversy, 76–77. In many cases, as Burns notes, where a plan similar in general form to Verot's plan was in force, it was based upon nothing more than a mutual understanding between the pastor and the civil and public school authorities, no formal contract being drawn up. The same tacit understanding lay at the basis of Ireland's Faribault Plan (see below). Burns, *Growth and Development,* 248, 261.

[73] The details of the Faribault Plan are given in Gobel, *Public Funds,* 495, and Reilly, *School Controversy,* Chapter III, "Archbishop Ireland's Plan," 67–106.

[74] See Reilly, *School Controversy,* 80–160.

[75] Gibbons' biographer thinks that the earlier plans of Savannah and Pough-keepsie went uncontroverted by conservative Catholics as long as they did because

Archbishop of New York, Bishop McQuaid of Rochester, and Bishop Nicholas Matz of Denver condemned the compromises as being unworthy concessions to "secularism," Matz saying, in an obvious play on Ireland: "May our right hand be withered if ever we give our approval to such a compromise."[76] Ireland, for his part, complained to Gibbons that "I have found myself in a singular predicament on this whole Faribault matter. I am between two enemies — one Catholic and one Protestant. If I placate one, I arouse the other . . . [but] public opinion favors us."[77] Catholic critics eventually became sufficiently aroused to send the matter to Rome, where condemnation of the school compromise movement was sought from the Roman Curia. Gibbons quickly wrote to Pope Leo XIII in Ireland's defense: "When we think that more than half of our children attend the public schools, and in spite of all we can do, will continue to attend them, we cannot refrain from praising Mgr. Ireland for what he has done and obtained."[78] He went on to cite school compromises that antedated the Faribault Plan in New York, Milwaukee, Albany, Buffalo, Erie, Harrisburg, Peoria, Rochester, and Savannah. "In the last named city, all the Catholic schools are in the same condition, and Mgr. Gross,[79] Archbishop of Portland, before his translation to Oregon, did not hesitate to say at our meeting [of the Archbishops in St. Louis, November, 1891] that he had always thanked himself for that state of things."[80] Ireland, too, cited the Savannah Plan in his own defense, telling the Vatican that "in the diocese of Savannah Bishop [Thomas A.] Becker[81] has it [the school compromise] in operation in all the Catholic schools of his Episcopal city."[82]

Impressed by the Ireland-Gibbons argument, the Vatican decided in April, 1892, that *tolerari potest* — "it can be allowed" — which Ireland exaggerated to mean a "full vindication" of the Faribault

---

no one with Ireland's "personality and language" had turned them into a national cause. John Tracy Ellis, *The Life of James Cardinal Gibbons* (Milwaukee: Bruce, 1952), II, 658. Cf. Curti, *American Educators*, 348–352.

[76] Quoted in Cross, *Liberal Catholicism*, 142.

[77] AAB, 89-B-2, Ireland to Gibbons; quoted in Reilly, *School Controversy*, 86.

[78] AAB, 89-O-1, Gibbons to Leo XIII, March 1, 1872, translated from the French and quoted in *ibid.*, 146.

[79] William H. Gross occupied the See of Savannah from 1873 to 1885.

[80] *Ibid.*, 147.

[81] Becker acceded to the See of Savannah in 1886 and died in 1899.

[82] Ireland's "Memorial" to the Sacred Congregation for the Propagation of the Faith, n.d., probably April, 1892; quoted in Reilly, *School Controversy*, 255.

Plan. Under the circumstances he was more correct than his shocked conservative critics, like Corrigan, who interpreted the decision to read: "Faribault system condemned. Special case tolerated." In the summer of that year Leo XIII dispatched Archbishop Francesco Satolli to the United States. Satolli took the side of the liberals, and, at a meeting of the American archbishops in November, 1892, presented a series of theses which actually did confer full vindication on Ireland and his plan.[83] A recent student of this affair has concluded:

> The liberals, with this timely aid from Rome, had won a great victory. . . . Instead of being forced to choose between an American culture bent on giving youth the finest possible secular education, and a Church which insisted that an inadequate parochial school, or no school at all, was better than a nonsectarian one, Catholics were freed to accept profitable compromises with the state schools. . . . The applause of education enthusiasts and the explicit toleration by the Pope seemed proof positive that the American Catholics did not need to make a costly choice between religious and secular loyalties.[84]

Ironically, very soon after this turn of events, American Catholics had to make that costly choice again: the Faribault Plan was annulled by city officials in 1893, and the Poughkeepsie Plan fell apart six years later. All around the country, as the Church entered the twentieth century, school compromises that had been worked out so laboriously by Catholic and municipal authorities were either annulled under Protestant pressure, or else allowed to lapse under conservative Catholic apathy. The longest history was written by the first major post-Civil War school plan in the country, at Savannah, where the Catholic public schools continued to operate until World War I. Then, in 1916, George Richter, a Savannah attorney, initiated a movement to obtain a cessation of the school agreement, on the ground that it violated State of Georgia laws forbidding the use of public funds for sectarian purposes. Richter wrote the board to that effect in August, 1916, and carried his objection to State Superintendent M. L. Brittain in the month following.[85] Brittain sought an opinion from Attorney

83 See Reilly, *School Controversy*, Chapter V, "Tolerari Potest," 134–171.
84 Cross, *Liberal Catholicism*, 145.
85 ASBE, Minutes, August 14, 1916, and November 13, 1916.

THE CATHOLIC PUBLIC SCHOOL 191

General Clifford Walker, who ruled on October 11, that while "such arrangements were entered into in utmost good faith and with the highest patriotic motives, it must appear to any impartial mind that it is a violation of our government. . . ." He stated furthermore: "I was never more clear or conscientious in the opinion that in our country even a slight connection of a church with the government will engender bitterness and prejudice as well as real resentment, and finally prove of great harm to that church; that the absolute and perfect separation of church and state will eventually be completely justified and prove beneficial to church, state and people."[86]

In compliance with this ruling the Savannah Plan was terminated at a meeting of the board of education on December 18, 1916.[87] Bishop Verot's "just and liberal union," as he had seen it, was broken. And the era of the Catholic Public School was over.

---

[86] Savannah *Morning News,* October 12, 1916.
[87] ASBE, Minutes, December 18, 1916.

CHAPTER VIII

AN AMERICAN AT THE VATICAN COUNCIL

IN A PUBLIC CONSISTORY at Rome on June 26, 1867, Pius IX announced his intention to call an ecumenical council of all the bishops of the Catholic Church. The first such assembly since the Council of Trent (1545–1563), it would open on December 8, 1869, and be known as the Vatican Council. The news electrified the Catholic world, particularly in Europe, where the Liberal Catholic movement, already burdened with anathemas from the Pope's *Syllabus of Errors* of 1864, suspected that Rome was about to use the council in a power play to reinforce the *Syllabus.*[1] Conservative European prelates were delighted, and many hoped that such a council would not only dogmatize the *Syllabus,* but would show the Church's defiance of the nineteenth century as a whole.

The news was not lost on America, either, but in the United States it lacked the ideological overtones. American prelates looked on the council simply as a means of reaffirming the Church's religious mission amid a new, and increasingly secular, form of civilization. An examination of the Catholic press for the period 1867–1869 reveals a universal Catholic pleasure at the prospects, and there was occasional editorial pride that the bishops of the United States were about to participate for the first time in a general council. The *Mirror* of Baltimore was intrigued by the

---

[1] Although some liberal European prelates like Bishop Dupanloup of Orléans, France, at first welcomed the idea of a general council, they shied away quickly after September 27, 1867, when the membership of a preparatory commission on faith and dogma meeting in Rome agreed to take the 1864 encyclical *Quanta Cura* of Pius IX with its annexed *Syllabus of Errors* as the foundation of its work. See James J. Hennesey, "James A. Corcoran's Mission to Rome: 1868–1869," *CHR,* XLVIII (July, 1962), 161.

changed character of the bishops who would attend the council, as opposed to those who went to earlier councils: ". . . how little they resemble the submissive subjects of Constantine, or the paramount lords of the episcopal towns of the Middle Ages, these sons of Paris and of New York, brought up at the school of popular sovereignty and democratic equality."[2] Bishop Verot's paper, the *Banner,* exulted that "there is life in the old Church yet,"[3] and Verot himself, in a lengthy pastoral letter on the subject, predicted that the council would be etched in the annals of the Church as "a glaring epoch and era where the finger of God . . . may be exhibited to the gaze of mankind with new luster and overpowering majesty for the . . . permanent reign of order everywhere in Church and State." He went on to urge the Catholics of Georgia and Florida to "enter into the views, desires and intentions" of the Pope. "For is it not supremely proper that the members should follow the direction of the Head?"[4] As things turned out, about the only Catholic in Georgia and Florida who balked at certain of those views, desires, intentions, and directions was, ironically, Verot himself. But that strange eventuality happened somewhat later, and against a fascinating background which can be described here only in part.

While the incipient liberal mind within the American hierarchy was exercising its fledgling imagination on the Negro and school questions during the period 1865–1870, full-blown Catholic liberals in Europe were eating stronger meat and mustering for a final assault on the conservative bastions of European Catholicity. Stung by the anathemas of the *Syllabus,* and in a virtual eclipse for several years following it, Liberal Catholicism was rebounding strongly toward the close of the decade.[5] There was nothing at all like it on the American side of the waters, where the prelates were still too bound up with practical matters to give much rein to ideology. But the American members of the hierarchy must have

---

[2] November 6, 1869.

[3] August 15, 1868.

[4] Pastoral Letter, September 8, 1869, in *Banner,* September 18, 1869.

[5] For the best recent studies of the Liberal Catholic movement and the controversies surrounding it, see Aubert, *Pie IX* (Paris: Bloud et Gay, 1952), 224–311; E. E. Y. Hales, *Pio Nono* (New York: Image, 1962), Chapter VII, "Pio Nono *versus* Liberalism," 266–306. Hales stresses the fact that, prior to the *Syllabus,* Pius IX had been friendly toward liberal programs. Also see Mosef L. Althoz, *The Liberal Catholic Movement in England* (London: Burns & Oates, 1962).

viewed with extreme fascination the news that was coming out of France, Germany, and England. Not all the protagonists were bishops, but some were, and those who were not had important episcopal connections. The names most frequently mentioned in the American papers were, from France: Félix-Antoine-Philibert Dupanloup, Bishop of Orléans, Georges Darboy, Archbishop of Paris, and Augustin Cochin, whom we have met before;[6] from Germany: Ignaz Döllinger, his country's leading theologian; from England: John Henry Newman, the brilliant convert from Anglicanism, and Lord Acton, historian and litterateur.

It is safe to say that these men and their followers held certain basic views in common which we may list as follows: (1) that liberal-minded Catholics, despite the strictures of the *Syllabus*, should continue to press for liberal institutions, including disestablishment of the Church, a free press, and official toleration of secular governments and Protestant religions; (2) that the Church should declare herself in favor of free intellectual inquiry and of the independent rights of history, reason, and science; and (3) that Catholics everywhere should resist any efforts of conservative factions to further centralize ecclesiastical thought and discipline at Rome. Darboy appealed to Pius IX: "You have distinguished and condemned the principal errors of our epoch. Turn your eyes now towards what she may hold that is honorable and good, and sustain her in her generous efforts."[7]

Bishop Verot was already, or would be later, connected very loosely with some of the liberal protagonists. Dupanloup had been his classmate at Issy. Cochin he had visited in Paris in 1865. With Darboy he would make common cause at the council. And during that event he would win the admiration of Döllinger and Acton. Verot was not, however, as the American prelates at large were not, a doctrinaire liberal of the continental variety. This would become apparent later, despite the fact that Verot's voice *in* the council closely resembled certain of the Liberal Catholic voices *before* the council, particularly on the issues of free scientific inquiry and papal infallibility. One such example will be apt.

The question of papal infallibility rose slowly to the surface during the preparatory years of the council, 1867–1869, and gained

[6] Chapter V, footnote 50.
[7] Quoted in Aubert, *Pie IX*, 261.

momentum as the date of assembly neared. Although the commission of theologians in Rome, who were in process of preparing
the *schema de ecclesia,* i.e., the agenda for discussions on the nature
and powers of the Church, did not include any chapters on infallibility, the rest of Europe was greatly exercised over the possibility of its definition as a *de fide* doctrine.[8] Conservatives in general were worried about the characteristic tendency of the times
to discredit the unique, supernatural, and miraculous element in
Christianity, and knowing that this was a concern of Pius IX,
they began to press him to have the council define his teaching
authority as infallible. Certain prelates, like Archbishops Henry
Edward Manning of Westminster (England) and Victor Auguste
Dechamps of Malines (Belgium), episcopal spokesmen for what
the liberals called "neo-ultramontanism,"[9] sought a definition of
the doctrine as a means of strengthening the Papacy against the
"exaggerations" of Dupanloup and his friends. For his part, Dupanloup, with the encouragement of Döllinger, decided to strike back
with a plea for nondefinition. On November 11, 1869, one month
before the council, he published a brochure entitled *Observations
on the Controversy Raised Over the Definition of Infallibility at
the Future Council,*[10] and sent copies to all the bishops who had
arrived in Rome. It caused a sensation, for it was the first public
expression from a prelate on the inadvisability of a definition.[11]

---

[8] Although the dogmatic commission did not mention infallibility in the draft
schema, it did discuss the matter at length in its meetings. Hennesey, "Corcoran's
Mission," 162.

[9] A term used to distinguish the conservative faction in the Church during the
1850's and 1860's, who were antiliberal, both religiously and politically, from the
old ultramontane group of Montalembert, Lacordaire, and their friends, who were
liberals in the 1830's and 1840's but strongly supported the Papacy ("beyond
the mountains" — *ultramontane*).

[10] *Observations sur la controverse soulevée relativement à la définition de l'in-
fallibilité au futur concile* (Paris, 1869).

[11] "It was a real misfortune . . . that Dupanloup, who would, and possibly
should have been the dominant figure at the Council, so spoilt his position by
publicly taking up his standpoint in advance." Hales, *Pio Nono,* 381. Cf. Henri
J. Icard's "Journal," kept during the council, and quoted in Aubert, *Pie IX,* 321.
"As to the Bishop of Orléans, the general opinion is that he has compromised
himself and lost the position which he would have had at the council." There was
no chance that Verot would tip his hand in a similar fashion, since the American
bishops were apparently not aware until their arrival at Rome of the lengths to
which the agitation for infallibility had gone. Bishop McQuaid wrote home on
December 1, 1869: "Since coming to Europe I have heard much of the question

Such a definition, Dupanloup reasoned, was "inopportune" because
of the two-fold danger of angering the secular governments and of
alienating still further the Protestants. It was also questionable,
he said, on doctrinal grounds, and possibly incapable of accurate
definition. These, basically, were the same positions taken later
in the council by Bishop Verot. But similarity in argument does not
mean identity in principle; neither is *post hoc* the same as *propter
hoc*. Verot would take these positions for his own reasons, and
he would argue them in his own way — not as a Liberal Catholic
but as an American Catholic.[12] The difference was subtle but it
was important.

Verot with the vicar-general, Peter Dufau, sailed for Europe
in October, 1869,[13] and took up quarters with sixteen other American prelates at the North American College in Rome.[14] Altogether,
there were forty-eight archbishops and bishops and one abbot
from the United States in attendance at the council, plus some
seventy other prelates from English-speaking countries.[15] The total
number in attendance at the opening ceremonies in the right
transept of St. Peter's Basilica on December 8 was about 700, or
seventy percent of the Catholic hierarchy.[16] Within the weeks that
followed, each national group came to be known for its peculiar
characteristics and bent of mind. The Italians and Spaniards were
quickly noted for their traditionalist and scholastic approach to

on the infallibility of the Pope, which with us in America was scarcely talked
of." Henry J. Browne, "The Letters of Bishop McQuaid from the Vatican Council,"
CHR, XLI (January, 1956), 412.

[12] Interestingly, Verot in his youth at Issy had been an admirer of the Abbé
de Lamennais, from whose writings the Liberal Catholic movement may be said
to have emanated. His classmate, Dupanloup, on the other hand, was critical of
Lamennais, as recorded in Dupanloup's "Journal" for those years: "The system
of M. de Lamennais occupied a great deal of our attention. . . . I was strongly
opposed to it; Verot was for it. Very subtle." L. Branchereau, *Journal intime de
Monseigneur Dupanloup, évêque d'Orléans* (2nd ed.; Paris: Pierre Tequi, 1910),
34, circa 1821–22.

[13] Savannah *Morning News*, September 27, 1869.

[14] *Catalogo Alfabetico di Tutti i Padri del Concilio I° Ecumenico Vaticano*
(Roma: Osservatore Romano, 1870), cf. *Catholic Mirror*, February 19, 1870.

[15] The figure of forty-nine American prelates is for the council as a whole.
Seven active bishops were excused from attendance; five others retired or were
on extended sick leave; five more were consecrated during the conciliar period
but never came to Rome.

[16] The difficulty of determining the exact total number of bishops is explained
in J. Fessler, *Das vatikanisches Konzilium* (2nd ed.; Vienna, 1871), 13.

things; the Germans for their intense interest in history, particularly of Christian antiquity; the Belgians for their diplomacy and conciliatory manner; the Austro-Hungarians for their splendor and panoply; and the French for their brilliant conversation and intellectual enthusiasm. As for the Americans, the universal judgment seems to have been that they were republican in principle, democratic in practice, and informal in manner.[17] A typical appraisal was the following in the *Conservatore* of Naples:

> The [Spanish bishops] are strict observers of the discipline of the Church. You never, by any chance, meet them . . . walking unattended in the public promenades. Their composed and grave demeanor [is apparent to all]. . . . The Italian bishops are more vivacious in their manner. . . . The French enter into the work of the Council with great zeal, and push their opinions to the extreme point. . . . They hold conference in gilded salons, receive on fixed days, and in a word, carry into Episcopal life the social character of their national customs. The English and German bishops are . . . cold and speculative [and] have been occupied in studying the bearings of the situation. . . . The American bishops . . . are a little more uncouth, and if I may speak on so delicate a matter, more careless of external forms. They pay less regard to ecclesiastical costume, they talk more loudly and gesticulate more freely, and do everything in a more offhand way than their European prototypes.[18]

How progressive, or liberal, were the American bishops thought to be on their arrival at Rome? It is difficult to answer, because of the scarcity of published views about them at the time, a scarcity that is not surprising since the Europeans knew little about them in the first place. The Roman correspondent of the American French-language *Courrier des États Unis* wrote, in early February, 1870, what may or may not have been a European view, depending on the nationality of the correspondent. Of the writer's own liberal outlook there can be no doubt:

> . . . The Bishops of America move as a unit in the way of progress and liberty. They comprehend that a liberal government, based upon an equality of rights, is most favorable to the development of proper and healthy ideas; and that the prosperous condition of Catholicism, amid the varied and opposing interests of social and political life in America, is entirely due to the enjoyment of a liberty

17 Cf. Aubert, *Pie IX*, 324.
18 Quoted in *Pittsburgh Catholic*, April 23, 1870.

which is perfect and unrestrained. The absolutists of Rome take deeply to heart this decided attitude of the American Bishops. Their republican boldness enforces respect; and they will insist that their rights as free citizens of a free state shall not be abridged because of their being Catholics.[19]

The Baltimore *Catholic Mirror,* although it granted that the *Courier's* editor was too well posted to "be deceived by his correspondence," nevertheless treated this report with contempt, saying that it was "boldly, nakedly untrue."[20] In the same issue, as will be shown later, the *Mirror* also denied as "absurd" reports that Verot defended the rights of physical science in the council — which, in fact, he did. The *Mirror's* criticism of the *Courier* account, therefore, loses something of its force, and suggests that perhaps the Europeans spotted a progressive bent in the American prelates' minds that was lost on their American counterparts. This suggestion may appeal more strongly to the reader when it is shown below that the majority of the Catholic papers in the United States were caught unawares — and unbelieving — when half the members of the American hierarchy came out publicly against the definition of infallibility. In Paris, *Le Monde* also spotted a liberal leaning among the American hierarchy, but erred concerning the bishop's attitude toward infallibility, and the extent to which they supported liberty of worship and education:

> There are no disputations among *them* about the infallibility of the Supreme Pontiff, and yet they are *liberal,* if that word means *friends of liberty,* but not in the sense of our liberal Catholics of Europe. They demand with energy civil liberties, liberty of worship, of education, etc.[21]

The most interesting part of the *Le Monde* appraisal was the distinction made between American attitudes and Liberal Catholicism properly so called. Largely because of the constitutional disestablishment of religion from the state in the United States, the American bishops did not have to contend with quite the same problems as those that faced their European colleagues. American Catholicism thrived within the isolated freedom conferred on it by

[19] February 12, 1870.
[20] February 19, 1870.
[21] Quoted in the *Vatican* of London, December 24, 1869. The *Vatican* was a pro-Manning periodical established in London for the duration of the council.

the Constitution, and experienced no need to theorize on the proprieties of Josephism, Napoleonism, Socialism, on the legal rights of the Papal States, or on the ideologies of the various left and right political groupings that were taking shape in Europe during the middle and last quarter of the nineteenth century.[22] The fact that some Catholics on the continent hoped, and as many others feared, that the Papacy, perhaps in the council, would make the temporal power of the popes a matter of dogmatic belief, heightened the nature of the politico-religious controversies from which American Catholics were for the most part spared. An index of the practical-minded American Catholic's reaction to the web of religious and political intrigue in Europe was expressed by James A. Corcoran, vicar-general of the Diocese of Charleston, whom the American bishops had dispatched to Rome in 1868 to represent them at the preparatory commission of theologians. Corcoran wrote back to Spalding that what he had seen of conciliar matters touching civil government offended "the fundamental principles of our (American and common sense) political doctrine. . . ."[23]

Bishop Verot's own views on the left or right leanings of the

---

[22] See Roger Aubert, Jean Baptiste Duroselle, and Arturo Jemolo, "Le Libéralisme religieux au XIXème siècle," *Relazioni,* Vol. V, Storia Contemporanea, X Congresso Internazionale di Scienze Storiche, Roma (Firenze: G. C. Sansoni, 1955): "The absence of the problem coincides therefore with an absence of theoreticians, except at the close of the century when we have the Americanism affair"; 308. Bishops Gibbons and Lynch, who contributed regular reports on the council to the *Catholic World,* from December, 1869, through August, 1870, said of the German mind that it was "clouded in hazy metaphysics," of the English mind that it was "given to doubt and uncertainty," and of the French mind that "on a minimum quantity of facts or principles it will construct a vast theory." From these abstract preoccupations, they said, Americans had been comparatively free. "We owe it, probably, to the fact that with us all men are so busy trying to amass fortunes that they have little time and less taste for such abstruse speculations." *Catholic World,* XI (June, 1870), 417–418.

[23] AAB, 33-M-12 Corcoran to Spalding, Rome, March 1, 1869. The relations of Church and State, though down for discussion in the council, were never in fact discussed, to the considerable relief of the European governments. Gladstone, of England, who worried about that possibility, wrote to Acton: "Of all the prelates at Rome, none have a finer opportunity, to none is a more crucial test now applied, than to those of the United States. For if there, where there is nothing of covenant, of restraint, or of equivalent between the church and the state, the propositions of the Syllabus are still to have the countenance of the episcopate, it becomes really a little difficult to maintain in argument the civil rights of such persons to toleration. . . ." John Morley, *The Life of William Ewart Gladstone* (London: Macmillan, 1903), II, 511. The American prelates were probably as relieved as anyone else when the Church-State matter was tabled.

American bishops were confided to Henri J. Icard, S.S., rector of the Sulpician Seminary at Issy, France, on the day after the opening session. They reinforce the judgment that the American bishops were not concerned with implementing abstract liberal principles; the extent of their liberalism lay rather in their desire to find some way of accommodating the Church to the exigencies of recent secular civilization. Verot must have heard with some surprise that, despite the doctrinaire sounds that came from Dupanloup, Darboy, *et al.*, the liberal French prelates held a position very close, in general, to the American position. Icard records that he went calling on Verot at the latter's invitation, and that "the purpose of his meeting with me was to obtain some information about . . . the bishops of France, and about the nature of the dissensions that existed among them. He asked me in particular if what he had heard about the liberal French bishops was true, as some of these bishops had told him, that the majority of them believed a definition of the infallibility of the Pope to be opportune." Icard responded that he did not understand Verot's use of the term "liberal." All the liberal French bishops were in fundamental agreement on basic issues, but differed in the way in which they expressed themselves. All were agreed, for example, that liberty of the press, of worship, and of assembly were not good things considered in themselves, but that such liberties were necessary in times like the present. Their disagreements came on the issue how the Church should conduct itself toward "the modern situation," some adopting a reserved approach, others wanting the Church to move forward actively and take advantage of opportunities offered it. Icard then records: "M. Verot told me that the theory that I have just presented on liberalism was the basic idea of the American bishops."[24]

Icard may have been mistaken in his appraisal of the liberal French bishops, attributing to them less devotion to theory than animated their leaders, Dupanloup and Darboy, but a recent authority seems to bear him out.[25] It is also apparent that most of the Americans did have close similarities with the liberal French prelates

[24]ASS, unpublished "Journal" of Icard, entry of December 9, 1869, pp. 32–33. Icard was later superior general of the Society of St. Sulpice (1879–1893).

[25] Aubert, *Pie IX*, 328. Cf. Jean-Remy Palanque, *Catholiques libéraux et Gallicans en France face au Concile du Vatican, 1867–1870* (Aix-en-Provence, Faculté des lettres, 1962).

in the attitudes they adopted toward issues that came before the council. But it would be a mistake to say that the two groups were motivated by identical outlooks and concerns.[26] Events in the council would demonstrate how difficult it was to compare the Americans with any of the other episcopal groups. The Americans, and Verot particularly, addressed themselves to subjects that no one else was concerned about. And when they spoke on matters of common interest to all — and here Verot was singular again — they spoke in a manner quite unlike anything that had been heard before in the highest councils of Catholicity. They spoke with a new kind of voice, a voice that was practical, disingenuous, courageous, and to the point. No one better exemplified this peculiar American quality than Augustin Verot. No one showed himself more aware of coming from a new society with new and distinctive problems than the prelate whom later authors, not understanding either the man or his background, could only describe as the *enfant terrible* of the council. Sometimes in exaggerated form, causing laughter or rebuke, sometimes careless of protocol and ceremony, but always straightforward and plain, Verot would give the assembled bishops a lesson in what it meant to be an American.[27]

Without entering into a detailed analysis of the proceedings of the council and of the many complex theological issues that came

[26] Aubert tends to seek the reasons for American positions at the council in the immigrant extraction or early education of the prelates in question. Thus he places Verot in the position of an antiultramontane by reason of his French and Sulpician background. He describes Kenrick of St. Louis as possessing "quite Gallican ideas." *Pie IX,* 329. Aubert misses the importance and significance of their American backgrounds. So did Emilio Campana, *Il Concilio Vaticano* (Lugano/Bellinzona: Grassi, 1926), II, 749. To Campana the fact that Verot was educated by the Sulpicians in Paris explained all.

[27] Pius IX received a taste of that certain difference when he visited the American College on January 29, 1870, for ceremonies honoring a candidate for canonization. Archbishop Spalding took the occasion to deliver a discourse in Latin in the name of the American Church. Gibbons and Lynch described the scene to the *Catholic World*: "Toward the end of his discourse, the good archbishop brought in a few touches of true American wit. This is what Italians would scarcely venture on, on such an occasion, and it was to them unexpected. Even the Pope looked for a moment puzzled, as if he could not conjecture what was coming; but as he caught the point, a smile spread over his countenance, and the smile developed into a hearty laugh. As for the Italian prelates, at first they wondered — as who would not, at an American joke in the language of Cicero? — but at last not all their stately dignity could resist its force, and they laugh yet, as they repeat it." *Catholic World,* XI, (April, 1870), 129.

before it, we can follow Bishop Verot's course in the council by beginning straightaway with the first public debates in which he participated.[28] The council opened on December 8. Discussion on the chapters of a prepared *schema de Fide Catholica* (outline of the Catholic Faith) began on December 28 and continued until the ninth congregation of January 10, when the *schema* was referred to committee for revision, together with the observations on it that came out of the public addresses.[29] Of the thirty-five Fathers

---

[28] Among the many volumes published on various aspects of the Vatican Council, the following have been found most valuable. All the official documents and transcripts of the debates are in Joannes D. Mansi, *Sacrorum Conciliorum nova et amplissima Collectio* (Leipzig, 1923–1927), Vols. XLIX-LIII, and *Collectio Lacencis Acta et Decreta Sacrorum Conciliorum Recentiorum* (Freiburg, 1870–1900), 5 vols. The pertinent passages have been translated by the author. The best of the older histories of the council is Theodor Granderath, S.J., *Geschichte des Vatikanischen Konzils von Seiner ersten Ankundigung bis zu Seiner Vertagung. Nach den Authentischen Dokumentum* (Freiburg im Breisgau, 1906), 3 vols. A recent summary of the debates on infallibility is Umberto Betti, O.F.M., *La Constituzione Dommatica "Pastor Aeternus" del Concilio Vaticano I* (Roma: Antonianum, 1951). A good general history in English (but definitely infallibilist in tone) is Butler, *Vatican Council* (London: Longmans, 1930), 2 vols. The definitive American account is now, James Hennesey, S.J., *The First Council of the Vatican: The American Experience* (New York: Herder & Herder, 1963). Father Hennesey's work replaces an earlier, less exhaustive study by Raymond J. Clancy, "American Prelates in the Vatican Council," *Historical Records and Studies,* XXVIII (New York: United States Catholic Historical Society, 1937), 7–135. On the generally hostile and misinformed secular press there is J. Ryan Beiser, *The Vatican Council and the American Secular Newspapers, 1869–70* (Washington, D. C.: The Catholic University of America, 1941). The most thorough recent work in French is Aubert, *Pie IX,* which is sympathetic to the Opposition party. Hostile to the Church, though favorable to Verot, is J. J. Ignaz von Döllinger, *Letters from Rome on the Council by Quirinus. Reprinted from the Allgemeine Zeitung* (London: Rivingtons, 1870), based on letters received by Döllinger ("Quirinus") from Acton and Johann Friedrich, theologian to Cardinal Hohenloe and agent of the Bavarian government; see Aubert, *Pie IX,* 346–347. Also hostile to the council and Church, yet laudatory of Verot's role is George Gordon Coulton, *Papal Infallibility* (London: The Faith Press, Inc., 1932).

[29] Good descriptions of the procedures followed in bringing matters before the council, and eventually to vote, were given on their return by Gibbons, *Catholic Mirror,* October 8, 1870, and Lynch, *Banner,* July 9, 1870. Lynch outlined the general sequence: ". . . A draft, or *schema,* of each subject to be considered was drawn up. This draft was submitted to each of the Bishops present for his criticism in writing. These criticisms were referred to a standing committee, who drew up a new draft, which was discussed in the Council, and amendments proposed. The discussion, carefully reported by the stenographers, as well as the amendments, was referred back to the standing committee, who reported on the amendments, and the *schema* thus amended was voted on by the Fathers, one by one. Subsequent to this vote, the *schema* was considered for the third time by the

(as the attending prelates were called) who spoke on the matter, two were Americans, Archbishop Peter Richard Kenrick of St. Louis and Verot of Savannah. Kenrick emphasized in his address that the council's business was doctrinal and not controversial, therefore that the constitution resulting from this *schema* ought to be simple and straightforward, according to the example of Christ.[30] On January 3, 1870, Augustin Verot mounted the ambo, or speaker's platform, for the first time. He could look out on an impressive scene. The right transept of St. Peter's was crowded with rows of wooden benches covered with Brussels carpet, which rose in eight tiers on either side. On the benches, in prelatial vestments, sat 700 bishops in council.[31] From the ambo sonorous Latin had been rolling out all day into the cavernous aula, and some of it was being lost.[32] But those who could hear well were about to hear an American employ Latin in the service of new ideas; and they would know at the conclusion of his effort what the speaker meant when he told the gathering, *venio de America* — "I come from America."

Eminentissimi praesides, reverendissimi patres. . . .

The doctrine of the schema about the harmony between science and faith is contained in Chapter X, and the doctrine is firm, and evident; since, indeed, there can be no opposition between reason and faith: God is the Author of both, and truth cannot be opposed to truth. But the manner in which that truth is expressed, or, if we may say, the tone of this chapter, seems to me to be, of its very nature, exasperating and irritating to patrons of natural science. And that is very annoying, because it is useful, it is very useful,

---

committee, in view of the vote, and it was then again reported to be voted on *viva voce* by one of the three formulas — *Placet* (I approve!), *Non Placet* (I disapprove!), *Placet juxta modum* (I approve conditionally!). The votes recorded according to the last formula must be accompanied in writing by the condition attached to the vote. The *schema* was then taken in charge by the committee, in conjunction with the conditional votes, and was by them afterwards submitted for the final vote . . . and promulgated in the next public session of the Council."

[30] Mansi, *Collectio,* Vol. L, col. 126.

[31] A detailed description of the refurbished transept appears in the *Catholic Mirror,* February 5, 1870. Seated in order of seniority, Verot sat in group VIII, bench 5, seat 2, or about halfway down the right side, as one faced the papal throne.

[32] Many of the bishops had difficulty in hearing the speakers. Early in December, an awning of 150 feet was placed over the assemblage to improve acoustics, but it did little good. See Butler, *Council,* I, 170–261.

to the Church to have the friendship of promoters and patrons of the sciences. And that chapter seems in some way to be an excuse or justification for a policy that certain theologians and Catholic doctors have followed in the past. And I adduce a few examples as proof. When Christopher Columbus proposed to sail west with the intention of reaching the Orient, doctors and theologians rose up against his scheme. Now I come from America, in which the major part of the population is Protestant; and our Protestants in America, in their elementary books of geography, show pictures of an illustrious assemblage of doctors in their skullcaps, bishops in green mitres, and cardinals all in red, seated before Columbus, who wanted to prove the globular shape of the earth and the existence of an opposite side to the planet. Those doctors reproached him, on the charge that what he said went against reason and Sacred Scripture, and because the pope had condemned the idea of a side of the earth opposite to ours. But the opposite side does exist, and there are bishops here who come from there, and more than two hundred bishops who come from [North and South] America, thanks to Columbus who discovered the continents. I offer another example, that of Galileo. This example I offer with heaviness of heart, because an earlier policy of certain Catholic doctors and theologians — Romans included — has brought opprobrium upon religion, upon the Church, and upon this Holy See, which was always the patron of knowledge. Galileo was twice cited and condemned, because he defended the system of Copernicus dealing with the motion of the earth.[33] The policy of those theologians whom I mentioned was a disaster for religion. Allow me to speak my mind on this point, because I was a professor of astronomy, and I have better insight on the matter than some others. Now I say that that page of history is a disgrace to religion, and I desire and petition that that page be erased, if it can be done. It will bring glory, great glory, to the Vatican Council, if due reparation is made to the memory of Galileo. I ask this rehabilitation of Galileo in the name of science, but especially in the name of the Roman See, which was always before a patron of the sciences.[34]

Verot proceeded then into a discussion of geology, and of the

[33] See George de Santillana, *The Crime of Galileo* (Chicago: University of Chicago, 1955).

[34] The oration is given in full in Mansi, *Collectio*, L, cols. 163–169. Leone Dehon, a stenographer at the council, complained that Verot's Latin was remarkable for "*nombreux barbarismes*" like the following: "Columbus discooperuit Americam." Vincenzo Carbone, ed., Leone Dehon, *Diario del Concilio Vaticano I* (Rome: Tipografia Poliglotta Vaticana, 1962), 44.

theory among geologists that, from evidence of earth strata, the earth existed for a much longer time than Scripture seemed to warrant. He concluded his remarks on science by proposing that a statement be added to Chapter X of the *schema* (1) assuring science that the council did not intend to condemn contemporary astronomy; (2) expressly rehabilitating the ecclesiastical reputation of Galileo; and (3) granting liberty to geologists to discover what they could about the age of the earth and about the actual duration of the "six days" of creation.[35]

Verot then turned to Chapter XV of the *schema* dealing with the unity of the human species. Here he was plainly annoyed that the preparatory commission had presented a chapter that was impractical and beside the point. It was shot through with anathemas against pantheism, rationalism, and every other sort of philosophical heterodoxy. The dualism of Anton Günther seemed to be under particular fire.[36] Corcoran had written home during the preparatory stage, protesting against the concentration placed on "some Professor Scratchemback in some German university."[37] Verot now contributed his bit, saying that all this abstruse material in the *schema* was "utterly useless" (*prorsus inutile*). He added: "These men don't care about our anathemas. But they do care about our reasoning, which is inserted into the *schema*." And that reasoning ought to get down to cases, and concern itself with questions that really matter — the Negro question, for example:

> But, most reverend Fathers, it seems to me that the material in this Chapter XV has not been treated plainly and adequately, because the author of the chapter saw only the errors of certain Germans, and so spoke of errors — perhaps grave errors — which are no problem in America, England, or France. An example is this question of the unity of the human race. . . . I come from a diocese in which there are many Negroes, more than a half-million Negroes, in fact. Now the Negroes are not generated from the whites, nor the whites from the Negroes. Perhaps there are some here who think that when men live in a hot climate they become Negroes,

---

[35] Mansi, *Collectio*, L, cols. 164–165.

[36] See Ladislaus Orban, *Theologia Guntheriana et Concilium Vaticannum*, Analecta Gregoriana XXVIII, "Series Facultatis Theologiae, Section B, No. 13A" (Roma: Gregorian, 1950), in which the council's obsession with Günther is examined exhaustively.

[37] Corcoran to Archbishop McCloskey, Rome, May 25, 1869, quoted in Hennesey, "Corcoran's Mission," *CHR*, XLVIII (July, 1962), 173.

and that Negroes in a cold climate become white. That is an error, most eminent Fathers, which only causes laughter in places where the facts are known. . . . And so, I want to say that in America [there are some books] in which it is stated that there was a two-fold creation of man in the beginning: one creation of white humanity in the person of Adam, and another creation of Negro humanity, the latter being, according to these writers, a grade of animal between beast and white man. . . . Furthermore, in my diocese there is a certain Methodist preacher, a Protestant minister, who teaches *ex professo* — and many come to hear him — teaches *ex professo* that Negroes do not have rational souls. . . . Errors of this kind are more deserving of condemnation than the Germanic errors set forth in the *schema*. These errors I speak of are under-stood by the average man, while the aberrations of certain German philosophers are only comprehended by other philosophers, not by the people at large. And so, in the *schema* it should be stated what exactly is understood by the "human species," namely, that those creatures are men who have language, who can speak. . . . Who does not have speech, that is, words, does not have intellectual ideas.[38]

But, Verot went on, Negroes *do* have speech, and therefore an addition must be made to the chapter in question, to this effect: "But especially do we condemn the inept error of those who dare to assert that Negroes do not belong to the human family, or that they are not endowed with spiritual and immortal souls."[39] As for the obvious physical and lingual differences that characterize the tribes of man, he concluded that "it is equally absurd and impious to assert that those differences, which are transmitted through generation, argue the existence of two sets of first parents"[40] — a double creation of white and Negro. How the differences originated, he did not know — "there is a great scientific difficulty in ex-plaining the diversity of human tribes"[41] — but he was sure that man did not evolve from the ape.[42] Verot closed his discourse with

[38] Mansi, *Collectio,* L, cols. 165–166.

[39] *Ibid.,* L, col. 166. Because there has been some confusion and error on what Verot actually said here, the original Latin is given as follows: "Specialiter autem condemnamus errorem ineptum eorum, qui asserere ausi sunt, nigros ad familiam humanam non pertinere, nec anima spirituali et immortali praeditos esse."

[40] *Ibid.,* L, col. 166.

[41] *Ibid.,* L, col. 166.

[42] *Ibid.,* L, col. 166. Darwin's *The Origin of Species* had appeared in 1859; his

a technical examination of original sin,[43] in which he went after the ambiguity of theological terms that the *schema* attached to that doctrine (e.g., *verum et proprium*), and proposed in their stead a marketplace terminology (e.g., *macula*) that would not need exegesis to make it intelligible. He obviously had checked out references to the matter in past councils, with the result that he demonstrated here, as elsewhere, his competence to speak not only on the broad questions but also on the more refined and technical matters that came before the council.

The reaction to this address on January 3 makes an interesting record. The Roman correspondent of the Chicago *Tribune* wrote his paper to say that Verot's address was "the most remarkable ever heard in the Eternal City since the days of Rienzi . . . not only eloquent" but a "warning and a rebuke . . . a demand for practical legislation adapted to the changed circumstances of the world and a vehement excoriation of those who were letting mankind perish while they discussed impractical and non-essential things." The correspondent declared that "such a speech could not be kept secret" for it had "electrified" its hearers and was the "subject of discussion in all circles of Rome."[44] A code of secrecy had been imposed by the council on all its proceedings and debates, excepting the public sessions, but news of the debates seems to have circulated rather freely in Rome,[45] and as Verot's was the first address of a sensational character, it may be presumed that knowledge of it did in fact spread widely, as the *Tribune* claimed. Of course, the intelligence probably lost some of its verisimilitude after several days, and this is probably about the time that the Boston *Advertiser* got hold of it: "Before I

The Descent of Man, explicitly applying the evolutionary process to man, did not appear until after the council, in 1871.

[43] Mansi, *Collectio,* L, cols. 166–169.

[44] Chicago *Tribune,* February 6, 1870. Cola di Rienzi was a fourteenth-century Italian demagogue.

[45] See Aubert, *Pie IX,* 346–347. Indiscretions were frequent enough to nullify almost completely the secrecy provisions. Döllinger in Germany received full reports on the debates, although they were not always accurate. Some bishops gave information willingly to journalists from their own lands, and Pius IX himself explicitly authorized certain infallibilist bishops to divulge what they thought would be useful. In speeches on their return home, cited later, the American prelates warned against the inaccuracy of all the accounts, in both secular and religious papers.

became a bishop," Verot was quoted as saying, "I was a mariner; before I learnt theology, I was taught the exact sciences. As a man of the age and of progress, I protest against the doctrines of the Jesuits, which are not those of the Church of Jesus Christ. The Church should not, cannot put science on the Index."[46] The most interesting reaction, however, was that of the *Catholic Mirror* in Baltimore, which appeared in the course of a wholesale assault on the veracity of reports appearing in the *Courrier des États Unis:*[47]

The other extracts we give without comment. Their absurdity is so patent that we will not insult the intelligence of our readers by needless criticism. We insert them only as instances of that malevolent spirit which is sure to err against truth and charity whenever Catholicity is in question. Who, for example, could believe the following? "The Bishop of Savannah delivered a discourse which was a curiosity in its way to us, who are behind the times. He demands a revision of the judgment in the case of Galileo, on the ground that there is no such thing as a revealed science; and that the plain duty of the Church is to abstain from imprudent meddling in things which do not concern her."[48]

Bishop Verot's amendments to the chapter on faith and morals, including that urging the rehabilitation of Galileo, were not accepted (as neither was his statement on the Negroes, but for the reason that the chapter dealing with unicity of the human species was not included in the Constitution finally adopted).[49] His efforts probably did help, however, to produce a statement in the Constitution that recognized the independent rights of physical science, so long as those sciences did not transgress the limits imposed by their own principles and methods, and "invade and disturb the domain of faith."[50] It was probably this statement that Archbishop Purcell had in mind when he returned home: "I am happy to say that never were the rights of science better vindicated than they were by the Bishops of that assembly."[51] Or he may simply have

---

46 Boston *Advertiser,* January 27, 1870.

47 *Courrier,* February 12, 1870.

48 February 19, 1870.

49 See this *Constitutio Dogmatica de Fide Catholica,* in Latin and English, in Butler, *Council,* II, 248–275. For the history of changes made in the original *schema,* see I, 269–283.

50 *Ibid.,* II, 267.

51 Cincinnati *Catholic Telegraph,* August 25, 1870.

referred to Verot's address, which he described at some length to a large crowd at Mozart Hall in Cincinnati:

> An American Bishop, who was my fellow student forty years ago, in Paris, now the Bishop of St. Augustine, in Florida,[52] was one of the first to speak. He is a sound theologian, and a sound natural philosopher [scientist]. . . . He rose . . . and reproached the congregation of Cardinals composing the Roman Inquisition for having done injustice to Galileo, and he emphasized: "You Roman Congregation, you condemned him as teaching a doctrine contrary to the Scriptures when he taught the motion of the earth. . . ." He also addressed himself to the Spanish Bishops who were there arranged and their predecessors, for the harm they [did] to religion as well as to humanity and science by their unwise arguments against the possibility of the American part of the globe. . . . I do not mention this as a reproach to the Church, but [as] a warning that science had its rights, and that they [the sciences] should never be interfered with; that scientific men should pursue with the largest liberty their investigations.[53]

When preliminary votes were taken on the original *schema* on April 1, 515 voted *Placet* and 80, including Verot and 16 other American prelates voted *Placet juxta modum*. In the written observations they were required to make, every American who explained his reservation specified that he opposed, among other things, the phrase *Sancta Romana Catholica Ecclesia* — "Holy Roman Catholic Church" — saying that the word "Roman" was given too much prominence in the formula. Verot argued that the Church should be known under the simple title "holy Catholic Church." As usual, he had a practical story to tell. Some years back, he said, a farm in his diocese had been left to the "Catholic Church," but it ended up in the hands of Episcopalians who contended before a court that theirs was the "Catholic" and Verot's the "Roman Catholic" Church![54] As a small concession to the

---

[52] Verot was transferred during the course of the council to the newly erected See of St. Augustine. He received notification to that effect on February 25; see ADSA, Sacred Congregation of the Propagation of the Faith to Verot, Rome, February 25, 1870. Formal appointment took place on March 11; *Catholic Mirror,* April 23, 1870.

[53] *Catholic Telegraph,* August 25, 1870.

[54] Mansi, *Collectio,* LI, cols. 377 ff, 395–396.

American view, also put forward by the English, *"Romana"* was moved from second to third in line.[55]

Beginning on January 25, a new schema, *de vita et honestate clericorum,* on the life and morals of the clergy, was put up for debate. Verot took the ambo on the first day, and ranged over a large area, finally settling on an issue which, although a common-place at this date, was very touchy ground in 1870 — the question of the veracity of certain homilies in the breviary. Verot particularly took exception to the Lesson from St. Augustine for the first Friday in Lent. In the passage St. Augustine gave a "mathematical" explanation for the thirty-eight years that the sick man at the Pool of Bethsaida had been in his infirmity. Verot's encounter with the saint showed, if nothing else, his concern for facts. "I must confess," he said, "that I can never read this without distraction."

> President [Cardinal Filippo de Angelis]: Let the Right Reverend speaker speak with greater reverence of the holy Fathers.
>
> Verot: Most Eminent Father, I wish to speak with all reverence, but even Homer nods sometimes, and I will say no more on that subject. My next point is . . . [that] it was with great pain that I saw on the Lateran Piazza a thing which certainly is a stumbling block to educated visitors of Rome; for there is an inscription, "Here Constantine was baptized by St. Sylvester." That is not true; and it is no more necessary to prove that in this assembly than it would be to offer proof of the earth's motion. . . .
>
> President: Our subject here is the life and decorous behavior of the clergy; and the Most Reverend Bishop has already expressed clearly enough his desire for a reform of the breviary, and this suffices for the present.[56]

But Verot had a great deal more to say on other subjects, including the universal catechism that was being proposed[57] and

---

[55] For a full treatment of this issue, see Butler, *Council,* I, 278–281, and Hennesey, *Council of the Vatican,* 153–161.

[56] Mansi, *Collectio,* L, col. 540.

[57] On February 8 and April 29 he spoke at length on the catechism. After pointing out his unique situation — "my diocese has as many or more varieties [of religions and races] than perhaps other dioceses of the world" — he gave the plan his guarded approval. *Ibid.,* L, cols. 539–549, 735. Verot had recently published his own catechism: *General Catechism of the Christian Doctrine, on the basis adopted by the first plenary council of Baltimore for the use of the Diocese of Florida . . .* (Baltimore: John Murphy, 1869), 108 pp. A copy is in the Manuscript Collections of The Catholic University of America, Washington, D. C. Verot published another, shorter, catechism in 1873, *Short Catechism of the*

papal infallibility. The latter, as we have seen, was the major question to come before the council. Although not originally on the agenda, it became clear shortly after the new year that clerical excitement within the council, and popular excitement without, might push the matter onto the council benches in the form of a *schema* chapter. Indeed, on New Year's Day a petition or *postulatum* to that end had circulated among the Fathers, and ten American prelates had signed it.[58] Twenty other American prelates countered, on January 12, 1870, with a *postulatum* of their own. Because this petition crystallized the reasons of "inopportuneness" brought out later by the Americans who spoke against the definition, it is worth quoting in greater part:

> Most Holy Father [Pius IX]: . . . We humbly and sincerely beg that the question of defining the infallibility of the Supreme Pontiff as a Dogma of Faith be not proposed to the Council of the Vatican. Allow us to adduce from many reasons only three, which seem to suffice:
>
> 1. because discussion of the question will clearly show a lack of union and especially of unanimity among the bishops;
>
> 2. because under the conditions prevailing in our regions, where heresies are not merely spread with impunity, but are actually prevalent, the definition, far from attracting to the Church, would only further alienate those whom we desire to win. . . .
>
> 3. because we foresee that interminable strife would arise from it, which we fear would impede the work of the ministry and perhaps destroy altogether the fruits of this Vatican Council among non-Catholics.[59]

Among the signatures affixed to this document were those of Kenrick, Purcell, McQuaid, Domenec, Whelan of Wheeling, Edward Fitzgerald of Little Rock, and Verot. This group would be particularly outspoken on the issue, all but Purcell and Whelan sticking it out, unwavering, to the end. There is no doubt, from their

---

Christian Doctrine on the Basis Adopted by the First Plenary Council of Baltimore for the Use of Catholics (Baltimore: John Murphy & Co., 1873), 32 pages. A copy is in ASLA. Neither catechism mentioned *papal* infallibility, although in answer to the question, "Is there a principle or bond of unity of doctrine in the Catholic Church?" the 1869 catechism answered: "Yes, if any question arise concerning faith, the decision of the Church, that is to say, of the Pope and Bishops in communion with him is final. . . . For Christ has clearly promised to his Church infallibility, that is, the gift of not erring in the faith" (57).

[58] Mansi, *Collectio*, LI, pp. 644–646. Altogether 380 Fathers signed it.

[59] *Ibid.*, LI, cols. 680–681.

postulatum, and from their speeches later in the council,[60] that these seven prelates in particular sensed the necessity of casting off the intransigence that had marked American Catholicism since the 1840's, and that was particularly apparent in the Catholic press. A review of the Catholic press for the period 1860–1870 reveals a universally nourished hostility toward Protestantism. The early 1870 press, as we shall show below, was no exception: the editors at home were clamoring for infallibility as a new weapon in the struggle with non-Catholic society. The prelates named above, however, felt, as their *postulatum* stated, that the definition would add an unnecessary obstacle to the integration of Catholic purposes into American life — "only further alienate those whom we desire to win." That they were serious in this judgment is borne out by actions taken in the months subsequent, after a general *schema de Ecclesia Christi* (on the Church, but not including infallibility) was distributed, on February 22, for comment. Verot, Lynch, and Whelan attacked a chapter where the Church was said not to be a *societas libera* — a free society — since the expression, they feared, was misleading; Verot and Whelan, objecting to another chapter, insisted that the council give explicit recognition to the good faith of many non-Catholics, and asked that the *schema* be worded so as to give as little offense as possible; Verot, Domenec, and Whelan protested against the harsh tone of the passages dealing with the coercive powers of the Church; and Verot and Whelan asked that it be made clear that the Church imposed punishments that were spiritual only, and never on those who were not Catholics.[61]

On March 7, in answer to the irresistible momentum of the infallibilist bishops, and at the instance of Pius IX, the chapter on papal primacy from the *schema de Ecclesia* was introduced out of turn.[62] Attached to it was a formula for the definition of papal infallibility. Oral debate began on May 13, and fifteen days later Bishop Verot had his turn at the ambo.[63] He began by expressing

---

[60] See *ibid.*, LI and LII, *passim*.

[61] For these observations see *ibid.*, LI, cols. 731–930. The portion of the *schema* under consideration in these remarks never came before the council for discussion or vote.

[62] The sequence of these events is described in Hales, *Pio Nono*, 311–318.

[63] Mansi, *Collectio*, LII cols. 289–302. Cf. Butler, *Council*, II, 52–54; Coulton, *Infallibility*, 160–164; Betti, *Pastor Aeternus*, 199–200.

his sorrow at having to speak on a subject so agitating in its nature that it threatened the peace of the bishops and the honor of the Holy See. But he has studied, he said, the whole question with great diligence, "not in newspapers, but in Church history, in the councils and in the history of the popes."

And it seems clear to me that we do not have here the most essential condition for defining any question; we do not have that constant tradition of the Church which would be required for defining papal infallibility. And here I hope to produce not words, but arguments. We are dealing here, according to the *schema,* with the "separate" [*signs of disapproval*], with the "absolute" infallibility of the pope. . . . I say therefore that this proposition has no foundation in Tradition, and I will begin with the first century. [*Murmurs.*]

He began with the Acts of the Apostles and worked steadily through the centuries, exposing what he called the "monuments of antiquity" with both learning and wit. When his exposition at points produced laughter, he said, "It is easier to laugh than to answer."

It is true that the Irish believe in the pope's infallibility; but they also believe in their priests' infallibility — and not only do they believe it, but they beat with sticks any who deny it.[64] But will the Cardinal of Dublin say that they believe Adrian IV was infallible when he handed over Ireland to the King of England?[65]

---

[64] "In that very learned speech of his, which remains thus far unanswered, the Right Reverend Bishop of St. Augustine in North America (than whom no man in this assembly is more worthy of the respect due, at all times, and from all persons whatsoever, to the Episcopal dignity) remarked that the Irish Catholics believe their own priests infallible, and therefore (as he asserted) it was no wonder that they should consider the Pope of Rome infallible. It seemed to some that he was using an exaggerated expression, rather in joke than in earnest." *Speech of Peter Richard Kenrick, Archbishop of St. Louis, in the United States of North America, 1870* (Naples: De Angelis Brothers Printers, 1870), 16. Kenrick was prevented from giving this speech in the council, owing to a peremptory halt to debate on June 3. He had the speech printed and distributed instead. It appears in Mansi, *Collectio,* LII, cols. 453–481.

[65] Cf. Kenrick and Purcell, letter to Dupanloup, translated and published in the *Banner,* June 4, 1870: "Our citizens of Irish birth, who are the majority and chief support of the Catholic Church in the United States, will have much difficulty, *de la peine,* in admitting that Pope Adran [*sic*] IV, who was an Englishman, was infallible when he gave Ireland to Henry II, King of England." One cannot help thinking that this argument was put forth facetiously, and without any real fear, since even the primitive chapter on infallibility clearly de-

. . . The question should be studied in the monuments of the Church and in the history of the Church, not in periodicals and newspapers. I say from this ambo to all editors of religious papers what I once said to one of them. He had been laughing at the practice of the Roman Church in blessing animals on St. Anthony's day, and when I defended it his answer was so absurd that I thought it right to answer a fool according to his folly. So I said: "I will let you know the day on which animals are blessed in Rome that you may go and get a blessing, which you badly need. For the biggest brutes [maximae bestiae] that I know are the editors, especially the lay ones, of religious periodicals." [Laughter.]

Cardinal Annibale Capalti, who was presiding, rang his bell. But Verot continued:

Allow me a few moments. I conclude that pontifical infallibility is not an apostolic tradition, but an opinion introduced by a piety and a zeal not based on knowledge. Therefore for me to give my vote for it would be a sacrilege — yes, a sacrilege. [Loud signs of disapproval.]
Cardinal Capalti: That should not be said. . . . Therefore I beg that if you have nothing more to say except jokes, there is no use occupying the ambo any longer. [Many Fathers: "Come down!"]
Verot: Allow me to speak. I did not mean that this was a sacrilege, far from it; I meant that it seemed sacrilegious for me, for me to give my vote to an opinion which I cannot see defended by Tradition. . . . And would that I could bring an olive branch into this august assembly! [Laughter.] . . .
Capalti: I cannot permit this. Be good enough to come down from the ambo, and make room for the Bishop of Temesvar.

Archbishop Giulio Arrigoni of Lucca recorded in his diary for that day that Verot "made one of his accustomed serio-comic discourses which held the firm attention of the Fathers for an hour and a half."[66] Bishop James Goold of Melbourne, Australia, an infallibilist, wrote into his: "May 28th — Another . . . prelate from the United States spoke absurdly on the same [Opposition] side. He had to quit the pulpit. He had outraged the patience of all."[67] Émile Ollivier, Prime Minister of France at the time, and, though

limited the pope's inerrancy to matters of faith and morals; see Betti, *Pastor Aeternus*, 546 and 548.
66 Quoted in Betti, *Pastor Aeternus*, 200, n. 2.
67 Quoted in Patrick Francis Cardinal Moran, *History of the Catholic Church in Australasia from Authentic Sources* (Sidney/Wellington: Oceanic, n.d.), 806.

a non-Catholic, author of one of the most instructive and impartial books on the council, described Verot on this occasion as a "sarcastic orator, full of good spirits and wit."[68] In the United States, the event went unreported, except by the secular Toledo *Blade,* which erroneously described a "violent scene" after Verot "assailed" infallibility. The majority, it said, gave "protesting cries, and the clamor became so furious" that the president rang his bell and demanded that Verot retract; but Verot, said the *Blade,* insisted that "he was a citizen of a country where every opinion was free," and that "he would preserve his independence even in the Ecumenical Council."[69]

Despite the general misinformation of this last report, it was true: Verot was the citizen of a free country. And he had learned there how much more could be accomplished for Catholicism by the free exchange of convictions than had been accomplished so far by hostile aloofness or by the imputation of unworthy motives to the Protestant majority. On June 6 he rose to ask the Fathers to recognize his different situation in America.[70] He noted the words in the *schema,* "the gates of hell rise up everywhere from day to day with greater fury," and said that this "increasing hostility" is not demonstrated at all in America:

> I live among Protestants, and I have a pretty good opportunity to see how they conduct themselves. And I can say that, in my view, it is not accurate to hold that, among American Protestants, who are numerous, that there is increasing hostility toward the Holy See. Granted, some years past there was a hostility manifested on many occasions in America against the Holy See: but that hostility was directed toward the temporal power of the Holy See. . . .

Then, in language that reminds one of Gibbons and Ireland twenty years later, Verot continued:

> Most reverend Fathers, I confess frankly that this council gave me high hopes of obtaining some reconciliation for the Protestants — high hopes, to be sure, if the exposition of doctrine made by this council were made plain, mild, and soothing — as far as the truth will bear — concerning those points which are subjects of controversy

---

68 Émile Ollivier, *L'Eglise et L'Etat au Concile du Vatican* (Paris: Garnier frères, 1879), 283.
69 Toledo *Blade,* June 23, 1870, quoted in Beiser, *Secular Newspapers,* 230–231.
70 Mansi, *Collectio,* LII, cols. 497–499.

between Catholics and Protestants. . . . It seems to me that if the
exposition on those points is softened and moderated by the council,
then at least the door will be open. . . .

This address, which was revealing of the social reasons that motivated Verot's attacks on infallibility, ended in one of his famous
scenes, brought on by a scathing mention of the "whims of ultra-
montanists. [*Noises and voices: No! No!*]" Cardinal Luigi Bilio,
who was presiding, cautioned the speaker not to continue in that
vein, and Verot, after a few final shots at the *schema*, assented to
Bilio's request that he step down. From Rome, Lord Acton and Dr.
Friedrich, who were always alert to say the worst about Roman
control over the council, described the event to Döllinger in this
fashion: "At this, murmurs arose, and Verot remarked that a previous speaker — Volerga — had been quietly listened to while he
talked for an hour and a half about the Gallican school . . . and it
was only fair, therefore, to let him call the other school by its
name.[71] Hereupon, Bilio, who has assumed the role of *ex officio*
blusterer and terrorist, interposed in his manner of a brawling
monk, saying this topic had nothing to do with the preamble. . . ."[72]

Speaking again on June 10, and after nearly an hour of historical
proofs, Verot came again to the possibilities of trouble in America
resulting from the definition:

> . . . Now let me say that about twenty years ago there was a com-
> motion in our America, a very vehement and acrimonious commotion
> against Catholics, and many of our churches were burned. It is my
> opinion, I may say, that if we are saddled with the obligation of
> promulgating the *Syllabus* [*of Errors*], then that will be a sign of
> widespread conflagration, and all our churches will be burned.
> [*Voices: No!*]

The "voices" were right in this instance, and Verot himself was
probably aware that he exaggerated. Besides this, the *Syllabus* was
not really at question. But he would make his point somehow, and
went on to propose the following canon: "If any man say that the
pope has such plenary authority in the Church that he can dispose

---

[71] This much was true; see *ibid.,* LII, col. 499.

[72] Döllinger, *Quirinus,* 665. The historian G. G. Coulton, also no friend of
infallibility (or of the Church, either, in his case), wrote in later years that
"Verot was interrupted by men of whom the majority possessed not half his
learning, nor half of his practical achievements for the Church;" *Infallibility,* 166.

all things at his will, let him be accursed. [*Murmurs and laughter.*]"
This brought Cardinal Capalti to his feet:

We are not in a theatre to hear buffooneries [*scurras*], but in the
Church of the Living God to deal with important affairs of the
Church; and nothing should be said in this discussion that is contumelious or foolish or erroneous. Let the Most Reverend Father
pardon me if, fired with zeal, I have been compelled to say this:
for as often as he mounts the ambo he detains the Fathers of the
council in listening to his pleasantries [*facetias*]. [*Hear! Hear!*][73]

On June 30 the battle was obviously lost. But on that date Verot,
the last American to address the council, rose to make one final,
and futile, effort against the definition.[74] "I have thought it best,"
he said apologetically, "to read this present speech, lest I should
indulge in prolixity at the expense of truth; and in order to avoid
incautious expressions. [*Laughter and signs of approval.*]" It was
a "learned and vigorous speech"[75] that carried the Fathers through
the centuries one last time: St. Paul, Polycarp, Irenaeus, Cyprian,
Augustine, Vigilius, Honorius, etc. He took issue with one of the prodefinition American speakers, Archbishop Joseph Sadoc Alemany
of San Francisco, who had charged at the general congregation of
June 20 that "I was contesting with my own self, since I had sub-
scribed to the decrees of the [Plenary] Council of Baltimore held
some years back [1866]."[76] It was true, Verot answered now, that

---

[73] Mansi, *Collectio*, LII, cols. 585–591. In the same speech, Verot expressed fear
that the chapter on papal primacy conferred an absolutist-centralist character on
the pope's episcopal office that was not justified by papal history and tradition.
Not enough attention, he felt, was given to the office of the other bishops, who
shared with the pope both the distinction of descent from one of the original
twelve Apostles, and powers that were ordinary and immediate within their
proper dioceses. See Gustave Thils, *Primauté Pontificale et Prérogatives Episcopales,*
"Potestas Ordinaria" au Concile du Vatican (Louvain: Warny, 1961), who
criticizes Verot's approach to the question (65, 77). The problem of delimiting
and reconciling papal and episcopal powers was never fully discussed by the
council, whose proceedings were interrupted before the chapters on the episcopacy
from the *schema de Ecclesia* could be introduced for debate. The problem lingered
as unfinished business until the second session of the Second Council of the
Vatican in the fall of 1963, when it was taken up again in a new *schema de
Ecclesia.*
[74] ". . . And then came Verot again, unsuppressed by previous experiences."
Butler, *Council*, II, 103.
[75] *Ibid.*, 104.
[76] Mansi, *Collectio*, LII, col. 792. In his discourse Alemany named several
of the American bishops in the Opposition who signed the Baltimore decrees of
1866. When he named Verot there was general laughter. Alemany said that the

the bishops at that council, himself included, had made a general profession of obedience to the Holy See, "but that involved no definition of infallibility." Indeed, the question of infallibility never came up, either directly or indirectly. Archbishop Spalding, who presided at that council, was in a position to know this best of all, and "from him, I may add (he is my metropolitan), I received an invitation and exhortation of specially studying this question, not by reading the books of Gallicans, if indeed there are any in the library now situated in our [North] American College, but in the books of ultramontanes. . . ." Verot claimed that he did use only standard sources and ultramontane commentaries, yet, to his surprise, came up with the same conclusions as had Bossuet and other Gallican theologians — because, he said, they represented the truth: "Consensus autem hic non potuit venire nisi a veritate. [*Murmurs and laughter.*]" Alluding to the scriptural texts that had been cited against his position, he said:

> I have heard Protestants argue in the same way against us from Sacred Scripture. We have in America Baptists, as they are called, who say that baptism is not valid unless given by immersion; and these Baptists can bring together texts, and can adduce weighty arguments from those texts and from the original meaning of the word "baptize." But what are we to say in answer? "We admit your texts; but the Church of the first centuries also knew those texts and yet baptized at least the sick and infirm by the pouring of water." And so, texts of Scripture are explained through history and through facts. And in the same way, all the subtle arguments that have been adduced here from texts of Scripture in order to prove papal infallibility must be explained through history and through facts. . . . It seems to me that ancient tradition and history go against this assertion [of infallibility]. I have already proved that, it seems to me, in the earlier discussion, and my arguments have called forth no answer [*laughter*], from which I judge that no answer could be given. [*Increased laughter.*] That dogma was unknown even to the first Christians who contended with Peter, and even to St. Paul. [*Increased laughter.*] . . . All men know what answer was given to me then, that "these were Protestant objections." But I say that even Protestants deserve to have their objections refuted. . . . Unless I am mistaken, there are in this hall more than a hundred bishops, from all parts of the world, not only

---

Baltimore decrees had been promulgated across the United States "from the possessions of the Russians to the regions of Florida and Savannah."

from France, but from Germany, England, Ireland, America, and Italy, who reject this doctrine. [*Cries of dissent.*] . . . In our American law, as in the English, we need the testimony of twelve jurymen for a capital sentence; if only one dissents, the penalty of death cannot be pronounced. [*Laughter.*] If one of the twelve Apostles had contradicted the rest, I doubt whether the world would have believed the Gospel. [*Murmurs and laughter.*]

And so on for about an hour and a half, finally halted by the shouts of many Fathers: "The hour is late!" The battle was over, and new decisions had to be made. On July 13 the chapters on the primacy and infallibility were put to a preliminary vote. Of the 601 Fathers present, 451 voted *Placet,* 62 *Placet juxta modum,* and 88 *non-Placet.* Seven Americans voted *non-Placet:* Verot, Kenrick, Domenec, McQuaid, Fitzgerald, William G. McCloskey of Louisville, and Ignatius Mrak of Marquette-Sault Ste. Marie.[77] When it was announced that a public session would be held on July 18 to enable the prelates to register their votes publicly, Verot, Kenrick, and Domenec signed their names to a protest letter to Pius IX (also signed by fifty-two other prelates), which read in part:

Thus confirming our votes by this writing, we have decided that we will not be present at the public session which is to be held on the eighteenth day of this month. For filial piety and reverence . . . will not suffer us, in a cause so proximately concerning the person of Your Holiness, openly and before a Father to say: *non-Placet.*[78]

As it happened, Fitzgerald was the only American to cast a *non-Placet* at the public session, one of the two cast in the assembly.[79]

[77] Purcell of Cincinnati, a member of the band of American "inopportunists," had left for home on June 30, hence was not present for the voting. Another member of the band, Whelan of Wheeling, had given up all hope of blocking the definition, and had either left Rome or abstained from further voting. Mansi, *Collectio,* LII, col. 915.

[78] *Ibid.,* LII, col. 1328. This letter was sent at the instance of Dupanloup, like his American colleagues who signed it, "inopportunist" to the last; see Hales, *Pio Nono,* 323.

[79] Mansi, *Collectio,* LIII, col. 967. The final voting took place amid the rumbling of a thunderstorm, which, as Hales says, was "variously interpreted according to the viewpoint of the witnesses"; *Pio Nono,* 323. The definition as approved is printed in Betti, *Pastor Aeternus,* 547. Verot had absented himself from the seat of these ceremonies: "Bishop Verot went to Naples this morning and will leave when he returns," Archives of the Archdiocese of Cincinnati, P. Geyer and P. H. Cusack to Purcell, Rome, July 20, 1870. Geyer and Cusack were recently ordained; Geyer had been one of the two American stenographers at the council.

The other American objectors, Verot included, had either left for home or absented themselves from the city. Verot stayed in the vicinity long enough to make his adherence to the new dogma, which he seems to have done quite willingly, since he was one of the first of the Opposition to declare his acceptance, on July 25:

> By these present letters I declare that I adhere to the constitution promulgated in the fourth public session.
>
> Augustin Verot
> Bishop of St. Augustine.[80]

While Verot and his American colleagues were accepting the decree — and all did without exception[81] — there was a similar shuffling of stance taking place at home in the editorial offices of the Catholic press. Probably never before, or since, was the Catholic press less knowledgeable about the mind of its leaders than it was during the first six months of 1870. At the first, when news that infallibility might be defined reached American shores, in January, 1870, the press in general came out strongly in the dogma's favor. Later, after it became apparent that certain of the American bishops opposed the definition, papers under the jurisdiction of several of the prelates concerned had to turn about sharply and begin writing about "inopportuneness," an idea that seems not to have troubled them before. Now, as the same bishops, one by one, professed faith in the dogma, their papers at home had to reverse course again, and speak in praise of something from which their enthusiasm only recently had been withdrawn. It is a curious episode. It is also an important episode, because it shows the extent to which the bishops, excluding those of Irish extraction, e.g., Kenrick, Purcell, Whelan, McQuaid, Fitzgerald, were in advance of their Catholic priests and people at home. It shows that the early development of a conciliatory Catholic approach to the American environment took place from the top down — that the Catholic hierarchy, customarily thought of in America at the time as an eminently conservative group and described even recently by an historian of the period as less advanced in their relationship with American conditions than the priests and people whom they gov-

---

[80] Mansi, *Collectio,* LIII, col. 1009.

[81] See the letters or other statements of adherence from Fitzgerald, Kenrick, Purcell, Domenec, McQuaid, and Mrak in Clancy, "American Prelates," 65–70.

erned,[82] actually took the lead in seeking a mitigation of the tensions existing between Catholicism and American life.

The upheaval in the Catholic press began with the discovery of two documents. The first was the American *postulatum* of January 15, 1870, in which twenty American prelates, Verot included, petitioned Pius IX not to allow infallibility to be defined. The second was a letter sent by Archbishops Kenrick and Purcell to Dupanloup, sometime between April 4 and 25. The Kenrick-Purcell letter was provoked by a communication from Archbishop Spalding to Dupanloup, on April 4, in which Spalding appeared to be speaking in the name of the American bishops. Widely printed in newspapers of both Europe and the United States,[83] the Spalding letter nettled some of the Americans in the Opposition, both because Spalding claimed to speak for them, and because they did not agree with him that infallibility ought to be defined, even implicitly.[84] Dupanloup received the Kenrick-Purcell letter sometime before April 21, and he wrote Verot asking him about the propriety of publishing it, together with the signatures attached (Kenrick, Purcell, McQuaid, Domenec, and Fitzgerald). Verot replied that "the names found on the letter are for your personal satisfaction, and the prelates would not like to see their names appear publicly, in the newspapers or elsewhere," but he recognized that it might be necessary in the end to publish them. "There are other prelates," he added, presumably including himself, "who would have signed except for their desire not to expose themselves to any publicity."[85] On April 28 the Kenrick-Purcell letter was released by Dupanloup to the *Gazette de France*, in Paris, but under the signature of Kenrick alone, as representing "plusieurs archevêques et évêques d'Amérique."[86] Subsequent news-

---

[82] Thomas T. McAvoy, "The American Catholic Minority in the Later Nineteenth Century," *The Review of Politics*, 14 (July, 1953), 299–301. McAvoy's study concludes that the bishops at the time were regarded as foreigners by most Americans, that they devoted all their energies to the perfection of the hierarchical organization and to purely spiritual enterprises, and that, while the bishops showed no parallel development with the course of American social life, "the Catholic population had been deeply affected by the political, economic and social conditions in which they lived" (300–301).

[83] This letter may be read in the *Banner*, May 21, 1870.

[84] Originally Spalding had favored a middle position, desiring the definition, but wishing it to be framed implicitly without the use of the word "infallible." His later switch to right of center is explained in his letter to Dupanloup.

[85] ASS, Verot to Dupanloup, Rome, April 21, 1870.

[86] Holdings of the *Gazette de France* are in the Bibliothèque Nationale, Paris.

paper coverage, throughout both Europe and the United States, carried the names of Kenrick and Purcell as authors.[87] The letter itself accused Spalding of having radically changed his mind on the "opportuneness" of a definition, first declaring it to be inexpedient to American Catholic purposes, and then afterward attempting to prove in his letter to Dupanloup that he never held any such thing: "Several among us would be able to declare, if needed, to have heard him more than once exhort and induce his colleagues in the episcopacy to oppose themselves to a definition absolutely inopportune." Spalding's letter, furthermore, "has no official authority to represent the views and convictions of the American prelates." Noting that Spalding claimed in his letter never to have doubted the general belief of the Church relative to infallibility, the Kenrick-Purcell letter replied: "In that case will it not be best to ask nothing more and to leave things where they are and where they have always been?"[88]

The American Catholic press was no less taken aback by this letter than it was by the earlier *postulatum,* and most papers began the process of switching sides. A comparison of editions published in January and February with those published in May and June reveals the extent to which they altered their viewpoint on the opportuneness of the definition.[89] Among the few papers which did not change colors, the *Freeman's Journal* and Verot's *Banner of the South,* edited by Abram J. Ryan, were most prominent. The former strongly attacked the Kenrick-Purcell letter and its authors, and engaged in a bitter controversy on the matter with Purcell's *Catholic Telegraph.*[90] The *Banner* remained stubbornly infallibilist;[91]

---

[87] A typical heading appears in the *Banner,* June 4, 1870: "Letter from Archbishops Kenrick and Purcell in behalf of several American Bishops in opposition to the Archbishop of Baltimore and in Defense of the Bishop of Orleans [Dupanloup]."

[88] *Banner,* June 4, 1870.

[89] See, e.g., *Pittsburgh Catholic,* February 19 and May 21, 1870; Cincinnati *Catholic Telegraph,* February 26 and June 16, 1870; St. Louis *Western Watchman,* February 12 and July 16, 1870; Detroit *Western Catholic,* May 7 and May 21, 1870; Baltimore *Catholic Mirror,* March 26 and April 9, 1870; New Orleans *Morning Star,* May 15 and May 29, 1870. No American paper, however, was more caught off guard than the infallibilist *Vatican* of London; see issues of March 25, April 8, May 27, June 17, July 15, 1870, in which the *Vatican's* appreciation of the American hierarchy turned gradually from glowing to glowering.

[90] *Freeman's Journal,* May 21, 1870 ff.; *Catholic Telegraph,* June 30, 1870 ff.

[91] See, e.g., issues of March 26, April 16, April 30, May 7, July 2, July 30, August 6, 1870.

for reasons unknown but probably unconnected with Abram Ryan's prodefinition stand, Verot fired the poet-priest as editor in March, 1870.[92]

On their return home to their proper dioceses during the summer and fall of 1870, most of the American prelates delivered lectures on the council. In simple and graphic language they described the workings of that body and the nature of the questions that came before it. Universally they tackled the question of division among the Fathers. To American Catholics who had never themselves been divided on doctrinal matters, and whose theological unity had, alone among the churches, survived the Civil War, this problem must have caused some concern. The bishops devoted a great amount of time to explaining it; and those among them who had been "inopportunists" spoke on it, understandably, at greatest length.[93] In October, 1870, Bishop Verot lectured on the council at St. Augustine, and complained that his position had been widely misrepresented in the popular press. The *Examiner* gave an account:

> The bishop stated that the reason of all these misrepresentations was in the secrecy which for the best reasons surrounded the deliberations and proceedings of the Council. Nearly all the newspapers of Europe had sent reporters to Rome in order to obtain some account of the doings of the Council, and it is a lamentable though an undeniable fact that the ignorance of those men, at least in ecclesiastical and theological matters, was surpassed only by their presumption and audacity. . . .[94] Thus he was . . . represented as hostile to the Church, and to the Holy See, because, using the privilege of a Bishop, and acting up to the desires and intentions of the Pope who wished all to say in all sincerity and liberty what they thought, he had ventured to defend Galileo, the staunch ad-

[92] MCND, Ignatius Persico to James McMaster (editor of the *Freeman's Journal*), Rome, May 30, 1870: "With regard to M. Ryan of Augusta, Ga., I must tell you that . . . Bp. Verot requested him to leave the Diocese." Cf. Charleston *Courier*, June 14, 1870: "We see it stated that Rev. Father Ryan better known as 'Moina,' one of the favorite poets of the South, will make Mobile his future home." Ryan wrote from Mobile on June 25: "At last, after some wanderings and pleasant meetings and from mournful goodbyes, at Savannah, Atlanta, and Macon, I have reached Mobile. . . . The *Banner of the South* must never furl its folds." *Banner*, July 9, 1870. The paper folded on October 29, following.

[93] See, e.g., Kenrick in the New Orleans *Morning Star*, January 15, 1871; Purcell in the *Banner*, September 3, 1870; Domenec in the Pittsburgh *Catholic*, September 17, 1870. The prelates all stressed the freedom of discussion that had been allowed, and proposed it to their hearers as a virtue instead of as a defect.

[94] Beiser, *Secular Newspapers*, does not say much more for the American

vocate of the true system of the world; for the condemnation of Galileo by a Roman Tribunal cannot be attributed to the Church herself, nor to the Pontiff speaking *ex cathedra*. Thus also with regard to the question of the infallibility of the Pope which occupied the Council for several months, there might be among the Bishops honest diversity of opinions, the question presenting itself under so many aspects; for no one ever dreamt that the Pope is infallible when he speaks as a private writer, or on questions of Grammar, Geography, History, or natural science. . . . But if there was a divergence of views during the protracted discussion which took place, there was none after the decision, and Bishop Verot with his flock and the Catholic world cheerfully subscribes and adheres to all the decrees of the Vatican Council.[95]

Contemporary opinion of the man varied according to the predispositions of the observer. Anti-infallibilists like the Acton-Friedrick-Döllinger combine admired him openly, saying that he was "a man of high character"[96] who was "compared in America with St. Francis de Sales."[97] Similarly, the New York *Herald* was impressed: "Rome has never felt such a rebuke as the American Bishops have administered, nor have the ears of the prelates heard such language as fell from the lips of Bishop Verot, of Savannah, and Archbishops Kenrick and Connolly. They uttered sentences that were new to the regions of Rome; and it will be wisdom if they are profited by."[98] On the other side there were those like Albert du Böys, a lay friend of Dupanloup, who said that Verot possessed "an audacity that was not always pleasing, and that sometimes went beyond the bounds."[99] Leone Dehon, a French priest-stenographer at the council, found him *"toujours plaisant,"* criti-

secular press, which was generally hostile toward the proceedings. It published, for the most part, "the type of news desired and the scraps were seized with little attempt at verification;" 298.

[95] St. Augustine *Examiner,* reprinted by exchange in the *Catholic Mirror,* November 26, 1870. Verot subsequently gave four additional lectures on the council at St. Augustine, as we learn from ADSA, Persico to Verot, Savannah, February 23, 1871, but reports on their content have not turned up in the author's research. Issues of the St. Augustine *Examiner* for the period are missing from all known holdings. Cf. "Episcopal Acts," 174.

[96] Döllinger, *Quirinus,* 631.

[97] *Ibid.,* 759.

[98] May 11, 1870.

[99] Manuscript notebooks in a private archives at St. Martin de la Place (Maine et Loire), France; citation courtesy of Professor Jacques Gadille of the Université de Dijon.

cized his "kitchen Latin," but occasionally conceded that he made good sense.[100] The blunt-spoken Verot was probably considered as something of an embarrassment by certain members of the Opposition with whom he made common cause. Apparently he now and then prematurely played a hand that Opposition leaders were holding in strategic reserve: Dehon said that he was "an *enfant terrible* who betrayed the small plots of his friends."[101] Bishop James Frederick Wood of Philadelphia, one of the few Americans to side with Spalding, must have been unimpressed by the man, judging from a letter he wrote after a visit with Verot in 1875: "He is full of conversation and loves and makes [*sic*] a joke. We did not discuss the infallibility nor allude to his peculiar '*Acta*' at the Vatican Council!"[102] Among the later accounts of the council that benefited from the published transcripts of the debates, the most interesting appraisal was that given in Theodor Granderath's multivolumed history of the council, published in 1903–1906. Granderath commented on Verot's discourse of January 3 on Galileo and the Negroes:

> The discourses already delivered had, in general, reflected the character of the country and of the people from which their authors came. This was even more noticeable in the case of Bishop Verot. In him was expressed the practical sense of the Americans. *It was the experience of life, of American life in particular, that furnished him with the material of his presentation, and it was on facts that he relied to drive home his proposals.*[103]

The difficulty in evaluating Verot at the council is founded in the various aspects under which he, like infallibility, can be considered. The title *enfant terrible* might seem to be an apt description of the man who told jokes from the ambo; but if that is granted, it should be added that there was some *enfantillage* demonstrated by his hecklers, too.[104] What the authors miss who give Verot that

---

[100] Carbone, ed., Dehon, *Diario del Concilio*, 66, 78, 164.

[101] *Ibid.*, 159.

[102] AAB, 42-U-51, Wood to James Roosevelt Bayley (Archbishop of Baltimore), Jacksonville, Florida, April 1, 1875.

[103] *Vatikanischen Konzils*, II, 285. Present author's emphasis.

[104] Hennesey, *Council of the Vatican*, argues that Verot deserved a fairer hearing than he received, since he had done his homework better than most and made a great deal of practical sense in his remarks: 235, 257, and *passim*. Hennesey also criticizes Cardinals (or Presidents) de Angelis and Capalti for their interruptions of Verot during the debates: 168, 237, 260.

title is the unaffected nature of his racy American style: he spoke what he thought, bluntly and candidly. It was an eminently American manner. His volatile nature, which had been demonstrated to his superiors as early as the years at old St. Mary's College, had not been much tempered by the open character of American society. Where he might have learned the restraints of diplomacy in the Europe that he left, in America there were as yet no such overriding imperatives. His sudden burst of oratory at the Vatican Council was as much a commentary on the society from which he came as it was on himself. As a theologian there is no doubt that Verot distinguished himself: his long dissertations on infallibility, with their exhaustive scriptural, patristic, and conciliar references, showed that he had made himself familiar with the pertinent theological materials — so much so that certain other speakers cited his discourses as references for their own. Was Verot a Gallican in theology? Certainly, he used some typically Gallican arguments, several times defended the Gallican Church, and in the frequent antitheses he drew between Gallicans and Ultramontanes he seems definitely to have included himself among the former. These terms, however, were not true descriptions of the opposing groups in the council. They were popular categories dating from older battles in the Church, and corresponded in 1870 not to any strict theological systems or parties, but to simple liberal-conservative groupings. That the Fathers of the council did not wish to have the controversy over infallibility categorized as a strict Gallican-Ultramontane encounter was demonstrated by the outcry raised when Verot used the terms. Was, then, Verot to the left? We would have to say that he was. Despite his hard conservative attitude on some other points (relating to the liturgy and to discipline of the clergy) he definitely chose conciliation over stubborn resistance as the proper response to the new species of problems facing the Catholic Church in the United States. He was not to the left ideologically, however, for he does not seem to have argued from any definite doctrinaire stance. He was not a rebel against Rome in the same way that he had been a rebel against Washington — seeking the decentralization of power as a matter of principle — rather, he argued from history and from *ad hoc* practice. And if he had any particular orientation, we would have to say — anticipating another council — that it was pastoral. No one at the council who took the trouble to find out the facts of his episcopal career could have doubted that here was one of the great pastors of the universal Church, and that what he said must have issued from his experience with souls. Finally, if one judges Verot by the success he obtained from his efforts in the council, then, surely, he was one of the minor figures. Yet, the nature of the things he proposed (e.g., on the questions of Galileo and the Negroes), the call he made for a conciliatory approach to Protestant society, his devotion to facts as opposed to the fabulous, and his sheer courage and perseverance should give him a permanent and major place in the history of the First Council of the Vatican; all the more so because these same sounds have been heard again, and louder, at the Second Council of the Vatican.

CHAPTER IX

THE LAST YEARS

ON MARCH 11, 1870, during the course of the Vatican Council, Pius IX elevated St. Augustine to the dignity of an episcopal see for all Florida east of the Apalachicola River, and on the same date transferred Augustin Verot from Savannah to the new diocese.[1] Bishop Ignatius Persico, a native of Italy with long experience among Englishmen and Americans, was named as fourth Bishop of Savannah.[2] The New Orleans *Morning Star* learned in advance of the actual appointment that Verot had been named to the lesser of the two dioceses "at his own request."[3] Verot confirmed the report on May 2 in a letter to the superior of the Sisters of St. Joseph in Le Puy, France: "I have chosen St. Augustine in preference to Savannah, principally because St. Augustine and Florida are the place where I was first sent, and also because in Florida there is more holy poverty as well as more good to be done in building churches and founding schools."[4] In Florida, the St. Augus-

---

[1] The original of the papal brief of March 11, 1870, *Quae Catholico nomini*, erecting the Diocese of St. Augustine is in the ADSA. A Latin transcription is in Donald C. Shearer, *Pontificia Americana: A Documentary History of the Catholic Church in the United States (1784–1884)* (Washington, D. C.: The Catholic University of America, 1933), No. 138, 349–351. The brief specified that the Diocese of St. Augustine would have the same geographic limits as the earlier vicariate. This had been recommended by the Tenth Provincial Council of Baltimore; AAB, 39-A-Ql, p. 33. Verot had hoped that the new diocese would include that part of Florida west of the Apalachicola River, then as now a part of the Diocese of Mobile; see above, Chapter VI. The apostolic letter translating Verot from Savannah to St. Augustine, dated March 11, 1870, is also in the ADSA.

[2] Persico resigned the See of Savannah in 1873 for reasons of health. He performed diplomatic missions for a time, then was named Bishop of Aquino in Italy in 1879. More diplomatic missions followed after 1887, and in 1893 he was created a cardinal. He died in 1896.

[3] February 13, 1870.

[4] ADP, Verot to Madame la Supérieure et très chère en N. S. (La Mère Léocadie Broc), Rome, May 2, 1870.

tine *Examiner* took appropriate satisfaction from the fact that Verot gave "preference to our little miniature City over the Emporium of Georgia" and predicted that, since "everywhere in this new land the erection of a City into a bishopric has been the signal of immense material improvement . . . beyond a doubt the population of the Ancient City will double in the next ten years."[5]

At the Tenth Provincial Council of Baltimore in 1869 Verot had pressed hard for St. Augustine's erection into a separate diocese. The province had sent on his recommendations to Rome with a strong endorsement, and had enumerated for the Holy See the major statistics for Catholic Florida at the turn of the decade: perhaps seven or eight thousand Catholics; eight priests; twelve cities or towns with either churches or mission chapels; three teaching orders of women; and a sufficiently large shell-rock church at St. Augustine to serve as cathedral. Prophetically, the Baltimore recommendations cautioned that jurisdictional difficulties might arise over the assignments of the Sisters of St. Joseph, now divided between the two dioceses, and that "doubt and uncertainty" might prevail over the divisions of real property and of the annual grants from the French Society for the Propagation of the Faith.[6] Verot himself seems to have glossed over these problems, if we may judge from the bland manner in which he described the change of command in his diary: ". . . In March, 1870 I was appointed Bishop of St. Augustine, Fla. A paper was drawn and signed by myself and the new Bishop of Savannah, dividing the property of the two dioceses and settling the questions that might have arisen from the division."[7] For the next several years, however, in controversies with Persico and with William H. Gross, Persico's successor, Verot would learn that the bishops at Baltimore had not been unwise when they intimated that the division of diocesan personnel and properties was not one of the calmer seas that the Barque of Peter traverses.[8]

[5] January 7, 1871. The United States Census rolls for St. Augustine in 1870 and 1880 show that the population actually increased during the next decade from 1760 to 2300.

[6] AAB, 39-A-Ql, 33–34.

[7] "Episcopal Acts," 174.

[8] A long and occasionally testy series of letters passed between Verot and Persico from January, 1871 through March, 1872, regarding, among other things, Central Railroad certificates, files of the Washington, Georgia, church property, Verot's claim on St. Patrick's Church, Savannah, past salaries for several priests, and a surplus in the Savannah "Cathedral fund." See, e.g., ADSA, Persico to

Verot left Rome on July 19, the day after the final public session of the Vatican Council. A second session was planned, but the council would never reconvene because of the outbreak of the Franco-Prussian War on July 15 and the occupation of Rome by Piedmontese troops under Victor Emmanuel on September 20 following. He traveled a crisscross course through the Italian peninsula, visiting in turn Pisa, Florence, Bologna, Loretto, Venice, Milan, Turin, Susa, and Mount Cenis. He was accompanied by a nephew, Joseph Leon Hugon, who had recently completed seminary studies for the priesthood and wished to serve under his uncle in the Florida missions. Verot passed into France and spent several weeks at Le Puy, where he made a retreat under the Jesuits, ordained his nephew to the priesthood, recruited a young Jesuit, Stephen Langlade, for Florida, and conferred minor orders on a number of Jesuit scholastics.

Meanwhile, three German armies were pushing into France from the Moselle, from the Palatinate on Metz, and from the upper Rhine on Strasbourg. Verot left for Paris as Marshal Marie Edmé Patrice Maurice de MacMahon led the cream of the French defenders against the Germans at Sedan, and he was in Paris when, on September 4, news reached the city that the French troops, with the Emperor Napoleon III, had capitulated. Mobs invaded the Palais Bourbon and obliged the reluctant members of the rump of the Legislative Assembly to join in proclaiming the fall of the empire. Verot recorded, laconically: "I was [there] when they proclaimed the republic."[9] Later, back in Florida, he would express his anguish at this turn in France's fortunes. With Father Hugon again for company, he sailed for New York on the *Ville de Paris,* arriving "toward the 20th of Sep., about the time the Italians were entering Rome."[10] He spent several days with Bishop John Loughlin of Brooklyn, and then left for Savannah, visiting briefly with his old Sulpician friends at Baltimore on the way. News of his impending arrival reached Savannah on about October 3, and, as the Savannah *Republican* recounted:

Verot, Savannah, October 31, 1871, and November 9, 1871. Verot's contributions to this debate are missing, but something of their tone can be learned from Persico's replies. Verot's altercation with Bishop Gross centered on jurisdiction over the Sisters of St. Joseph; see Chapter V.

[9] "Episcopal Acts," 174.
[10] *Ibid.*

In consequence of this intelligence a number of our citizens hastily
projected measures for his reception at the depot on the arrival of
the Charleston train. The members of the different Roman Catholic
Churches selected a committee of twenty gentlemen, whilst the St.
Patrick's Total Abstinence Society appointed a committee of ten
persons. These two committees were driven in carriages to the
depot, where they awaited the arrival of the train. The committee
of the Total Abstinence Society wore regalia.

The cars reached the city at the usual hour in the afternoon,
and as Bishop Verot stepped upon the platform he was surprised,
nay, quite overcome by emotion, to find himself the recipient of
a most hearty welcome from many of his old parishioners who
remember him as one dear, honored and loved among the eminent
divines of the Catholic Church.[11]

Verot spent the first week in Savannah packing. On the 14th he
lectured to a large audience on "Rome and the Council," and the
next day greeted the arrival of Ignatius Persico, the new ordinary.[12]
Persico's installation took place on the 16th, and Verot took his
official leave of the diocese on the 18th. As he rode out of the
famous old Confederate stronghold, the Savannah *Republican* for
that day was eulogizing Robert E. Lee, whose death had occurred
six days before. In its pages the newspaper printed a poem, "The
Sword of Lee," by Verot's ertswhile friend, Abram J. Ryan. The
coincidence symbolized the end of an era for both the "rebel
bishop" and the "priest-poet of the Confederacy":

> *And they who saw it gleaming there*
> *And knew who bore it, knelt to swear*
> *That where that sword led, they would dare*
> *To follow and to die.*

The new Bishop of St. Augustine entered his episcopal see "with
tolerably great pomp" on October 22 and the next day, Sunday,
delivered an inaugural sermon in the cathedral church. He predicted to his hearers that the elevation of Florida to the dignity
of a diocese would prove an incalculable advantage to the priests
and Catholic people of that ancient mission territory. At the same
time he warned that more should not be expected of him at the
present time than his few material resources would allow him to

---

[11] October, 7, 1870.
[12] Savannah *Morning News,* October 17, 1870.

accomplish. He pointed out that Catholic Florida had long been dependent on the French Society for the Propagation of the Faith, and that now all aid from that source had been cut off by the political and military upheavals in France. If the disasters in France had been foreseen, he said, Rome would probably not have created the new diocese. Given the present impoverished state of France, it was doubtful that the Society would be able to disburse funds to Florida for several years to come. "Still the Bishop made this remark," explained the local *Examiner*, "not by way of creating in the minds of the faithful despondency and gloom, but in order that too much should not be anticipated from the new administration."[13] This matter properly dispatched, but the troubles of France still on his mind, the bishop launched then upon an excoriation of Napoleon III that for diction and directness must rank among the more remarkable of his utterances. It would be obvious to anyone in attendance that this had suddenly become no ordinary inaugural sermon, and, indeed, the *Examiner* reported afterward that "the remarks of the Right Rev. Bishop were all the time listened to with breathless attention":[14]

A great calamity has befallen the Holy See and indeed the whole Catholic Church. The source of the misfortune is to be traced to Catholic France. The greatest misfortune that can befall a nation is to have a ruler without capacity, without honesty, and without virtue. It is the method employed by Divine Providence to chastise nations, and it is a dreadful chastisement, as also He exalts and blesses nations by giving them rulers gifted with integrity, ability, and disinterestedness. France has had the misfortune of having at its head an adventurer without principles, without honesty, without ability, who has turned everything to the selfish and mean purposes of self-aggrandizement, whilst hypocrisy, corruption, and imbecility have had the sway of the country for many years. The gaudy bubble has burst, exhibiting to the world the ludicrous spectacle of a so-called great Emperor, so much deprived of all military ability and chivalrous propensities, as to ignominiously surrender himself to his foes at the head of an army of one hundred and twenty thousand men.

This has been the signal of appalling calamities, which have fallen not only upon France, which represented Catholicity in the cabinet

---

[13] St. Augustine *Examiner*, November 5, 1870.
[14] *Ibid.*

of European powers, no matter how wicked and impious the rulers might be, but also upon the whole Church and specially upon the Holy See. The miserable wretch who hides his shame in the palatial dungeons of Germany seems, during the course of his reign, to have done all that could be done to humble and impair Catholic influence and Pontifical supremacy. He stripped Austria, a great Catholic power, of her ascendancy, robbing her of several provinces and consenting to her degradation in the scale of European Powers during her late struggle with Prussia. He introduced division and discord in Italy, and, as all indications point out, contributed to the installation of anarchy in Spain. But the Holy See received most violent blows from him; so much the worse as they seemed to come from a friend, and were cloaked with hypocritical deference and reverential sacrilege. He was ashamed to rob the Holy See of the feeble remnant of temporal power which it exercised under his patronage, but as soon as the defeat of Weissenburg [August 6] and the surrender of Sedan became known, the bastard government he had created in Italy shook off the yoke of the imperial juggler, and marched on Rome, which it took after a slight resistance from the Papal soldiers who opposed the invading army — just enough to avoid bloodshed, and enter a solemn protest in the face of the civilized world.[15]

Verot also took the occasion of his first sermon to announce his adhesion to the constitutions promulgated by the Vatican Council. He sent copies of the statement to "many Prelates in America and out of it, disclaiming many errors that had been attributed to me,"[16] and later, in February of 1871, he delivered four lectures on the council before large crowds in the cathedral.

Verot's cathedral had been constructed in 1793–1797 during the second Spanish occupation of Florida. Designed by a royal engineer, Mariano de la Rocque, and paid for in greater part by the Spanish crown, it was a handsome building fronting on the city's central plaza. Its façade and walls were formed from large blocks of coquina, a shell rock indigenous to the area. The façade faced toward the south where its buff-colored stucco finish was almost continually in the sunlight; its edges swept upward in ogee curves to a belfry, a design typical of most churches built by the Spanish in the eighteenth century. Bishop Verot loved the old church, and

---

15 *Ibid.*
16 "Episcopal Acts," 174. See Chapter VIII.

had been on familiar terms with it since first coming to the city in 1858. Now that it was a cathedral he determined to restore and repair it where age had worked its ravages. Between 1870 and 1872, accordingly, he installed a new tin roof to replace the original shingle roof that had decayed, redecorated the sanctuary, and replaced most of the woodwork in the interior. In 1872 he staged a fair in the city to raise funds for this work, and realized $600; later the same year he made a fund-raising tour of Baltimore, Brooklyn, and Augusta from which he brought home an additional $2,100.[17] A tongue-in-cheek appeal for funds appeared under his name in the *Examiner*:

> The people of St. Augustine have always been poor, and are likely to continue to be so. The Lord in his all-wise Providence in granting them the ancient faith has also granted them exemption from *thorns,* as our Saviour calls the riches or wealth of worldlings. Their lot will not perhaps excite much envy among outsiders, as some seem to like exceedingly the pricking of those thorns. The people of St. Augustine therefore make an appeal to all those who during the winter come from the frozen zones of the North to enjoy the genial heat, the beautiful sun and the bracing sea-breeze of St. Augustine to rid themselves of some of those thorns in behalf of the old cathedral that no doubt they have visited, and admired, and contemplated with surprise and awe.[18]

It should be recorded that some people in the city, namely the Episcopal congregation of Trinity Church across the plaza, were accustomed to contemplate the cathedral with something less than surprise and awe — at least at twelve o'clock noon on Sundays, when what one visitor to the city called an "uproarious" Angelus sounded from the cathedral belfry.[19] In earlier days the cathedral sacristans mounted a wooden balcony behind the belfry and sounded the bells by pulling on ropes attached to the clappers. In Verot's time young boys performed this task, but instead of ropes and clappers used sticks. St. Augustine was a city where the Angelus was not rung, but rattled. An English visitor recorded: "On Sundays the Episcopalians, who have their pretty little semi-Gothic church on the opposite side of the square, are brought to a summary

---

[17] *Ibid.,* 175.

[18] MCND, clipping from *Examiner,* date excised, but probably 1872.

[19] An English visitor (Therese Yelverton), *Saint Augustine, Florida* (New York: James Miller, Publisher, 1871), 22.

standstill in their devotion. The minister has usually arrived at the peroration of his sermon when the rub-a-dub-dub commences in the Cathedral. The congregation cannot hear another syllable to save their souls, and the ringing or rattling continues often for half an hour."[20]

The cathedral was heir to a long parochial history dating from 1565. No relics remained, however, of the parish during the sixteenth and seventeenth centuries. Verot thought that the early parish registers were probably in Cuba, where many of the Spanish residents of St. Augustine resettled after Florida was ceded to England in 1763. He resolved to find out, and in the spring of 1871 he wrote to ask permission from the Bishop of Havana to search through his archives. On May 10 a diocesan official in Havana replied that Verot was very welcome to see "if perhaps you might find ancient documents relating to the religious history of Florida" in the holdings of the diocese.[21] Accordingly, Verot sailed for Cuba from Key West sometimes in the early summer of that year, and in Havana, he said, "I found the old records of St. Augustine for three hundred years."[22] It was a notable find. The first extant page of the registers, which numbered 1340 pages in fifteen folio volumes, was dated June 25, 1594, only twenty-nine years after the founding of the pioneer parish. The first entry recorded the baptism of an infant girl and was signed by the pastor of the time, Diego Escobar de Sambrana. When, after negotiations involving the historian, John Gilmary Shea, and two of Verot's successors in the See of St. Augustine, the old records were finally returned to their proper parish in 1906, they constituted the oldest written records of American origin preserved in the United States.[23]

During the latter part of the 1860's Verot had learned something of the history of a plot of ground slightly north of the city that

---

[20] *Ibid.*, 23.

[21] ADSA, Benignus Merino et Mendi (Benigno Merino y Mendi) to Illustrissime Domine, Havana, May 10, 1871, in Latin.

[22] "Episcopal Acts," 174.

[23] A missing volume was discovered in Havana and returned to St. Augustine in 1939. In the same year the individual pages were laminated by the National Archives in protective sheaths of acetate foil. The registers are preserved today in the ADSA. In *Sadlier's Catholic Directory . . . for 1872*, 317, Verot wrote of his cathedral, "it is the *unique* privilege of that church to have a full set of church records of baptisms, marriages, etc., from the year 1594, in a perfect state of preservation."

was variously called by residents "Nombre de Dios" and "Nuestra
Señora de la Leche." This was the site where Menéndez de Avilés,
founder of the city, landed in 1565, and where Mass was first offered
in the pioneer settlement on the same date — as the early Spanish
themselves took pride in pointing out.[24] Verot also heard, erroneously, that this was the same site where a Franciscan missionary,
Fray Blas Rodriguez, had been slain during the Guale Indian revolt
of 1597.[25] What was true was that on this site Spanish priests had
founded the country's first Indian mission, Nombre de Dios, and
later, probably in the early seventeenth century, had erected a hermitage to Nuestra Señora de la Leche y Buen Parto — "Our Nurs-
ing Mother of Happy Delivery." A succession of chapels had stood
on the site but all had been destroyed either by storm, or fire, or
English gunfire.

The property had fallen into private hands as farmland with the
change of flags in 1763 and again in 1821, but in August of 1868
Verot had managed to buy it back from one John McGuire for the
sum of one dollar.[26] McGuire had reverently preserved the spot, a
slight elevation of about twenty feet square, where one of the
original Spanish chapels had stood. Fragments of coquina from the

---

[24] See map of the city by Juan Joseph Elixio de la Puente, dated 1769, preserved in the Museo Naval in Madrid. The key indicates the site and reads in
part: "Place called Nombre de Dios, which is the same where the first Mass was
said on September 8, 1565, when the Spaniards under the command of the
Adelantado Pedro Menéndez de Avilés set out to conquer these provinces; and
afterward an Indian village was built there, with a chapel in which was placed
an image of Maria Santisima de la Leche." Translated from the original by the
author.

[25] Verot wrote in Sadlier's Catholic Directory . . . for 1872, 317: "The spot
is hallowed from the fact that a missionary priest, more than two hundred years
ago, was put to death there by the Indians, from whom he asked and obtained
permission to say Mass, which they attended in silence, and at the end of which
they massacred him." This was obviously the Franciscan Rodriquez, whose
martyrdom was related by Fray Luís Gerónimo de Oré, O.F.M., in his Relación
de los mártires que ha habido en las Provincias de la Florida published sometime between 1617 and 1620; see Maynard Geiger, O.F.M., The Martyrs of
Florida, Franciscan Studies No. 18 (New York: Joseph F. Wagner, Inc., 1936),
xiii. Geiger establishes that Rodriquez was slain, not at Nombre de Dios, but at
Tupiqui, an Indian village in present-day McIntosh County, Georgia; cf. John
Tate Lanning, The Spanish Missions of Georgia (Chapel Hill: University of
North Carolina Press, 1935), 4.

[26] St. John's County, Deed Book "R," 423, warranty deed, John McGuire to
Augustin Verot, August 17, 1868.

chapel lay about the ground, which, for half an acre around, McGuire had left unplowed and undisturbed.[27]

In 1871 Verot undertook the restoration of the site, including reconstruction of the last Spanish chapel, whose foundations he excavated. The work was completed in 1875 and blessed by Verot on November 14 of that year.[28] (Unhappily, only a few years later this chapel, like one or more others before it, was destroyed in a storm.) In 1875, while on a trip to Europe, the bishop commissioned a painting of the first Mass offered at Nombre de Dios, which he installed on the east wall of the cathedral shortly before his death.[29] In the lower right-hand corner of the painting Verot had the artist paint symbols of the civilization brought to Florida by Menéndez and his men: a printing press; a staff entwined by serpents (for medicine); a world globe and books; a harp and a painter's palette; a scythe, a sickle, and a spade; various vegetables; and an anchor. Five hundred photoengraved reproductions of the painting were distributed by Verot throughout the diocese and the country; on them he printed over his name the following legend: "With Religion came to our shores Civilisation, Arts, Sciences and Industry. 'Piety is profitable to all things, having promise of the life that now is, and of that which is to come. (I *Timothy* 4:8.)' "[30]

His restoration work at Nombre de Dios whetted Verot's interest in the Indians of Florida who had learned Christianity and the rudiments of European arts and crafts from early Spanish missionaries. Particularly, he wondered what had happened to the nearly 35,000 Indians whom the Spanish had baptized before the end of the seventeenth century. From his friend, the noted Florida historian Buckingham Smith, Verot learned that the Spanish chain of missions, or *doctrinas*, that once stretched along the coast from Nombre de Dios north to St. Catherine's Island, Georgia, and in a second line westward from Nombre de Dios to Tallahassee, had been systematically and almost totally destroyed by English raiders under Colonel James Moore of Carolina in 1702–1704. The Chris-

[27] Anon., "Our Ancient City," *Lippincott's Magazine*, I (January, 1868), 100.
[28] ADSA, ms. page from journal kept by Miss Eugenia Sanchez of St. Augustine, dated November 14, 1875.
[29] The artist was a French priest, Louis M. Lambert. Verot's estate paid $94 for the work. Lambert's receipt, dated October 10, 1876, is in the ADSA. The painting was destroyed in the fire that gutted the cathedral in 1887.
[30] Copy in the ADSA.

tian Indians, those who escaped capture and enslavement, had fled into the surrounding woods, where most subsequently abandoned the practice of their religion. Despite valiant efforts, the Spaniards had not been able to restore the missions to their former influence.[31] As for the Indians, they had lost all remaining confidence in the white man during the Seminole Wars of the early nineteenth century when Florida was an American territory. Moved by this history of tragedy and neglect, Verot decided to make an effort to win back the Indians' confidence, to provide them again with the opportunity to secure an education, and to restore them to the practice of the Catholic Faith. Most of the remaining Indians — perhaps now only 600 in number — lived at the time in the Everglades at the bottom of the peninsula. To these survivors of the ancient Christian tribes Verot in February, 1872, sent an emissary, his vicar-general, Peter Dufau, armed with a letter as poignant as it was solicitous:

> The Bishop of St. Augustine to the Chief and the whole tribe of the Indians of Florida, greeting and benediction from God and His Son, Jesus Christ.
>
> Beloved Children: We have always had a great desire of promoting your welfare in every respect, and with this view we send to you our beloved representative and Vicar, Father Peter Dufau, who will hand you this letter, and will state to you by word of mouth our good will towards you.
>
> You may, perhaps, remember that in former times your ancestors lived in settlements and villages in various parts of the country, and specially around St. Augustine, on friendly terms with those who then governed the country, and were Spaniards. Many among you had become Christians, like the Spaniards, and professed the religion which the Black Gowns had preached to you. The country has since passed into other hands, but I profess the same religion which was then preached to your fathers, and the Great Chief of Religion on earth, the Pope, who dwells in Rome, has appointed me Chief of Religion for this country. I felt it then a duty, as well as a great happiness, to offer to your nation the help of religion; for we have a soul which does not perish with the body, and there is another life after the present, of eternal happiness for the good and eternal misery for the bad. To enable you, therefore, to save your immortal souls, and teach you the way to obtain eternal happiness, is the object of the present step we take. We are not

---

[31] See Mark F. Boyd, Hale G. Smith, and John W. Griffin, *Here They Once Stood* (Gainesville: University of Florida Press, 1950).

connected in any way with the Civil Government of Florida, and have not the remotest intention of changing or disturbing your present state or relation with the Government, and our efforts are solely for the benefit of your souls. If you are willing to make some necessary arrangements and promise peace and your co-operation, we are willing to send you Sisters of Charity, who will teach your children how to read and write, and how to please the great Spirit, and obtain eternal happiness for them after the present life. A Priest or Black Gown, of the same religion with those who formerly taught your fathers, will accompany the Sisters, and you will enjoy, in this, a great consolation and great advantage.

May the God of Heaven bless you.[32]

In Miami, at the eastern perimeter of the Everglades, Father Dufau searched for a guide who would take him to the Great Chief Taskanooga, "but at any price," he wrote back to the bishop, "I could not find a man, either white, black, or red, who dared or wished to take me in a canoe, and sail with me through the Everglades, from the Miami to Lake Okeechobee, whereabouts the Great Chief resides, no one who would deliver your letter to him." Dufau explained that the Indians who lived on the borders of the Everglades were under the strictest discipline not to introduce white men into the heart of the Indian territory, nor to bear any messages for them. Still, Dufau was able to communicate with a large number of Indians on the borders, and he set down what he learned about them in his letter to Verot. It was a remarkable report, filled with detailed and colorful accounts of the Indians' home life, dress, personal habits, morals, and general character. He described, in one amusing passage, how he lived for a time with a subchief and somehow screwed up the courage to eat with the whole household out of the same wooden spoon: "This I should do in order not to disgrace myself in the Everglades." As for Verot's hopes that the Indians might wish to return to the faith of their fathers, Dufau was not able to report any signs that this was likely:

They have been so unjustly and so shamefully deceived and robbed of the fruits of their labors by unprincipled men that they fear to be deceived again, and they mistrust newcomers should they be angels clothed with human nature. Taught by a long experience not to trust every man that meets them for the first time by chance

[32] Printed in the Savannah *Daily Republican*, April 17, 1872. The letter was dated January 28, 1872.

or otherwise, they stand before him with studied and well-composed, almost freezing coldness, answering questions without opening their lips, by inarticulated sounds. . . . It is my impression that the Indians of the Everglades would have long ago taken serious steps toward civilization and Christian faith if justice had been done them. . . . The Indians have the knowledge of some fundamental truths of morality and justice. They profess to believe in a Supreme Spirit, who rewards the Indians in a place they call the happy hunting ground, and chastises the wicked somewhere down in the earth. Some of them know that Our Lord Jesus Christ came down from heaven and was put to death by the Jews. They call Him Teossee, and consider Him as something more than an ordinary man. This knowledge of Him must have come to them by tradition. I could not know what kind of worship they have.[33]

The Bishop Verot story would be incomplete were not something more said about Peter Dufau. Born at Bayonne, France, he had come to the Florida missions in 1859, and was fifty-four years old at the time he went as Verot's emissary to the Indians. Dufau had been the bishop's favorite right arm since the war years in Savannah. Father Clavreul described him as a man of distinguished dress and bearing, and said that, of the two men, he was often thought by strangers to be the one who was the bishop. He was of average height and slender build with shoulders somewhat stooped, over which draped locks of hair turned prematurely white. His facial features were ascetic, his nose aquiline, his eyes bright and piercing, and his forehead broad — "all in him," wrote Clavreul, "bespoke intelligence and refinement. In spite of his delicate health and of his twenty-two years of mission work in Georgia and Florida, his wonderful energy enabled him to do such an amount of work as might have staggered one of a more robust constitution."[34] Dufau was named pastor of Immaculate Conception Church at Jacksonville in 1874, where he completed construction of a new church to replace the one burned by federal troops during the Civil War.[35] The body of the church was constructed of white brick imported from Le

---

[33] *Ibid.* Cf. AAB, 72-H-10, Verot to Bishop James Gibbons (Vicar Apostolic of North Carolina), St. Augustine, February 12, 1872: ". . . my Vicar General Fath. Dufau is gone to the Indians out of the pale of civilization." Cf. "Episcopal Acts," 175.

[34] *Notes,* 22.

[35] See Chapter III. Cf. *ibid.,* 22, and *Sadlier's Catholic Directory . . . for 1876,* 301.

Havre, France. A basement school and an adjoining rectory were also completed. (The entire complex would be destroyed in the fire that swept Jacksonville in 1901.) Dufau stayed at Immaculate Conception after the bishop's death, serving as administrator of the diocese until the consecration of Verot's successor, John Moore, in May, 1877. He died in May, 1881, in Savannah while on his way to France to recuperate from a long illness.

Father Clavreul was also closely associated with the bishop during these years, and often left his post in St. Augustine as rector of the cathedral to accompany Verot on his travels. In his diary for the spring of 1872 he recorded: "Out early in March, riding my horse, accompanying the Bishop in a buggy to Green Cove Springs, Middleburg, Starke. I fall sick on the way between Middleburg and Starke and we stop at the latter place for the night with the Pace family.[36] Day after I go to Waldo; sick, I receive the attention of John Mularki at Waldo, where I remain, whilst the Bishop goes alone to Orange Creek and Morrison's Mill [Hawthorne]...." In April he was off to New York with Verot: "In New York go with the Bishop to the office of R[obert]. Murphy, agent for the 25 Papal Bonds Bishop Verot had invested and of which nothing could be heard. To the query about the Bonds, Murphy answered the Bishop that he had been secured more than he had secured. That was the last of the Bonds."[37] Verot's loss at Murphy's hands amounted to $1,589.01. In 1873 and 1874 he conducted a long correspondence with the New York law firm of Lowe and Thompson, whom he engaged to handle the matter of Murphy's "embezzlement." Verot did not prosecute, but he urged his attorneys to hold Murphy to the latter's promise to pay back the sum in regular installments.[38] Father Clavreul recorded another loss sustained by Verot two years later: "Namely, the Church property [at St. Augustine], which had hitherto been considered exempt from taxation, was sold at public auction during one of [Verot's] Episcopal Visitations of the Diocese, which lasted three months, from April to

[36] This was the family of George E. Pace, whose son, Edward Aloysius, was later rector of the Cathedral of St. Augustine (1886–1888) and well-known professor and vice rector at The Catholic University of America (1891–1935). The young Edward Pace entered the seminary from Starke in September, 1876, two months after Verot's death.

[37] "Clavreul's Diary," 71–72.

[38] ADSA, E. Louis Lowe to Verot, New York, various dates in 1873–1874.

July, 1874. In order to save the property the Bishop bought it back at a considerable loss."[39]

On January 15, 1874, in St. Augustine, Verot blessed and laid the cornerstone of a new convent for the Sisters of St. Joseph. A large crowd attended the ceremonies, at which Verot announced that the structure would house a novitiate, a grade school, and a normal institute for the training of teachers. He went on to add that the completed building would be "a solemn protest against the false, foolish, and injurious idea of modern times to separate education from religion, to exclude what they call *sect* from schools, to proclaim a divorce between Christ and knowledge."[40] Verot's remarks about the public school system were published without comment in the local *Examiner,* in consequence of which Reconstruction government patronage was withdrawn from the editor. Verot, on learning of this, offered to compensate the editor for his loss by writing a special series of spiritual "conferences." These writings appeared weekly in the *Examiner* from August, 1874, to August, 1875. Father Clavreul states, however, that "publication of the Conferences failed to prove a financial success."[41]

Early in 1876 Verot entered upon a publishing venture of his own — the St. Augustine *Instructor* — what the *Morning Star* of New Orleans called "the smallest Catholic newspaper in America, and so far as we know in the world."[42] The *Instructor* was about the size of four sheets of note paper, and numbered eight pages. Besides being the official organ of the bishop, the paper announced itself as being "devoted to religion, good education, morality, and Christian politics." It was edited by Father Clavreul and published weekly by Matthias R. Andreu. Each issue contained a sermon by Verot, and the front page carried this advice to readers: "The four

---

[39] *Notes,* 22. Verot's "Episcopal Acts" adds these details: "During my absence on the visitation of the diocese the church property was sold for non-payment of taxes. At my return I had to take steps to have this cancelled, and I obtained a judgment . . . to this effect. The adverse party obtained in September leave to open the case again, and in March, 1875, the former decision was repealed, and I had to pay the whole, which made an expense of more than 12 hundred dollars" (177).

[40] Reported in the *Catholic Mirror,* February 14, 1874.

[41] *Notes,* 20. Except for a few scattered issues, files of the *Examiner* for this period are missing from all known holdings. Clavreul quotes a lengthy paragraph from one of the conferences in *ibid.,* 20.

[42] March 12, 1876.

inner pages of this paper contain a sermon, or part of a sermon, suited to the times and to the country, making the paper a useful Sunday Visitor. Detach those four inner pages, join them to the following issue, and you will have at the end of a year a volume of sermons."[43] The paper lasted for about four months and then died with Verot on June 10.[44] During its brief life it had been the first Catholic newspaper in Florida.

In addition to Immaculate Conception Church in Jacksonville, Verot built new churches during the 1870's at Mill Creek and at Fernandina. The Mill Creek church was dedicated in honor of St. Leopold on July 6, 1873. The church at Fernandina was a substantial brick building, with steeple and stained-glass windows, probably the finest small church in the diocese. Verot dedicated it on February 8, 1874, under the patronage of St. Michael to honor a Spanish missionary priest, Miguel de Auñon, who was slain by Indians — Verot mistakenly thought at that site — in 1597.[45] In 1873 he had "a sort of seminary" in operation at St. Augustine, "where I teach English and theology to three young men," and in September of that year he preached the retreat to the minor seminarians at St. Charles College near Baltimore, "taking along the boy, John Carrera, to study at St. Charles, where he will be kept for 160? dol. a year."[46] Renovations in the sanctuary at his cathedral were completed in 1873 and Verot blessed two new lateral chapels dedicated to St. Monica and to St. Benedict the Moor. For the national Catholic directory in 1874 Verot listed the Negro organizations in the cathedral parish: for the men St. Benedict's Colored Catholic Benevolent Association; for the women, under the direction of the Sisters of St. Joseph, three societies, St. Monica's Society for the care of the sick, St. Frances' Society for married women, and St. Cecilia's Society for single girls; for the young boys a Society of St. Joseph. Verot added proudly that, "The colored Catholic population of St. Augustine is large enough to require for their accommodation an enlarge-

---

[43] Copy in the ADSA. Cf. AAB, 40-T-2, Peter Dufau to Archbishop James Roosevelt Bayley, St. Augustine, July 2, 1876: "He [Verot] had begun this year to publish some of his sermons in the 'St. Augustine Instructor,' and he was about to publish 50 lectures."

[44] ADSA, receipt from Clavreul to Dufau, St. Augustine, July 12, 1876, for $100 for liquidation of the *Instructor*.

[45] "Episcopal Acts," 177. Lanning, *Missions of Georgia,* establishes that Auñon was slain at the Indian village of Asopo on St. Catherine's Island, Georgia (89).

[46] "Episcopal Acts," 176.

ment of the Cathedral; this is now being executed." As for the Negro apostolate elsewhere in Florida, he was compelled to admit that in most cases "the Church has not made any gain."[47]

In the annual issues of *Sadlier's Catholic Directory* during the 1870's Verot devoted the last part of his entries on the diocese of St. Augustine to advertisements for Florida's healthy climate and material resources. Excerpts from his promotional material in the 1874 *Directory* read:

> Catholic gardeners and farmers who would like a pleasant and healthy place to settle in would do well to try the neighborhood of St. Augustine. . . . The country in St. Augustine, and probably throughout Florida, is well adapted to the cultivation of the vine. The natives of this place have, from time immemorial, cultivated two species of grape vine, probably imported from Spain by their ancestors, and to which they give the names of black grape and purple grape. The black grape, which gives a red wine, very good for the table, and the purple grape, which gives a white wine similar to the Sauterne and the Champagne, grow in St. Augustine with astonishing luxuriance, and the people do not remember a year in which there has been a scarcity of grapes in St. Augustine, or a general failure of that crop. . . . It is also believed that the orange-tree insect, which had for some years back blighted the prospects of Florida, has now disappeared, and that delicious oranges can now be obtained everywhere as heretofore. An unusual frost, however, on two different years at Christmas, has killed innumerable orange saplings, without injuring old trees. Honest, industrious settlers, furnished with a reasonable capital, can scarcely meet with failure.[48]

Verot entertained Archbishop James Roosevelt Bayley of Baltimore at St. Augustine from February 11 to March 26, 1873, who had as his traveling companion the celebrated Paulist, Isaac Hecker.[49] In the spring of 1875 Bishop James Frederick Wood of Philadelphia visited "the quaint old city of St. Augustine," for a convalescent stay at the elegant resort hotel, Florida House. He

---

[47] *Sadlier's Catholic Directory* . . . *for 1874*, 318.
[48] *Ibid.*, 319–320.
[49] AAB, Bayley Journal, p. 4 ff. Cf. Sister M. Hildegarde Yeager, C.S.C., *The Life of James Roosevelt Bayley, First Bishop of Newark and Eighth Bishop of Baltimore, 1814–1877* (Washington, D. C.: The Catholic University of America, 1947), 356.

wrote to Bayley: "Visitors very many, hotels all crowded, fare *fair*, rooms excellent, prices aristocratic. I think my convalescence is confirmed. The good Bishop exceedingly kind. We dine with him tomorrow *on oysters and other refreshments!*"[50] From Jacksonville while on his way home on April 1, and under the headline, "Thermo: 76°, Sun scorching hot," Wood wrote again to Bayley saying of Verot: "He is in fine health and spirits and works with an energy and perseverance quite edifying. He is full of conversation and loves and makes [*sic*] a joke. We did not discuss the infallibility nor allude to his peculiar *'Acta'* at the Vatican Council!"[51]

Verot himself traveled a great deal outside his diocese during these last years. He made four trips to the northern states in 1871–1873 for fund-raising or episcopal consecrations or to give retreats and dedicate churches.[52] In the summer of 1875 he made one final journey to Europe.

> I started after Corpus Christi from St. Augustine, joined with Rev. I. S. Beauchamp through New York and Brooklyn, Havre, Paris, Lyons, Puy, the Trappe of Aiguebelle, Marseilles, Genoa, Pisa, Rome. I had an interview with the Pope on the 31st of July, spent a little more than two weeks at the American College, returned by way of Ancona, Loretto, Bologna, Pavia, where I visited the mausoleum of St. Augustine, Milan, Turin, Chambrey, The Grande Chartreuse, where I spent 4 days, Annecy, where I saw my old friends and professors, Lyons, Puy, where I got the assistant to come to visit Florida for the Sisters of St. Joseph, Clermont, Paris, Havre and New York.[53]

This condensed account of a long journey is typical of his "Episcopal Acts," or diary, which covers in lapidary fashion trips and adventures and difficulties that were obviously more interesting and involved than they read in the record. Verot apparently did keep detailed records of all his activities at the time of their occurrence, but later entered them, less minutely, in the "Episcopal Acts." The original accounts have since been lost or destroyed, all save one written under the title: "Notes of the Mission to Tampa in a private conveyance." As entered in the "Episcopal Acts" this mis-

---

[50] AAB, 42-U-51, Wood to Bayley, St. Augustine, March 11, 1875.
[51] AAB, 42-U-51, Wood to Bayley, Jacksonville, April 1, 1875.
[52] "Episcopal Acts," 174–177.
[53] *Ibid.*, 178.

246   REBEL BISHOP

sionary journey taken in the spring of 1874 read as follows:
". . . Pilatka, Tampa, where I went with horse and buggy accompanied by Father Clavreul, Pinellas, Manatee, back to Tampa, and
returning to Pilatka. . . ."[54] In the extant original notes we learn
how much lay between those two lines:

> Started Monday from Pil[atka]. Stopped at Deep Creek for
> dinner 16 miles, got to Orange Springs 7 P. M. Started for Ocala
> next morning, got to Silver Springs by sundown, and by 8 o'clock
> to Ocala, having gone 2 or 3 miles out of the way which turns to
> the right before you come to Silver Springs. Started from Ocala
> Wednesday morning, went to dinner at Mr. Gerigan or Gettigan,
> and stopped on the road at Crenshaw's 4 or 5 miles from Carrey
> which we could not reach. Next morning went to Caruther's after
> dinner and did nothing there the man not being a Catholic, although
> his wife, the daughter of the late Gough, is. Many children not
> baptized. Next morning left for Columbus. Gough 1½ miles whom
> it would have been better to visit the night before, and from there
> went to Mrs. Stanley on the Sumter road following the telegraph
> wire 7 miles beyond Sumterville; there we dined and I confirmed
> Michael Gough next morning and left for Brooksville through
> Smith's ferry: arrived at 8 P. M. at Brooksville, road very sandy.
> Sunday morning said Mass in the hotel at Cat Bottom and started
> at 10 A. M. for Tampa through David Hope's, 5 miles from
> Brooksville, stopped at a pond for dinner. Missed Wekter 26 miles
> from Brooksville and arrived at Mrs. Ellis at 10 P. M. Went from
> Tampa to Point Pinellas and afterwards to Manatee and on foot
> to the left bank of the river to Mrs. Griffin and Foggerty. Left
> Tampa on Pentecost Monday, came to Wekter's, the next day to
> David Hope, the next day to Bayport, having missed our road near
> Bayport so as to reach the beautiful river of Bayport beach, we
> had taken the left instead of the right hand road at 7 miles from
> Bayport. From Bayport, going out of the Big Swamp, took the
> Homosassa road to the left 3 miles to Stafford, 15 miles to Wiggins.
> Next day from Wiggins went to Homosassa, where we should have
> taken the right hand road to Ho'm's bridge, then to Monroe's, then
> to Crystal river. There we were to take Fertooth's ferry 10 miles;
> but we took the road for Jesse Smith 10 miles which we missed
> and Wednesday 15 miles where we arrived at 1½ A. M. Then that
> same day went to Harrison's ferry and at Mr. Bon. to Boughs
> and Thomas, and at Mr. Grigg's missed the road, went to John

---

[54] *Ibid.*, 176. Pilatka was a common spelling for this St. John's River town in
the past century. It is currently spelled Palatka.

Night's, said Mass, and came to Ocala Sunday. Then went to old Town or place of Tim Ward and Tim Guilfoyle came; went next day to Dann's on Disla road, to Owen's 6 miles through Camp Ground, then to Cabbage Hammock 6 miles having passed through Mrs. Harris' place, then to Evekirk, to Simmon's where we spent the night and to Orange Springs . . . [and returning to Pilatka].[55]

It was after just such a trip, a lengthy visitation of the diocese undertaken in the spring of 1876, that Verot was visited by the "mild indisposition" that carried off his life. Advancing age never tempered his missionary zeal nor his willingness to take on arduous travel. On the last trip of his life through Florida's thinly settled wilderness he suffered fatigues and inconveniences that beggar the imagination of missionaries who cover that same ground today. It was a trip, wrote Father Clavreul, that consisted of "sleepless nights, protracted fasts, exposure, long and interminable rides through roads often impassable, in wretched and incommodious stage coaches."[56] It brought him back to St. Augustine on June 6 in mortally weakened condition. He had fully intended to carry on the journey several days later to Pilatka and other points up the St. John's River. But it was not to be. Four days later his visitation was interrupted by the last fatigue — the final inconvenience. Death alone could strip him of his harness. Jean-Pierre Augustin Marcellin Verot had promised to God a lifetime service, and well did he keep his word.

News of the bishop's death was flashed across the country by telegraph. Father Dufau sent special messages to Archbishop Bayley and to Bishops Lynch, Gibbons, and Quinlan inviting them to attend the funeral.[57] In the meantime he caused Verot's body to be packed in ice that had just arrived in barrels aboard ship from the north. The ice, however, did not keep, and neither did the bishop's remains. As Dufau wrote later: "It was expected that his remains could be kept till the day when some Bishops of the neighboring Dioceses, the Clergy of Florida, and some faithful from the various parishes of the Diocese should be present to celebrate with due

---

[55] The original of this document is in the ASLA. A transcription is printed in Roth, ed. *Churches of the Diocese,* Part 6, 180.

[56] "A Sermon Delivered in the Cathedral of St. Augustine, on Sunday, July 16th, A.D. 1876 by Rev. Father Clavreul, Rector of the Cathedral," *ibid.,* Part 4, 77.

[57] ADSA, receipts from The Western Union Telegraph Company, June 10, 1876.

honor his obsequies, but all means that had been taken to that purpose failed, and the ceremony of his burial could be delayed no
longer than last Monday, June 12th."[58] On that date the body was
placed in an $80 "metallic case" and carried into the cathedral for
a requiem Mass offered by Father Dufau. A hastily improvised
burial followed at Tolomato Cemetery in the city, where Verot's
body was placed in a mortuary chapel vault already containing
the body of a Cuban patriot-priest, Félix Francisco José Maria de
la Concepcion Varela. In order to make a place for Verot's body the
bones of Varela were put into a pillow and moved to one end of
the vault.[59]

Four days later Father Clavreul delivered a eulogy before a
large crowd in the cathedral. It was a beautiful tribute, lasting
close to an hour. Because he spoke of Verot not from manuscripts
and old letters as we must speak here, but from the very flesh, we
may forgive him if he failed to notice Verot the theorist on slavery,
or Verot the Confederate, or Verot the champion of freedmen, or
Verot the school compromise deviser, or Verot the council orator.
Clavreul spoke of him as the man, and he called upon the example
of his life as a means of teaching virtue, for virtue above all is what
Clavreul thought he saw:

    Methinks I hear the saintly Bishop address us in the words of
    St. Paul: "Be ye, therefore, my imitators as I am of Christ." All

[58] ADSA, "Circular Letter to the Clergy and Laity of the Diocese of St.
Augustine, P. Dufau, Pastor of Im. Con. Church, Jacksonville, St. Augustine,
Fla., June 13, 1876."

[59] Varela was born in Havana in 1788. After ordination he lectured and
wrote on economics and philosophy. In 1821 he was elected one of three Cuban
representatives to the Spanish Cortes, or parliament. His advocacy of Cuban
rights in that body angered Spain and made it necessary for him to go into
exile. He went to New York where he became pastor of the Church of the
Transfiguration and vicar-general of the diocese. Father Varela was attracted by
the Spanish atmosphere of St. Augustine, which he visited on three occasions.
During his last visit in 1853 he died and was buried at Tolomato. Two years
later Cuban admirers exhumed his body and placed it in a mortuary chapel vault,
the same in which Bishop Verot's remains were placed in 1876. In 1911 Varela's
bones were removed to Cuba to be enshrined in a monument reverencing him as
a national hero. In 1949 doubt was raised by certain parties in Cuba whether
Varela's admirers had brought home the right bones. Varela (or Verot?) was
therefore moved again, this time to a laboratory at the University of Havana,
where a team of scientists decided that this was Varela indeed, and that Augustin
Verot remained at St. Augustine. The findings were published in a weird book:
Julio Morales Coello, et al., Los Restos del Padre Varela en la Universidad de la
Habana (La Habana: La Imprenta de la Universidad de la Habana, 1955), 208 pp.

the precepts commanded in the Gospel, all the virtues which should adorn the Christian, were reflected in his action. For his life was, what he liked so well to tell us, speaking of the lives of the Saints, the Gospel in practice. Where could be seen more humility, patience, forebearance, mortification, more complete mastery over self? Who ever heard him boast, speak of himself; who knew him proud, self-conceited; when did he ever complain, show even indignation, except when the cause of God and the Church was in question; what duty however painful did he not fulfill? What was it which he knew God or the Church demanded of him that he did neglect? Who knew him ever to lose time, and indulge in anything which Religion or reason did not approve? What authority do not like examples give to the invitation he is addressing us to be his imitators as he was of Christ?[60]

It would be unwise to say that Father Clavreul's emphasis was not the correct one. As Bishop Verot had inscribed under the Lambert painting of the first Mass: "Piety is profitable to all things, having promise of the life that now is, and of that which is to come (I *Timothy* 4:8)." The available evidence leaves little doubt that, if he did not lead an altogether blameless life — descending below the horizon without a single cloud to darken his fair name, as Bishop James Gibbons remarked — he did in fact *strive* to let piety and the needs of piety form the sole principle of all his actions. The extant record discloses no exception to a lifetime's dedication to the things of God. Neither does the record say that the integrity of his character was ever put into question by those who knew him well, even by those for whom the bishop's political views or outspoken manner may have been distasteful.

Sometimes, it is true, men who did not know the man personally, as for example General Gillmore during the cemetery episode, doubted the spiritual character of his motives; and certain of the prelates at the Vatican Council judged him to be a comic interloper on the scene of sacred deliberations. But these were men who may have changed their minds when (or if) they had the chance to know him well. Obviously, our own attempt to know him here, in these pages, suffers not only from the absence of the man himself, but also from the long interval of ninety-odd years since his death and from the loss of many of the pertinent documents. As nearly

---

[60] "Sermon," *Churches of the Diocese*, Part 4, 80.

as we can re-create him, though, his image bears out the judgment of Father Clavreul that he was a man on whom anyone might profitably pattern his life. Save perhaps for that brief period of frustration and petty grievance that Verot allowed to mar his last years at St. Mary's College, and a few notable examples of intemperate speech, his life appears to have been a constant pursuit of perfection in selfless service to God and man. His labors for souls in the poor and sparsely settled flatlands of Florida, his wartime travels and ministrations throughout two Confederate states, his compassion for the suffering enemy at Andersonville, his earnest advocacy of the human dignity and of the rights of the Negro freedmen, his zealous rebuilding of the war-shattered Church, and the arduous missionary travels that he undertook in the autumn of life, when he might easily have rested on the "well done" of a faithful servant — these were not the deeds of a mere politician or comic interloper.

In the course of the social and political causes that attracted his attention in the 1860's Verot conducted himself at all times honorably, doing credit both to himself and to his Church. He never compromised religion or the dignity of his episcopal office. At the same time, when he decided to take a public position, he did so with no timidity or procrastination. Verot's early call to link arms with the Confederate adventure made it possible for Catholics in the South to declare that they were not alien "come lately's" in the conflict, but men who had stood with their neighbors from the beginning. If there had been doubt in the South before the Civil War that Catholics made good Americans, there could have been no doubt after 1861 that they certainly made good Confederates. Verot's ringing sermon on slavery, his Peace Pastoral of 1863, and his spirited articles in the *Pacificator* went far to work this change in the Church's image, although that was never their express purpose.

In Verot's other great public moment, the First Council of the Vatican, he again acted from wholly sincere and honorable motives. He revealed openly that he had come to certain unconventional conclusions about the manner of approach that the Church should make toward Protestant and secular society. His fame at the council came partly from his bold insistence that the universal Church ought straightaway to adopt the same conclusions. The remaining share of the notoriety that attached to his name after the council resulted from his firm and outspoken conviction that papal infallibility was neither an opportune doctrine nor one even possible of definition. The unpretentious and practical speeches that he delivered on these matters came as a surprise not only to European but also to many of his fellow American bishops, a number of whom felt that he was lacking in good manners, if not in good sense. But Verot was never a man for pretense. He spoke his mind honestly at all times. Whatever was in his mind was sure to come out, with no apologies, with no dissimulation. On occasion he exaggerated the truth, or used arguments that were beside the point, or debated *ad hominem* in place of the issue, but such mistakes may be forgiven men who dare the passion of battle. It is a fair guess that Augustin Verot would not have felt any special need to stand ashamed before the "thought for the week" that appeared in the Baltimore *Catholic Mirror* on June 10, 1876, the day on which he died: "As words can never be recalled, speak only such words as you would never wish to recall."

He was a warm and lovable man, a selfless and dedicated man, a keenly perceptive man, a spiritual man, an altogether colorful and exciting man. He was a character in the best sense of that word. He seemed to combine in his person most of the qualities that make men worth remembering. In a way, he was one of a kind. And there were probably those who asked at his passing, will we ever see his like again?

INDEX

Abolitionism, criticized by Verot, 123; linked with nativism, 39, 39 *n;* sermon on, 1861, 31 ff; Verot's changed attitude toward, 116

Acton, John Emerich Edward Dalberg (Lord Acton), and Liberal Catholic movement, 194; reports on Verot's speech to Döllinger, 216

Acts of the Apostles, 213

"Address to the People of the United States in Behalf of Peace, An," three-part article by Verot in *Pacificator,* 77 f

African Colonization Society, 129 f

African Methodist Episcopal Church, 130, 139

African Methodist Episcopal Zion Church, 139

Alabama, defeatist group in, 85

Alabama Baptist Convention, 117 *n*

Albany, Ga., church used as hospital, 107; Verot visits in 1864, 107

Albany, N. Y., school plan in, 189

Alemany, Joseph Sadoc, Archbishop, criticizes Verot, 217 f, 217 *n*

Alexandria, *see* Natchitoches

Alvord, John W., Freedmen's Bureau, visits Negro school of Sisters of St. Joseph, 134 f

Amedia Island, *see* Fernandina

American Freedmen's Union Commission (New York branch), 129

Americus, Ga., 1869 mission at, 157; visited by Verot, 94

Anderson, Edward C., on Savannah city council, 182

Andersonville prison, Clavreul, Fr., describes, 97, 102 f; execution of raiders at, 100 f; Hamilton, Fr., describes, 95 f, 99 f; history and description of, 94 f; priests minister at, 90; Verot describes, 97 ff, 100; Verot leaves for, 91; visited twice by Verot, 94; Whelan, Fr., describes, 96, 100 ff

Andreu, Matthias R., publisher of *Instructor,* 242

Angelis, Filippo de, Cardinal, rebukes Verot, 210

Annonay, France, Basilian college at, 6

Apalachicola River, northwest boundary of vicariate, 25

Arkansas, defeatist group in, 85

Arnold, Richard D., M.D., chairman of Savannah board of education, 174

Arrigoni, Giulio, Archibshop, comments on Verot's speech, 214

Assumption, Church of the, Macon, Ga., 95

Athens, Ga., Verot visits in 1864, 107

Atlanta, Ga., Catholics attempt to follow Savannah school plan, 187; new church started, 149; proposed school for Negroes criticized, 141; public school system, 170; Redemptorist mission in, 155; residents driven from, 81; Verot visits after burning of city, 109; visited by Verot, 91

Aubril, Edmund, C.P.M., stationed at St. Augustine, 25, 91

Augusta, Ga., *Banner of the South* published at, 140; 1869 mission at, 157; *Pacificator* published at, 75 f; priests stationed at in 1864, 92; Redemptorist mission in, 155; Verot publishes wartime catechism at, 91; Verot speaks on civil war, 65; Verot visits in 1864, 107; visited by Verot, 90

Augusta *Chronicle and Sentinel,* prints *Banner of the South,* 140

Augusta *Daily Constitutionalist,* on demoralized South, 116; on means to end war, 87; praises Verot's *Pacificator* article, 82

Aulance, John Bernard, Father, recruited from France, 29; tries to stop fleeing Catholics, 66

Baker, William H., superintendent of education, Savannah, Ga., 185

Baltimore, Md., Verot allowed to remain at, 16; Verot consecrated at, 21; Verot learns of new appointment in, 63 f; Verot's arrival at, 7; Verot's slavery tract published at, 49; visited by Verot in 1870, 230

253

258 INDEX

Gallicanism, Verot on, 216; and Verot's
studies, 218
Galveston, diocese of, 60
Garnier, Antoine, S.S., promises to Verot
recalled, 14 f; Sulpician Superior General, 6
Gartland, Francis X., Bishop, body reinterred, 114; body rescued, 110;
death noted, 19
Gaston, William, Judge, 37 n
Gazette de France, prints Kenrick-
Purcell letter, 221
Genoa, Italy, two priests recruited from,
157
Georgia, Catholics number 8000 in
1861, 63; described by Fr. Wissel in
1868, 154; devastated condition of,
in 1865, 108 f; growth of Church in,
164; origin of public school system,
170; poverty of people after war,
147; status of Catholicism in 1861
and 1870, 145; under diocese of
Savannah, 60
Georgia, Confederate warship, 90
Gibbons, James, Cardinal, defends Ireland's school plan, 189 f; epitomizes
late nineteenth-century Catholicism,
4; favors public schools, 173 f; informed of Verot's death, 247; on
Verot's death, 1
Gibbs, George Gordon, Circuit Court
Judge, opinion on Negro education,
142, 142 n
Gillmore, Quincy A., Major General,
complains to Archbishop Spalding
about Verot, 112 f; complains to War
Department about Verot, 112; meets
Verot, 113; receives apology from
Verot, 113; receives protest from
Verot on desecration of cemetery, 110;
receives second protest from Verot,
112; replies to Verot, 110
Gladstone, William Ewart, on U. S.
bishops, 199 n
Glass, Gallow, description of Verot,
18, 18 n
Goold, James, Bishop, comments on
Verot's speech, 214
Granderath, Theodore, on Verot at Vati-
can Council, 225
Gregory XVI, Pope, prohibited slave
trade, 45; on slave trade, 34
Green, Duff, General, Whig politician,
56 n
Gross, William H., C.SS.R., Bishop, con-
troversies with Verot over Sisters of
St. Joseph, 229, 229 n; describes
Savannah in 1868, 154; description
of Verot, 18; gives missions in 1868,

153 f; and Savannah school plan,
189; and Sisters of St. Joseph, 135 n

Halpine, Charles G., Major, 80 n
Hamilton, William J., Father, administrator during Verot's absence, 134 n,
135; appointed negotiator with school
board, 183; attends federal officers at
Macon, Ga., 100 n; cares for sick at
Macon, 105; first visit to Anderson-
ville, 95 f; in Jacksonville, 25;
praised by prisoner, 104; transferred
to Georgia, 92
Hammond, Nathaniel, Congressman,
187 n
Hampton Roads Conference, 85
Hardie, James A., Major General, In-
spector General, rebukes Verot, 11
Harrisburg, Pa., school plan in, 189
Harrison, G. P., on Savannah school
commission, 171
Hartford, diocese of, 29
Hassett, Thomas, Father, started free
school in St. Augustine, 165 n
Hassler, Ferdinand, founder of Coast
and Geodetic Survey, 7 f
Hecker, Isaac, Father, accompanies
Archbishop Bayley to St. Augustine,
244; and public school question, 169,
169 n, 179 n, 180 n, 180 f; quoted in
Banner of the South, 164
Henry, Joseph, director of Smithsonian
Institute, 7 f
Hierarchy of North and South, pro-
posed as peace commissioners, 86
Hierarchy of the South, praised for pa-
triotism, 148; praised for support of
Confederacy, 75, 82
Hierarchy of U. S., abstained from
national politics before war, 31, 56 ff;
in advance of priests and people,
220 f; described at Vatican Council,
197 ff; liberalism of bishops at Vati-
can Council, 200 f; number attend-
ing Vatican Council, 196; *postulatum*
vs. infallibility, 221
Hillaire, Emile, Father, recruited from
France, 29
Hilton Head, S. C., headquarters of
Military Department of the South,
110; Verot meets Gen. Gillmore, 113
Horne, Henry, loaned money to Fr.
Whelan, 102
Howard, O. O., General, Freedmen's
Bureau Commissioner, 134
Hughes, John, Archbishop, contribution
to Brisbane, 107 n; description of
Channing, Parker, *et al.,* 37; epit-
omizes early middle period Catholi-